ABOUT THE EDITOR

Joseph Mersand, Ph.D., has devoted himself throughout his long career as a teacher to the theatre and its literature. He has written and edited books about the drama over a period of twenty years. Among these are *The American Drama, 1930–1940; The Play's the Thing* and *The American Drama Since 1930.* Dr. Mersand was chairman of the Editorial Committee of the National Council of Teachers of English, which authorized the publication of *Guide to Play Selection,* a standard work.

For ten years Dr. Mersand served as chairman of the English and Speech departments at Long Island City High School, in New York City. Highly regarded in his field, he has been an instructor at Cornell University, Queens College, Teachers College, Columbia University, Syracuse University and New York University. He is past president of the National Council of Teachers of English and is presently chairman of the English department at Jamaica High School, in New York City.

THE  ANTA SERIES OF DISTINGUISHED PLAYS

Fifteen American One-Act Plays: The Lottery, The Devil and Daniel Webster and thirteen other outstanding plays (46867 75¢)

Three Comedies of American Family Life: I Remember Mama, Life with Father, You Can't Take It with You (46853 75¢)

Three Dramas of American Realism: Idiot's Delight, Street Scene, The Time of Your Life (W0652 60¢)

Three Plays About Business in America: The Adding Machine, Beggar on Horseback, All My Sons (46852 75¢)

Three Plays About Marriage: Craig's Wife, They Knew What They Wanted, Holiday (W0659 60¢)

Three Plays About Crime and Criminals: Arsenic and Old Lace, Kind Lady, Detective Story (W0934 75¢)

Three Plays About Doctors: An Enemy of the People, Men in White, Yellow Jack (46855 75¢)

Three Plays by Maxwell Anderson: Valley Forge, Joan of Lorraine, Journey to Jerusalem (W0670 60¢)

Three Plays by Victor Hugo: Hernani, Ruy Blas, The King Amuses Himself (W0662 60¢)

Three Classic Spanish Plays: The Sheep Well, None Beneath the King, Life Is a Dream (W0660 60¢)

Three Scandinavian Plays: The Father, The Lady from the Sea, The Wild Duck (W0657 60¢)

Three Dramas of W. Somerset Maugham: The Letter, The Sacred Flame, For Services Rendered (47487 90¢)

Four Plays by Bernard Shaw: Caesar and Cleopatra, The Devil's Disciple, Man and Superman, Candida (W•935 75¢)

THE ANTA SERIES OF DISTINGUISHED PLAYS

Three Comedies of
American Family Life

I REMEMBER MAMA
by John van Druten

LIFE WITH FATHER
by Howard Lindsay and Russel Crouse

YOU CAN'T TAKE IT WITH YOU
by Moss Hart and George S. Kaufman

Edited and with Introductions by JOSEPH MERSAND

WSP

WASHINGTON SQUARE PRESS, INC. • NEW YORK

THREE COMEDIES OF AMERICAN FAMILY LIFE

A *Washington Square Press* edition

1st printing....................December, 1960
13th printing......................January, 1969

L

Published by
Washington Square Press, Inc., 630 Fifth Avenue, New York, N.Y.

WASHINGTON SQUARE PRESS editions are distributed in the
U.S. by Simon & Schuster, Inc., 630 Fifth Avenue, New
York, N.Y. 10020 and in Canada by Simon & Schuster
of Canada, Ltd., Richmond Hill, Ontario, Canada.

Standard Book Number: 671-46853-7.

CONTENTS

I REMEMBER MAMA

INTRODUCTION

In 1943, a collection of seventeen short stories about a Norwegian family living in San Francisco appeared under the title of *Mama's Bank Account*. Its author, Kathryn Forbes, was acclaimed for the warmth and sympathy of her treatment of life in the comparatively halcyon days of 1910. Each of the seventeen sketches centered around a different episode in the efforts of Mama to preserve her home in the face of illness, strikes, prejudice and a hard life in general. Throughout the series she remains strong, resolute, understanding of the foibles of others—a person compounded of one part nobility, one part humility, one part gentility. Perhaps it was the anxieties of those dark days of 1943 that won the hearts of so many readers to this book.

It was not surprising that the book was soon adapted into a play by the skillful craftsman John van Druten, who had been a successful playwright for almost twenty years, and whose *Voice of the Turtle* was having a big success at the time. The dramatic version of Miss Forbes's book, *I Remember Mama*, was also fortunate in having as its producers Rodgers and Hammerstein, who were breaking records with their *Oklahoma!* The cast included such distinguished stars as Mady Christians as Mama, Oscar Homolka as Uncle Chris and Joan Tetzel as Katrin. Superb direction by John van Druten and unusually flexible and original staging combined to make the play one of the most memorable of the year; Burns Mantle included it among the best plays of the 1944–1945 season.

Plays from sketches or short stories are no novelty on the

Broadway stage; the fabulously successful *Life with Father* was built out of exactly such a collection. But there was a tenderness and simplicity about *I Remember Mama* that won the hearts of the audience. Even after a period of more than fifteen years, certain scenes are as vivid to this playgoer as they were in 1944. Mama's working her way into Dagmar's ward as a scrubwoman, the death of that kind old reprobate Uncle Chris, Mama's exchange of a recipe for Miss Moorhead's advice about Katrin's writing—these are among the memorable moments of several decades of theatregoing.

Simplicity, sincerity and struggle are the keynotes of this saga of a Norwegian family transplanted from their homeland to San Francisco, where life for them was always a question of making ends meet. In a world of neurosis, psychosis and hysteria, it was a stabilizing experience in 1944 to meet a woman who could face all life's problems with courage and balance, whether it was managing to send her son to high school or helping her uncle die in peace. Pervading the household was the love and respect that Papa and Mama felt for each other and for their children. The latter knew their place and kept it—no juvenile delinquency here! Getting into high school was a privilege and a responsibility. No underachievers and drop-outs in this household! Rather, they were eager for the joy of an education, even though it meant deprivation and sacrifices.

The family portrayed might very well have been duplicated by millions of Slavic or Italian or other Continental stock who had left their homelands to establish new roots in a beautiful and free land. Many who saw the play must have remembered similar situations in their own families.

There was also the interest in Katrin's struggle for literary self-expression and for maturity, as revealed in her exchange of the dresser set for her mother's brooch.

In a world that becomes more complex each year, more frustrating and soul-destroying, it is comforting to be brought back to a period half a century ago when living seemed so much simpler, and yet so enjoyable. This was long before talking pictures, radio and television, and all the other inexpensive means of entertainment that form such an important part of our lives. The one kind of entertainment available to Mama's family was the age-old one of reading aloud from the classics. From the boarder, Mr. Hyde, reading from *A Tale of Two Cities,* to a prominent author or actress reading on television, the circle has now been completed. The more it changes, the more it is the same.

Some of the pleasure of the original production was due to the novelty of the staging. As the curtain went up, Katrin, seated in front of the curtain, was reading from the book about her family. When she came to the line about Papa's Saturday-night pay envelope, the curtain was opened and the family revealed. Spectators welcomed this unusual method of narrative asides by Katrin and the use of revolving stages. The play might be realistic in content, but it was by no means realistic in its staging, and the audience enjoyed both.

For those who had read the original sketches, there was additional delight in contemplating the artistry with which John van Druten discarded material that was not dramatic and heightened other scenes so that his play kept one's interest from the opening to the closing lines.

THE PLAYWRIGHT

John van Druten was born in London, England, on June 1, 1901. He prepared for the law at the University College of London, but soon gave up the practice of his profession. His next career was that of university lecturer on English law and legal history at the University of Wales. In 1926 he came to the United States on a lecture tour and eventually turned to writing—his third career and the one that would bring him fame.

By 1944, when he undertook the adaptation of *I Remember Mama,* he was already one of our most accomplished dramatists. Such plays as *Young Woodley* (1925), *There's Al-*

ways Juliet (1931), *The Distaff Side* (1933) and *Old Acquaintance* (1940) had enjoyed long runs, frequently on both sides of the Atlantic. His acknowledged masterpiece—and greatest success—*The Voice of the Turtle* (1943), demonstrated his ability to sustain audience attention and sympathy by using only three characters. This play, with a radiant performance by Margaret Sullavan, had one of the longest runs in Broadway history.

After the adaptation of *I Remember Mama*, he wrote *The Mermaids Singing* (1945), *The Druid Circle* (1947), *Bell, Book and Candle* (1950), *I Am a Camera* (1951) and *I've Got Sixpence* (1952).

For those who would gain an insight into his methods of work, his *Playwright at Work* (1953) will prove illuminating. Seldom has a successful playwright opened his mind and heart so completely to his readers. This work has a place on the small shelf of books on dramaturgy that are truly revealing and helpful. The charm and wit that delighted so many playgoers from behind the footlights are evident on page after page. On December 19, 1957, after more than thirty years in the theatre, John van Druten died.

ADDITIONAL READING

Brown, John Mason. *Seeing Things,* pp. 217–223. New York: McGraw-Hill, 1946.

Kunitz, Stanley J., and Haycraft, Howard. *Twentieth Century Authors,* pp. 1444–1445. New York: Wilson, 1942.

Kunitz, Stanley J. *Twentieth Century Authors.* First Supplement, p. 1025. New York: Wilson, 1955.

Morris, Lloyd B. *Postscript to Yesterday.* New York: Random House, 1947.

Nathan, George Jean. *The Theatre Book of the Year, 1944–1945,* pp. 109–112. New York: Knopf, 1945.

van Druten, John. *Playwright at Work.* New York: Harper, 1953.

I REMEMBER MAMA

BY JOHN VAN DRUTEN

ACT I

The period of the play is around 1910.

SCENE: *On either side of the stage are two small turntables
on which the shorter scenes are played against very simpli-
fied backgrounds. As each scene finishes the lights dim and
the table revolves out, leaving an unobstructed view of the
main stage. The main stage is raised by two steps, above
which traveler curtains open and close.*

When the curtain rises, KATRIN, *in a spotlight, is seated at a
desk on the right turntable, facing the audience. She is
writing and smoking a cigarette.* KATRIN *is somewhere in
her early twenties. She should be played by an actress who
is small in stature, and capable of looking sufficiently a child
not to break the illusion in subsequent scenes. She is a
blonde. Her hair, when we see her first, is in a modern "up"
style, capable of being easily loosened to fall to shoulder
length for the childhood scenes. She wears a very short
dress, the skirt of which is concealed for the prologue by
the desk behind which she is seated.*

KATRIN *writes in silence for a few moments, then puts down her pen, takes up her manuscript, and begins to read aloud what she has written.*

KATRIN (*reading*): "For as long as I could remember, the house on Steiner Street had been home. Papa and Mama had both been born in Norway, but they came to San Francisco because Mama's sisters were here. All of us were born here. Nels, the oldest and the only boy—my sister Christine —and the littlest sister, Dagmar." (*She puts down her manuscript and looks out front.*) It's funny, but when I look back, I always see Nels and Christine and myself looking almost as we do today. I guess that's because the people you see all the time stay the same age in your head. Dagmar's different. She was always the baby—so I see her as a baby. Even Mama—it's funny, but I always see Mama as around forty. She couldn't always have been forty. (*She puts out her cigarette, picks up her manuscript and starts to read again.*) "Besides us, there was our boarder, Mr. Hyde. Mr. Hyde was an Englishman who had once been an actor, and Mama was very impressed by his flowery talk and courtly manners. He used to read aloud to us in the evenings. But first and foremost, I remember Mama." (*The light dims down, leaving KATRIN only faintly visible. Lights come up on the main stage, revealing the house on Steiner Street—a kitchen room. It has a black flat, with a dresser, holding china. On either side of the dresser is a door, one leading to the pantry, the other to the rest of the house. The wall on the left is a short one. It is the wall of the house, and contains a door leading into the street, being presumably the back door of the house, but the one most commonly used as the entry door. Beyond it the street is visible, with a single lamppost at left, just outside the house. Behind the room rises the house itself with upper windows lighted, and behind it a painted backdrop of the San Francisco hills, houses, and telegraph posts. The furniture of the kitchen is simple. A center table, with two chairs above it, armchairs at either end, and a low bench below it. Against the right wall, a large stove, below it another armchair. The window*) *is below the door in the left wall and has a low Norwegian chest under it.* KATRIN's *voice continuing in the half-dark, as the scene is revealed.*) "I remember that every Saturday night Mama would sit down by the kitchen table and count out the money Papa had brought home in the little envelope."

(*By now the tableau is revealed in full, and the light on* KATRIN *dwindles further. The picture is as she described.* MAMA—*looking around forty—is in the armchair at right of the table, emptying the envelope of its silver dollars and smaller coins.* PAPA—*looking a little older than* MAMA—*stands above her. His English throughout is better than hers, with less accent.*)

MAMA: You call the children, Lars. Is good they should know about money.

(PAPA *goes to door at the back and calls.*)

PAPA: Children! Nels—Christine—Katrin!
CHILDREN'S VOICES (*off, answering*): Coming, Papa!
MAMA: You call loud for Katrin. She is in her study, maybe.
PAPA: She is where?
MAMA: Katrin make the old attic under the roof into a study.
PAPA (*amused*): So? (*shouting*) Katrin! Katrin!
KATRIN (*still at her desk*): Yes, Papa. I heard.
PAPA (*returning to the room*): A study now, huh? What does Katrin study?
MAMA: I think Katrin wants to be author.
PAPA: Author?
MAMA: Stories she will write. For the magazines. And books, too, maybe, one day.
PAPA (*taking out his pipe*): Is good pay to be author?
MAMA: I don't know. For magazines, I think maybe yes. For books, I think no.
PAPA: Then she become writer for magazines.

MAMA: Maybe. But I like she writes books. Like the ones Mr. Hyde reads us. (DAGMAR *enters from the pantry. She is a plump child of about eight and carries an alley cat in her arms.*) Dagmar, you bring that cat in again?

DAGMAR: Sure, she's my Elizabeth—my beautiful Elizabeth! (*She crosses to the chest under the window, and sits, nursing the cat.*)

PAPA: Poor Elizabeth looks as if she had been in fight again.

DAGMAR: Not poor Elizabeth. *Brave* Elizabeth. Elizabeth's a Viking cat. She fights for her honor!

PAPA (*exchanging an amused glance with* MAMA): And just what is a cat's honor, little one?

DAGMAR: The honor of being the bravest cat in San Francisco. (CHRISTINE *comes in. She, like* KATRIN, *should be played by a small young actress, but not a child. Her hair is to her shoulders, her dress short, her age indeterminate. Actually, she is about thirteen at this time. She is the cool, aloof, matter-of-fact one of the family. She carries a box of crayons, scissors and a picture-book.*) Aren't you, Elizabeth?

CHRISTINE (*sitting above the table and starting to color the picture-book with the crayons*): That disgusting cat!

DAGMAR: She's not disgusting. She's beautiful. Beautiful as the dawn!

CHRISTINE: And when have *you* ever seen the dawn?

DAGMAR: I haven't seen it, but Mr. Hyde read to us about it. (MR. HYDE *comes in from back door. He is a slightly seedy, long-haired man in his fifties. Rather of the old-fashioned English "laddie" actor type. He wears a very shabby long overcoat, with a deplorable fur collar, and carries his hat. His accent is English.*) Didn't you, Mr. Hyde? Didn't you read to us about the dawn?

MR. HYDE: I did, my child of joy. The dawn, the rosy-finger-tipped Aurora . . .

DAGMAR: When can I get to *see* the dawn, Mama?

MAMA: Any morning you get up early.

DAGMAR: Is there a dawn every morning?

MAMA: Sure.

I Remember Mama

DAGMAR (*incredulous*): It's all that beautiful, and it happens every *morning?* Why didn't anyone *tell* me?

MR. HYDE: My child, that is what the poets are for. To tell you of *all* the beautiful things that are happening every day, and that no one sees until they tell them. (*He starts for the door.*)

MAMA: You go out, Mr. Hyde?

MR. HYDE: For a few moments only, dear Madam. To buy myself a modicum of that tawny weed, tobacco, that I lust after, as Ben Jonson says. I shall be back in time for our nightly reading. (*He goes out and disappears down the street.*)

MAMA (*who has gone to the back door, calls with a good deal of sharpness and firmness*): Nels! Katrin! You do not hear Papa call you?

NELS (*from upstairs*): Coming, Mama!

KATRIN (*at her desk*): Yes, Mama. I'm coming. (*She rises. In her few moments in the dark, she has loosened her hair to her shoulders, and we see that her skirt is short as she walks from her desk, and up the steps into the set. As soon as she has left it, the turntable revolves out. Immediately after her, NELS comes in from the back. He is a tall, strapping young fellow—old enough to look eighteen or nineteen, or fifteen or sixteen, according to his dress, or demeanor. Now, he is about fifteen. KATRIN, to CHRISTINE.*) Move over. (*She shares CHRISTINE's chair at the table with her.*)

PAPA: So now all are here.

MAMA: Come, then. (*CHRISTINE, NELS and KATRIN gather around the table. DAGMAR remains crooning to ELIZABETH, but rises and stands behind PAPA. Sorting coins.*) First, for the landlord. (*She makes a pile of silver dollars. It gets pushed down the table from one member of the family to the next, each speaking as he passes it. PAPA comes last.*)

NELS (*passing it on*): For the landlord.

KATRIN (*doing likewise*): For the landlord.

CHRISTINE (*passing it to PAPA*): The landlord.

11

PAPA: For the landlord. (*He dumps the pile at his end of the table, writing on a piece of paper, which he wraps around the pile*).

MAMA (*who has been sorting*): For the grocer.

(*The business is repeated. During this repeat, DAGMAR's crooning to the cat becomes audible, contrapuntally to the repetitions of "For the Grocer."*)

DAGMAR (*in a crescendo*): In all the United States no cat was as brave as Elizabeth. (*Fortissimo.*) In all the *world* no cat was as brave as Elizabeth!

MAMA (*gently*): Hush, Dagmar. Quietly. You put Elizabeth back into the pantry.

DAGMAR (*in a loud stage whisper, as she crosses to pantry*): In Heaven or HELL no cat was as brave as Elizabeth! (*She goes out with the cat.*)

MAMA: For Katrin's shoes to be half-soled. (*She passes a half dollar.*)

NELS: Katrin's shoes.

KATRIN (*proudly*): *My* shoes!

CHRISTINE (*contemptuously*): Katrin's old shoes.

PAPA: Katrin's shoes.

CHRISTINE (*rising and coming to* MAMA): Mama, Teacher says this week I'll need a new notebook.

MAMA: How much it will be?

CHRISTINE: A dime.

MAMA (*giving her a dime*): For the notebook. You don't lose it.

CHRISTINE: I won't lose it. (*She wraps it in her handkerchief.*)

MAMA: You take care when you blow your nose.

CHRISTINE: I'll take care. (*She returns to her seat.*)

PAPA: Is all, Mama?

MAMA: Is all for this week. Is good. We do not have to go to the Bank. (*She starts to gather up the few remaining coins.* KATRIN *leaves the group, comes and sits on steps.*)

NELS (*rising*): Mama . . . (*She looks up, catching an urgency in his tone.* PAPA *suspends smoking for a moment.*) Mama, I'll be graduating from grammar school next month. Could I . . . could I go on to High, do you think?

MAMA (*pleased*): You want to go to high school?

NELS: I'd like to . . . if you think I could.

MAMA: Is good.

(PAPA *nods approvingly.*)

NELS (*awkwardly*): It . . . it'll cost a little money. I've got it all written down. (*Producing a piece of paper from his pocket.*) Carfare, clothes, notebooks—things I'll really need. I figured it out with Cy Nichols. He went to High last year.

(PAPA *rises and comes behind* MAMA *to look at the paper* NELS *puts before them.*)

MAMA: Get the Little Bank, Christine.

(CHRISTINE *gets a small box from the dresser.*)

KATRIN (*from the steps—herself again, in the present—looking out front*): The Little Bank! That was the most important thing in the whole house. It was a box we used to keep for emergencies—like the time when Dagmar had croup and Papa had to go and get medicine to put in the steam kettle. I can *smell* that medicine now! The things that came out of the Little Bank! Mama was always going to buy herself a warm coat out of it, when there was enough, only there never was.

(*Meanwhile,* MAMA *has been counting the contents.*)

NELS (*anxiously*): Is there enough, Mama?

MAMA (*shaking her head*): Is not much in the Little Bank right now. We give to the dentist, you remember? And for your roller skates?

NELS (*his face falling*): I know. And there's your warm coat you've been saving for.

MAMA: The coat I can get another time. But even so . . . (*She shakes her head.*)

CHRISTINE: You mean Nels can't go to High?

MAMA: Is not enough here. We do not want to have to go to the Bank, do we?

NELS: No, Mama, no. I'll work in Dillon's grocery after school.

(MAMA *writes a figure on the paper and starts to count on her fingers.* PAPA *looks over, and does the sum in his head.*)

PAPA: Is not enough.

MAMA (*finishing on her fingers against her collarbone*): No, is not enough.

PAPA (*taking his pipe out of his mouth and looking at it a long time*): I give up tobacco.

(MAMA *looks at him, almost speaks, then just touches his sleeve, writes another figure and starts on her fingers again.*)

CHRISTINE: I'll mind the Maxwell children Friday nights. Katrin can help me.

(MAMA *writes another figure.* PAPA *looks over—calculates again, nods with satisfaction.*)

MAMA (*triumphantly*): Is good! Is enough!

NELS: Gee! (*He moves beside* PAPA *and starts to play with a wire puzzle.*)

MAMA: We do not have to go to the Bank.

(DAGMAR *returns, without the cat.*)

DAGMAR (*hearing the last line*): Where is the Bank?

CHRISTINE (*leaving the table, cutting out the picture which she colored*): Downtown.

DAGMAR: What's it look like?

CHRISTINE: Just a building.

DAGMAR (*sitting on the bench, below the table*): Like a prison?

CHRISTINE (*sharply*): No, nothing like a prison.

DAGMAR: Well, then, why does Mama always say "We don't want to go to the Bank"?

CHRISTINE: Because . . . well, because no one ever wants to go to the Bank.

DAGMAR: Why not?

CHRISTINE: Because if we went to the Bank all the time, there'd be no money left there. And then if we couldn't pay our rent, they'd turn us out like Mrs. Jensen down the street.

DAGMAR: You mean, it's like saving some of your candy for tomorrow?

MAMA (*busy with coffee and cups at the stove and the dresser*): Yes, my Dagmar. Is exactly like saving your candy.

DAGMAR: But if . . . if all the other people go to the Bank, then there won't be any money left for us, either.

NELS (*kindly*): It isn't like that, Dagmar. Everyone can only get so much.

DAGMAR: How much?

NELS: However much you've got there . . . put away. You see, it's *our* money that we put there, to keep safe.

DAGMAR: When did we put it there?

NELS: I . . . I don't know when. A long time back, I guess. Wasn't it, Mama?

MAMA: Is enough about the Bank.

DAGMAR: How much money have we got in the Bank?

NELS: I don't know. How much, Mama?

MAMA: Enough. (*During the last speeches* AUNT TRINA

appears from the wings. She is a timid, mouselike little woman of about forty, with some prettiness about her. She wears her hat and coat and a pathetic feather boa. She comes up the street and knocks on the house door. MAMA, *hearing the knock.*) Was the door?

CHRISTINE (*quickly moving*): If it's the aunts, I'm going to my boodwar.

KATRIN (*rising, entering the scene*): And I'm going to my study.

MAMA (*stopping them*): You cannot run away. We must be polite to the aunts. (*She opens the door.*) Why, is Trina!

PAPA: Trina, and all by herself!

MAMA: Say good evening to Aunt Trina, children.

CHILDREN (*together*): Good evening, Aunt Trina.

TRINA: Good evening, children. How well they all look. (*She comes to the table.*)

MAMA: You have a feather boa. Is new. (*Inspecting it.*) Beautiful.

TRINA (*simpering a little*): It was a present.

MAMA (*smiling*): A present! Look, Lars. Trina has a present.

PAPA (*feeling it*): Is fine. (*He puts* TRINA's *hat, coat and boa on the chest under the window.*)

MAMA: Jenny and Sigrid don't come with you, Trina?

TRINA (*embarrassed*): No, I . . . I didn't tell them I was coming. I want to talk to you, Marta.

MAMA (*smiling*): So? Sit then, and we talk. (*She puts her in* PAPA's *chair, at the left of the table.*)

TRINA (*nervously agitated*): Could we talk alone?

MAMA: Alone?

TRINA: If you wouldn't mind.

MAMA: Children, you leave us alone a little. I call you. Dagmar, you go with Katrin.

KATRIN (*protesting*): Oh, but, Mama . . .

MAMA (*firmly*): Katrin, you take Dagmar!

KATRIN: Yes, Mama. (*Pushing* DAGMAR *resentfully.*) Come on.

(*The* CHILDREN *go out the back.*)

MAMA: Now—what is it, Trina?

TRINA (*looking down, embarrassed*): Marta . . .

MAMA (*helpfully*): Yes?

TRINA: Oh, no, I can't say it.

MAMA (*anxiously*): Trina, what is it?

TRINA: It's . . . something very personal.

MAMA: You want Lars should go outside?

TRINA: Would you mind, Lars? Just for a minute?

PAPA (*good-humoredly*): No, I go. I know what women's secrets are. (*Teasing.*) As your Uncle Chris say—"Vomen! Pff!"

MAMA: You have your pipe, Lars? Is fine night. (PAPA *takes
out his pipe—then lays it down.*) What is it?

PAPA. I forget. I give up tobacco.

MAMA: Is still some tobacco in your pouch? (PAPA *nods.*)
Then you do not give up tobacco till you have finish. You
give up *more* tobacco—not the tobacco you already have.

PAPA: Is not right, Marta. (*He pats her, takes his pipe, and
goes out, standing outside the house, under the lamppost,
and looking up at the stars, smoking.*)

MAMA: So, Trina. Now. What is it?

TRINA: Marta . . . I want to get married.

MAMA: You mean . . . you want to get married, or there is
someone you want to marry?

TRINA: There's someone I want to marry.

MAMA: Does *he* want to marry *you?*

TRINA (*sitting on bench*): He says he does.

MAMA (*delighted*): Trina! Is wonderful! (*She sits beside her.*)

TRINA (*crying a little*): I think it is.

MAMA: Who is?

TRINA: Mr. Thorkelson.

MAMA: From the funeral parlor? (TRINA *nods.* MAMA *nods,
speculatively, but with less enthusiasm.*)

TRINA: I know he isn't very handsome or . . . or tall. I know
it isn't what most people would think a very nice profession, but . . .

MAMA: You love him, Trina. (TRINA *nods ecstatically.*) Then
is good. (*She pats* TRINA's *hand.*)

17

TRINA: Marta, will you . . . will you help me tell the others?

MAMA: Oh . . . Jenny and Sigrid . . . they do not know?

TRINA: No. I was afraid they'd laugh at me. But if *you* tell them . . .

MAMA: Jenny will not like you tell me first.

TRINA (*desperately*): I can't help that. You've got to tell them not to laugh at me. If they laugh at me, I'll . . . I'll kill myself.

MAMA (*with decision*): Jenny and Sigrid will not laugh. I promise you, Trina.

TRINA: Oh, thank you, Marta. And . . . Uncle Chris?

MAMA (*with some seriousness*): Ah!

TRINA: Will you talk to him?

MAMA: It is Mr. Thorkelson who must talk to Uncle Chris. Always it is the husband who must talk to the head of the family.

TRINA: Yes. I know, but . . . well, Uncle Chris is so very frightening. He's so big and black, and he shouts so. And Mr. Thorkelson is (*gesturing a very small man*) . . . well, kind of timid, really.

MAMA (*gently*): But, Trina, if he is to be your husband, he must learn not to be timid. You do not want husband should be timid. *You* are timid. Is not good when *both* are timid. (*Then firmly.*) No! Jenny and Sigrid I speak to, but Mr. Thorkelson must go to Uncle Chris.

PAPA (*re-enters the house*): Marta, Trina, I do not want to interrupt your talk, but Jenny and Sigrid are coming.

TRINA (*alarmed*): Oh, dear! (*She rises, quickly.*)

PAPA: I see them get off the cable car. They come up the hill.

TRINA (*in a flurry*): I'd better go to your room for a minute.

(*She starts for the door, turns back, gets her things from the chest, and runs out, carrying them. Meanwhile, MAMA has been whispering the news to PAPA.*)

MAMA: The coffee is ready—I get more cups.

(*During the above*, AUNTS JENNY *and* SIGRID *have entered from the front.* JENNY *is a domineering woman in her fifties,* SIGRID, *whining and complaining.*)

SIGRID (*in the street*): Wait, Jenny, I must get my breath. This hill kills me every time I climb it.

JENNY: You climbed bigger hills than that in the old country.

SIGRID: I was a *girl* in the old country.

(*They march to the door and knock*—SIGRID *following* JENNY.)

MAMA (*opening the door to them*): Jenny. Sigrid. Is surprise. (*to* SIGRID) Where's Ole?

SIGRID: Working. He's always working. I never see anything of him at all.

MAMA (*crossing to the stove for coffeepot*): Is good to work.

SIGRID: It's good to see your husband once in a while, too. (*Sits near table.*)

JENNY (*no nonsense about her*): Has Trina been here? (*At the left of table.*)

MAMA (*at right of table*): Trina?

JENNY: She's gone somewhere. And she doesn't know anyone but *you*. . . .

MAMA: That is what *you* think.

JENNY: What do you mean by that?

MAMA: Give Lars your coat. I give you some coffee. Then we talk about Trina.

SIGRID (*as* PAPA *helps with coats*): She *has* been here?

MAMA: Yes, she has been here. (*Pouring coffee and passing cups.*)

JENNY: What did Trina want?

MAMA: She want to talk to me.

JENNY: What about?

MAMA: Marriage.

SIGRID: What?

MAMA (*pouring calmly*): Marriage. (*Passing* SIGRID's *cup.*) Trina wants to get married.

JENNY (*seated at left of table*): That's no news. Of course she wants to get married. Every old maid wants to get married. (*She rolls up her veil.*)

MAMA: There is someone who wants to marry Trina.

JENNY: Who'd want to marry Trina?

MAMA: Mr. Thorkelson.

SIGRID: Peter Thorkelson? Little Peter? (*She gestures a midget.*)

MAMA: He is not so little.

SIGRID: He's hardly bigger than my Arne—and Arne is not ten yet.

MAMA: So he is hardly bigger than your Arne. Does every husband have to be big man?

JENNY: Trina's making it up. That happens with old maids when they get to Trina's age.

MAMA (*firmly*): No, Jenny—it is true. Mr. Thorkelson wants to marry Trina.

JENNY (*changing her tactics slightly*): Mr. Thorkelson. She'd be the laughing stock. (*She laughs, rising and moving to the left.*)

MAMA (*moving to her*): Jenny, Trina is here. She will come in in a minute. This is serious for her. You will not laugh at her.

JENNY: I shall do what I please.

MAMA: No, Jenny, you will not.

JENNY: And why won't I?

MAMA: Because I will not let you.

JENNY: And how will you stop me?

MAMA: If you laugh at Trina, I will tell her of the time before your wedding when your husband try to run away.

SIGRID (*rising, intrigued*): What is that?

JENNY: Who told you that?

MAMA: I know.

SIGRID (*intrigued—stealing around and below the table*): Erik . . . tried to run away?

JENNY: It's not true.

MAMA: Then you do not mind if I tell Trina.

JENNY: Uncle Chris told you.

SIGRID (*tenaciously*): Tried to run away?

MAMA: It does not matter, Sigrid. Jenny will not laugh at Trina now. Nor will you! For if *you* laugh at her, I will tell her of your wedding night with Ole, when you cry all the time, and he send you back to Mother.

PAPA (*with sudden enjoyment*): This I do *not* know!

MAMA (*reprovingly*): Is no need you should know. I do not tell these stories for spite—only so they do not laugh at Trina. Call her, Lars. You like more coffee, Jenny? Sigrid?

(PAPA *goes to the back door, calls,* "Trina." MAMA *pours coffee for* JENNY. MR. HYDE *reappears and lets himself into the house. The* AUNTS *rise, standing in line with* MAMA.)

MR. HYDE (*seeing company*): Oh, I beg your pardon. I was not aware . . .

MAMA: Mr. Hyde, these are my sisters.

MR. HYDE: Enchanted, ladies, Madame, Madame. The Three Graces. (*He bows.* SIGRID *giggles coyly. He turns to leave the room.*) You will excuse me?

MAMA: Sure, Mr. Hyde.

MR. HYDE: I shall be in my room. (*He goes out.*)

JENNY (*moving to table again*): So *that's* your famous boarder. Has he paid you his rent yet? Three months he's been here, hasn't he?

MAMA (*at the other side of the table*): Is hard to ask. Surely he will pay soon.

JENNY (*with a snort*): Surely he won't! If I ran my boarding house the way you run this place . . .

PAPA: Maybe your boarders wouldn't always leave you.

JENNY: If Marta thinks she's going to get the warm coat she's always talking about out of *that* one . . .

MAMA: Jenny, Mr. Hyde is a gentleman. He reads to us aloud. Wonderful books . . . Longfellow, and Charles Dickens, and Fenimore Kipling. (TRINA *steals back.* MAMA, *seeing her hesitant in the doorway.*) Come in, Trina. The coffee

21

is getting cold. (*She pours a cup. There is a silence.*) I tell them.

JENNY: Why did you come to Marta first?

PAPA (*beside her*): She thought Marta would understand.

JENNY: Aren't Sigrid and I married women, too?

PAPA: You have been married longer than Marta. She think maybe you forget.

JENNY: What sort of a living does Mr. Thorkelson make?

TRINA (*on bench near table*): I . . . I haven't asked.

SIGRID (*at right of table*): Can he keep you?

TRINA: I don't think he would have asked me to marry him if he couldn't.

JENNY: Maybe he thinks you are going to keep *him*.

MAMA (*warningly*): Jenny!

SIGRID: Maybe he thinks Trina will have a dowry like the girls at home.

TRINA: Well, why shouldn't I? You all had dowries. . . .

JENNY: We were married in Norway. And our parents were alive. Where would your dowry come from, I'd like to know?

TRINA: Uncle Chris. He's head of the family.

JENNY: And who will ask him?

TRINA: He won't need asking. When Mr. Thorkelson goes to see him . . .

JENNY: Uncle Chris will eat him!

SIGRID (*giggling maliciously*): Little Peter and Uncle Chris!

MAMA (*with meaning*): Maybe Uncle Chris will tell him some family stories. He knows many, does Uncle Chris.

(*The* AUNTS *put down their cups, discomfited.*)

JENNY (*to change the subject*): Where are the children? Aren't we going to see them before we go?

PAPA: Of course. I'll call them. (*He goes to the door and does so, shouting.*) Children! Your aunts are *leaving!*

CHILDREN'S VOICES (*eagerly shouting back*): Coming, Papa!

I Remember Mama

JENNY: You come with us, Trina?

MAMA: I think maybe Trina like to stay here and listen to Mr. Hyde read to us. You like, Trina?

TRINA: Well, if I wouldn't be in the way. I asked Mr. Thorkelson to call for me here. He'll see me home. I'll help you with the coffee things. (*She takes the tray of coffee cups and goes into the pantry.*)

(KATRIN *returns from her study. She carries her diary.* DAGMAR *follows her, and behind them,* CHRISTINE.)

KATRIN *and* DAGMAR (*curtseying*): Good evening, Aunt Sigrid. Good evening, Aunt Jenny.

(CHRISTINE *sketches a perfunctory curtsey without speaking.*)

JENNY: Where have *you* all been hiding yourselves?

DAGMAR (*going into the pantry*): We've been in Christine's boodwar.

JENNY: Her *what?*

MAMA: Christine makes the little closet into a boudoir. I give her those bead portieres, Jenny, that you lend us when we come from the old country.

SIGRID: And what does she do there?

CHRISTINE (*impertinently*): What people usually do in boudoirs.

MAMA: Christine, that is rude. It is her little place to herself.

(NELS *enters.*)

NELS: Hello, Aunt Sigrid. Hello, Aunt Jenny.

SIGRID (*shaking hands*): Good evening, Nels. My, how tall he is getting!

MAMA (*proudly*): Yes, is almost as tall as his Papa.

(NELS *sits on the chest under the windows.*)

23

SIGRID: He looks to me as if he was outgrowing his strength. Dagmar was looking pale, too. (DAGMAR *returns now, carrying the cat again.* SIGRID, *jumping.*) Goodness, what a horrid-looking cat.

DAGMAR: She's not. She's beautiful.

PAPA: Is her new friend. She goes with Dagmar everywhere.

CHRISTINE (*seated, above table*): She does. First thing you know, she'll have the cat sleeping with her.

DAGMAR (*eagerly*): Oh, Mama, can I? Can I, Mama? (*She comes to the bench and sits.*)

JENNY: Certainly not. Don't you know a cat draws breath from a sleeping child? You wouldn't want to wake up some morning *smothered,* would you?

DAGMAR: I wouldn't care. Elizabeth can have *all* my breath! (*She blows into the cat's face.*) There!

JENNY (*putting on gloves*): Elizabeth—what a very silly name for a cat.

NELS (*rising*): It's a very silly name for *that* cat. It's a Tom.

MAMA: Nels, how you know?

NELS: I looked!

DAGMAR: How can you tell?

NELS: You can.

DAGMAR: But how?

MAMA (*quickly warning*): Nels, you do not say how!

NELS (*to* DAGMAR): So you'd better think up another name for him.

DAGMAR: I won't. He's Elizabeth. And he's going to *stay* Elizabeth.

PAPA: We could call him *Uncle* Elizabeth!

DAGMAR (*laughing delightedly*): Uncle Elizabeth! Do you hear, Elizabeth? You're called *Uncle* Elizabeth now!

JENNY: Such foolishness! Well, good-by, all. Marta. Lars.

(*Good-bys are exchanged all around, the* CHILDREN *curtseying formally.*)

MAMA: Good-by, Jenny. Good-by, Sigrid. Nels, you go tell Mr. Hyde we are ready for the reading.

(NELS *goes off. The* AUNTS *leave and* MAMA *stands in the doorway, waving good-by.*)

SIGRID (*as they go*): Well, I never thought we'd live to see Trina get married.

JENNY: She's not married yet. She's got Uncle Chris to deal with first.

(*They disappear into wings.*)

MAMA (*returning to the room and calling into the pantry*): Trina, they have gone. Dagmar, you put Elizabeth out for the night now.

DAGMAR (*correcting her*): *Uncle* Elizabeth!

MAMA: *Uncle* Elizabeth. (DAGMAR *goes out into the pantry with the cat.* TRINA *comes in as* MR. HYDE *and* NELS *return.*) Mr. Hyde, this is my sister Trina.

MR. HYDE (*bowing*): Enchanted!

MAMA (*seating herself at the table*): Mr. Hyde reads to us "The Tales From Two Cities." Is beautiful story. But sad.

TRINA (*brightly*): I like sad stories. (*She gets out her handkerchief.*)

(*The whole family group themselves around the table,* MAMA *near the table in her old chair—*PAPA *behind her.* TRINA *at one side behind table,* NELS *on the other side behind table.* DAGMAR *returning and seating herself on the floor in front of* MAMA. MR. HYDE *takes the armchair at left of table.* CHRISTINE *sits on the floor in front of table.* KATRIN *is on the steps.*)

MR. HYDE: Tonight, I would like to finish it.

MAMA: Is good.

MR. HYDE: Are you ready?

CHILDREN: Yes, please, Mr. Hyde.

MR. HYDE: I will go on from where we left off. (*He starts to read.*) "In the black prison of the Conciergerie, the doomed of the day awaited their fate. They were in number as the weeks of the year. Fifty-two were to roll that afternoon on the life-tide of the City to the boundless, everlasting sea. . . ."

(*The lights dim down slowly, leaving spots on* KATRIN *and* MR. HYDE *only.*)

KATRIN: I don't think I shall ever forget that night. It was almost midnight when he came to the end, and none of us had noticed. MR. HYDE (*reading from the last page*): "It is a far, far better thing that I do than I have ever done; it is a far, far better rest that I go to than I have ever known." (*He closes the book.*) "The End."

(*The turntable revolves in again.* KATRIN *rises from the step and crosses to her desk on the turntable.*)

KATRIN: I wrote in my diary that night before I went to bed. (*She reads aloud from it.*) "Tonight Mr. Hyde finished *The Tale of Two Cities*. The closing chapters are indeed superb. How beautiful a thing is self-sacrifice. I wish there were someone *I* could die for." (*She sits looking out front.*) Mr. Hyde read us all kinds of books. He thrilled us with *Treasure Island* and terrified us with "The Hound of the Baskervilles." I can still remember the horror in his voice as he read. . . .

MR. HYDE (*still on the main stage in his spot, reading*): "Dr. Mortimer looked strangely at us for an instant, and his voice sank almost to a whisper as he answered: 'Mr. Holmes, they were the footprints of a gigantic *hound!*'" (*He closes the book.*) We will continue tomorrow night. If you are interested.

KATRIN (*looking out front*): If we were interested! You

couldn't have kept us from it. It meant a lot to Mama, too, because Nels stopped going nights to the street corner to hang about with the neighborhood boys. The night they got into trouble for breaking into Mr. Dillon's store, Nels was home with us. And sometimes Mr. Hyde read us poetry. "The Lady of the Lake" . . . and the "Rime of the Ancient Mariner."

MR. HYDE (*reading*):

> "About, about, in reel and rout
> The death-fires danced at night.
> The water, like a witch's oils,
> Burnt green and blue and white."

(*His spot goes out, and the traveler curtains close on the kitchen scene.*)

KATRIN: There were many nights I couldn't sleep for the way he had set my imagination dancing. (*Reading from her diary again.*) "What a wonderful thing is literature, transporting us to realms unknown." (*To herself.*) And all the time my schoolteacher kept telling me that I ought to write about things I knew. I did write a piece for her once about Uncle Chris, and she said it wasn't nice to write like that about a member of one's own family. Papa called Mama's Uncle Chris a black Norwegian, because of his dark hair and fierce mustache, but there were others in the family who claimed that he was black in a different way. The aunts, for example.

(*Spot goes up on turntable, representing* JENNY's *kitchen.* JENNY *and* TRINA *are discovered.* JENNY *is rolling pastry.* TRINA *is crocheting.*)

JENNY: Black! I'll say he's black. Black in his heart. Cursing and swearing. . . .

TRINA: Marta says that's only because it hurts him to walk.

JENNY: Rubbish. I know all about his limp and the accident

back in the old country—but has anyone ever heard him complain? Marta's always making excuses for him.

TRINA: I know . . . but he *is* good to the children. All those oranges he's always sending them. . . .

JENNY: Oranges! What good is oranges? Turn 'em yellow. They're the only things he's ever been known to give away, anyway. He's got other uses for his money.

TRINA: What you mean?

JENNY: Bottles! And that woman he lives with!

TRINA: He *says* she's his housekeeper.

JENNY: Well, he couldn't very well come right out and call her what she is, could he? Though *I* will one of these days. And to his face, too.

(SIGRID *comes through the curtains. She crosses to* JENNY *and* TRINA.)

SIGRID: Jenny. Trina. What do you think? What do you think Uncle Chris has done now?

TRINA: What?

JENNY: Tell us.

SIGRID: You know my little Arne's knee—that fall he had two months ago? The man at the drugstore said it was only a bruise, but today it was hurting him again, so I left him home when I went to do the marketing. I asked Mrs. Schultz next door to keep an eye on him, and who should turn up, not ten minutes after I'd gone, but Uncle Chris. And what do you think?

JENNY: Well, tell us, if you're going to. Don't keep *asking* us.

SIGRID: He took one look at Arne's knee, bundled him into that rattletrap old automobile of his, and rushed him straight off to the hospital. I've just come from there . . . and what do you think? They've operated! They've got him in plaster of Paris!

JENNY: Without consulting you?

SIGRID: It seems the doctor is a friend of his . . . that's why he did it. No, this time he's gone too far. To put a child

28

of Arne's age through all that pain. They wouldn't even let me *see* Arne. I'm going to tell Uncle Chris exactly what I think of him. . .

JENNY: That's right.

SIGRID: I'm going to tell him right now. (*Weakening a little.*) Come with me, Jenny.

JENNY: Well, I . . . No, I can't leave my baking.

SIGRID: You must, Jenny. We must stand together. You come, too, Trina, and ask about your dowry. *Make* him give it to you.

TRINA: Oh, but . . . Marta said Mr. Thorkelson should do that. . . .

JENNY: Well, then, go and get Mr. Thorkelson. Go down to the mortuary and get him now. Sigrid is right. We girls have got to stand together!

(*Blackout. Turntable revolves out.*)

KATRIN (*at her desk*): Nobody knew where Uncle Chris lived. That was part of the mystery about him. He used to roam up and down the state buying up farms and ranches that had gone to pieces, and bullying them back into prosperity. Then he'd sell at a profit and move on again. Two or three times a year he'd descend on the city in his automobile and come roaring and stamping into our house.

(*Her light dims. The sound of a very old and noisy Ford car changing gears is heard in the distance. A grinding and screaming as it comes to a standstill. Then UNCLE CHRIS' VOICE, shouting.*)

UNCLE CHRIS' VOICE: Marta! Lars! Children—vere are you?

(*The curtains part on the kitchen again. Outside in the street is UNCLE CHRIS' car—an antique model. A woman is seated beside the empty driver's seat. UNCLE CHRIS is knocking on the house door. He is an elderly, powerful, swarthy man*

29

with a limp. In the kitchen, NELS *and* CHRISTINE *are cowering.*)

UNCLE CHRIS: Marta! Lars!

CHRISTINE (*scared*): It's Uncle Chris.

NELS (*equally so*): I know.

CHRISTINE: What'll we do?

UNCLE CHRIS: Is nobody home? Hey, there—is nobody home? (*Banging on the door.*) Hey—someone—answer the door. (*He tries the door handle, it opens and he strides, limpingly, in. He has a strong accent, and uses the Norwegian pronunciation of the children's names.*) So, vat is—you do not answer the door? You do not hear me calling? (*The* CHILDREN *cower silently.*) I say, you do not hear me calling? I do not call loud enough?

CHRISTINE: Y-yes, Uncle Chris.

UNCLE CHRIS: Which yes? Yes, you do not hear me—or yes I do not call loud enough?

NELS: We heard you, Uncle Chris.

UNCLE CHRIS: Then why you do not come?

NELS: We . . . we were just going to.

(KATRIN *has left her desk and come up the steps.*)

UNCLE CHRIS: Let me look at you. You too, Katrinë, do not stand there—come and let me look at you. (*They line up as though for inspection. He thumps* NELS *between the shoulder blades.*) Stand tall! (*They all straighten up.*) Um-hum. By the dresser, where the marks are. (NELS *goes to the wall by the dresser.* UNCLE CHRIS *compares his mark with the previous one—and makes a new one on the wall, writing by it.*) Two inches. Two inches in . . . (*examining the date*) six months. Is good. Christinë. (CHRISTINE *replaces* NELS.) Show me your teeth. (*She does so.*) You brush them goot? (*She nods.*) Nils, there is a box of oranges in the automobile. You fetch them in. (NELS *goes out.*

UNCLE CHRIS *measures* CHRISTINE.) Where is the little von? Dagmar?

KATRIN: She's sick, Uncle Chris.

UNCLE CHRIS (*arrested*): Sick? What is the matter with her?

KATRIN: It's her ear. She's had an earache for two days. Bad earache. Mama sent for the doctor.

UNCLE CHRIS: Goot doctor? What he say?

KATRIN: He's in there now. (*She points off. Meanwhile* CHRISTINE *has remained standing by the wall, afraid to move.*)

UNCLE CHRIS: I go in. (*He starts to the door, but* MAMA *and* DR. JOHNSON *come into the room as he does so. During this* NELS *has gone to the car, and with nervous smiles at the woman seated by the driver's seat, has heaved out a huge box of oranges. He returns with the oranges during the ensuing scene.*)

MAMA (*greeting him*): Uncle Chris.

UNCLE CHRIS: How is with Dagmar?

MAMA: Is bad. Doctor, this is my uncle, Mr. Halvorsen.

DOCTOR: How do you do, sir? (*He goes for his hat and bag which are on the bench in front of the window.*)

UNCLE CHRIS: What is with the child?

DOCTOR: We must get her to a hospital. At once. We'll have to operate.

MAMA: Operate?

DOCTOR: I'm afraid so.

MAMA: Can wait? Until my husband comes home from work?

DOCTOR: I'm afraid not. Her best chance is for us to operate immediately.

MAMA (*after a second*): We go. (*She goes to the dresser for the Little Bank.*)

UNCLE CHRIS (*who has watched her decision with approval, turns to the doctor, moving to him*): What is with the child?

DOCTOR: I'm afraid it's a mastoid.

UNCLE CHRIS: Ah . . . then you operate immediately.

DOCTOR (*resenting this*): That's what I said.

31

UNCLE CHRIS: Immediately!

MAMA (*who has poured the contents of the Little Bank onto the table*): Doctor . . . is enough?

DOCTOR (*at table*): I was thinking of the County Hospital.

MAMA: No. No. We pay. Is enough?

KATRIN: If there isn't, we can go to the Bank.

CHRISTINE: We've got a bank account.

MAMA: Is enough without we go to the Bank, Doctor? My husband is carpenter. Make good money.

UNCLE CHRIS: If there is need of money, *I* pay.

DOCTOR (*mainly in dislike of* UNCLE CHRIS): It'll be all right. We'll take her to the clinic. You pay what you can afford.

UNCLE CHRIS: Goot. Goot. I have a patient there already. My nephew, Arne. They operate this morning on his knee.

DOCTOR: Are you a physician, sir?

UNCLE CHRIS: I am better physician than most doctors. Nils, there, my other nephew, he become doctor when he grow up.

(NELS, *who has just returned, looks up, surprised.*)

DOCTOR (*chilly*): Oh, indeed . . . very interesting. Well, now, if you will have the child at the clinic in . . . shall we say an hour's time. . . .

UNCLE CHRIS (*striding in front of table*): The child will be at the clinic in *ten minutes'* time. I haf my automobile.

DOCTOR: I can hardly make arrangements in ten minutes.

UNCLE CHRIS (*at table*): *I* make arrangements. I know doctors.

MAMA: Uncle Chris, Dr. Johnson arrange. He is good doctor.

DOCTOR (*ironically*): Thank you, Madam.

MAMA: You go, Doctor. We come.

DOCTOR: Very well, in an hour, then. And Dagmar will be well taken care of, I promise you. I will do the operation myself.

UNCLE CHRIS: I watch.

DOCTOR: You will do no such thing, sir.

UNCLE CHRIS: Always I watch operations. I am head of family.

DOCTOR: I allow no one to attend my operations.

UNCLE CHRIS: Are so bad?

DOCTOR (*to* MAMA): Mrs. Hanson, if I am to undertake this operation and the care of your child, it must be on the strict understanding that this gentleman does not come near either me or my patient.

MAMA: Yes, Doctor, I talk to him. . . . You go to hospital now, please.

DOCTOR: Very well. But you understand . . . nowhere near me, or I withdraw from the case. (*He goes.*)

UNCLE CHRIS: I go see Dagmar.

MAMA (*stopping him above table*): Wait. Uncle Chris, is kind of you, but Dagmar is sick. You frighten her.

UNCLE CHRIS: I frighten her?

MAMA: Yes, Uncle Chris. You frighten everyone. . . .

UNCLE CHRIS (*amazed*): I?

MAMA: Everyone but me. Even the girls. . . . Jenny, Sigrid, Trina . . . they are frightened of you.

UNCLE CHRIS: The girls! Vomen! Pff!

MAMA: And the children, too. So Nels and I get Dagmar. You drive us to hospital in your automobile, but you do not frighten Dagmar. And you leave doctor alone. Dr. Johnson is *fine* doctor. You come with me, Nels. You carry Dagmar.

(NELS *and* MAMA *go out.* UNCLE CHRIS *stands in amazement and puzzlement. The* TWO GIRLS *watch him, hardly daring to move.*)

UNCLE CHRIS (*coming to table*): Is true? I frighten you? Christinë . . . Katrinë . . . you are frightened of me? Come, I ask you. Tell me the truth. You are frightened of me?

KATRIN (*tremulously*): A . . . a little, Uncle Chris.

UNCLE CHRIS (*on bench*): No? And you, Christinë?

CHRISTINE: Y . . . yes, Uncle Chris.

UNCLE CHRIS: But Nils . . . Nils is a boy . . . he is not frightened?

CHRISTINE: Not . . . not as much as we are. . . .

UNCLE CHRIS: But he is frightened?

CHRISTINE: Yes, Uncle Chris.

UNCLE CHRIS (*with a roar*): But why? What is there to be frightened of? I am your Uncle Chris . . . why do I frighten you?

CHRISTINE: I don't know.

UNCLE CHRIS: But that is bad. Very bad. The aunts, yes, I like to frighten them. (*The* GIRLS *giggle.*) That makes you laugh. (*He crosses to them.*) You do not like the aunts? Come, tell me. You do not like the aunts? Say!

KATRIN: Not . . . very much, Uncle Chris.

UNCLE CHRIS: And which do you not like the most? Jenny. . . Sigrid . . . Trina. . . . Tell me—huh?

KATRIN: I think I like Aunt Jenny least. She's so . . . so bossy.

CHRISTINE: I can't stand Aunt Sigrid. Always whining and complaining.

UNCLE CHRIS (*with a great roar of laughter*): Is good. Jenny, bossy. Sigrid, whining. Is true! But your Mama, she is different. And she cook goot. The aunts, they cannot cook at all. Only you do not tell your Mama we have talked of them so. It is a secret, for us. Then you cannot be frightened of me any more . . . when we have secret. I tell you my secret, too. *I* do not like the aunts. And so that they do not bother me, I frighten them and shout at them. You I do not shout at if you are goot children, and clean your teeth goot, and eat your oranges. (*He takes out a snuffbox and partakes of its contents.*)

(*As he says "You I do not shout at," the posse of* AUNTS *appears, in outdoor clothes, accompanied by* MR. THORKELSON, *a terrified little man. They come in at the left and start up to the house.*)

SIGRID (*stopping in the street*): Jenny. Do you see what I see? A woman, in his automobile.

JENNY: How shameful!

SIGRID: Ought we to bow?

JENNY: Bow? To a woman like that? We cut her. That's what we do. I'll show you. (*She strides to the front door, ignoring the woman in the car, and enters the house. The others follow.* JENNY, *entering*.) Uncle Chris, Sigrid has something to say to you.

SIGRID (*with false bravery*): Uncle Chris, you took Arne to the hospital. . . .

UNCLE CHRIS (*at table*): Yes, I take Arne to the hospital. And now we take Dagmar to the hospital, so you do not clutter up the place.

JENNY (*on the other side of table*): What's the matter with Dagmar?

CHRISTINE: It's her ear. Dr. Johnson's going to operate.

SIGRID (*catching her favorite word*): Operate? This is some more of Uncle Chris' doing. Did you hear what he did to Arne?

UNCLE CHRIS (*turning on her*): Sigrid, you are a whining old fool, and you get out of here. . . .

SIGRID (*deflating*): We'd better go, Jenny. . . .

JENNY (*stoutly*): No . . . there has been enough of these high-handed goings-on. . . .

UNCLE CHRIS: And you, Jenny . . . you are a bossy old fool, and you get out of here, too, and we take Dagmar to hospital. (NELS *enters, carrying* DAGMAR *in his arms, wrapped in a blanket.*) You got her goot, Nils?

NELS: Sure, Uncle Chris.

UNCLE CHRIS: We go.

JENNY (*getting between him and the door*): No! You are going to hear me out. (*Weakening.*) That is, you are going to hear *Sigrid* out. . . .

UNCLE CHRIS: If you do not get out of the way of the door before I count three, I trow you out. And Sigrid, too, as big as she is. Von. . . . (SIGRID *moves.*) Two. . . . (JENNY *moves. He looks back at the children with a wink and a smile.*) Is goot! You put her in back of the car, Nils.

(NELS *goes out carrying* DAGMAR, *and lifts her into the car.* UNCLE CHRIS *follows and starts cranking.*)

TRINA (*running to the door after him, with* MR. THORKELSON): But, Uncle Chris, I want to introduce Mr. Thorkelson. . . . (*But* UNCLE CHRIS *ignores her, continuing to crank. She returns crestfallen into the room with* MR. THORKELSON. MAMA *re-enters, wearing hat and coat and carrying a cheap little overnight case.*)

MAMA: Jenny . . . Trina, we go to hospital. (*She goes to* KATRIN *and* CHRISTINE.) You will be good children until Mama comes home?

THE GIRLS: Sure, Mama.

UNCLE CHRIS (*calling from the car*): Marta, we go!

MAMA (*calling back*): I come! (*She turns to the children again.*) There is milk in the cooler, and fruit and cookies for your lunch.

CHRISTINE: We'll be all right, Mama. Don't worry.

MAMA: I go now. (*She starts for the door.*)

SIGRID (*stopping her*): Marta!

MAMA: What is it?

SIGRID: You *can't* go in his automobile.

MAMA: Why not?

UNCLE CHRIS (*calling again*): Marta, we go!

MAMA: I come!

SIGRID: Because . . . because *she's* in it. The . . . the woman!

MAMA: So it will kill me, or Dagmar, if we sit in the automobile with her? I have see her. She looks nice woman. (*Calling off, as she goes.*) I come!

UNCLE CHRIS: We go! (MAMA *climbs into the rear of the car, which backs noisily off during the next speeches.*)

MR. THORKELSON (*in a low whisper to* TRINA): Is that woman his wife?

TRINA (*nervously*): Yes. . . .

MR. THORKELSON: Yes?

TRINA (*whispering back, loudly*): No!

JENNY (*to the* GIRLS): Don't stand there gaping like that, girls. (*She shoos them into the pantry.*) Go away! Go away! (*The* GIRLS *go.* JENNY *turns and sees the disappearing car through the open door.*) Oh! They've gone! We go after them! SIGRID, you lead the way! (*She gives* SIGRID *a push and the four go out, with* JENNY *dragging* MR. THORKELSON, *and* TRINA *following. Blackout. The travelers close.*)

(*Spot on turntable, representing a kind of closet room. Roller skates hanging on the wall.* KATRIN *is seated on the floor and* CHRISTINE *on a small kitchen stepladder with glasses of milk, and cookies on plates.*)

KATRIN: How long have they been gone now?

CHRISTINE: About three hours. And I wish you wouldn't keep asking that.

KATRIN: How long do operations take? I heard Aunt Sigrid telling about Mrs. Bergman who was five hours on the table.

CHRISTINE: Aunt Sigrid's friends always have everything worse than anyone else. And it gets worse each time she tells it, too.

(KATRIN *smiles—drinks some milk and eats a cookie.*)

KATRIN (*with a certain melancholy enjoyment*): The house feels lonesome, doesn't it—without Mama? It's like in a book. "The sisters sat huddled in the empty house, waiting for the verdict that was to spell life or death to the little family."

CHRISTINE: Oh, don't talk such nonsense.

KATRIN: It's not nonsense.

CHRISTINE: It is, too. In the first place, we're not a little family. We're a big one. And who said anything about life or death, anyway? Always trying to make everything so dramatic!

KATRIN: Well, it *is* dramatic.

CHRISTINE: It's not. It's just . . . well, worrying. But you don't have to make a tragedy out of it.

(*Pause*)

KATRIN: You're not eating anything.

CHRISTINE: I know that.

KATRIN: You're not drinking your milk, either. Aren't you hungry?

CHRISTINE: No. And you wouldn't be, either, if you'd any feeling for Mama and Dagmar, instead of just heartlessly sitting there eating and enjoying making a story out of it.

KATRIN: Oh, Chris, I'm not heartless. I do have feeling for them. I can't help it if it goes into words like that. Everything always does with me. But it doesn't mean I don't feel it. And I think we *ought* to eat. I think Mama would want us to.

(*Pause.* CHRISTINE *hesitates a moment, then takes a bite of a cookie. They both eat in silence. The light dims on them, and the turntable revolves out. The travelers part on the hospital corridor. A wall runs diagonally up from the front of the main stage towards the back. In front of this is a bench, on which* MAMA *and* NELS *are sitting, holding hands, looking off. Below the bench is the elevator, and above the bench, set back a little, is a closet for brooms and mops, etc. The reception desk, at which a nurse is sitting, is towards the front. The wall goes up into darkness, and behind the nurse's desk is darkness. As the curtains open, there is a hubbub down by the nurse's desk, where the* AUNTS *are haranguing* UNCLE CHRIS. MR. THORKELSON *stands slightly behind them.*)

SIGRID: But, Uncle Chris, I tell you I must see him!

UNCLE CHRIS (*storming*): You don't understand English? No visitors for twenty-four hours.

SIGRID: But *you've* seen him.

UNCLE CHRIS: I am not visitor. I am exception.

SIGRID: Well, then, his mother should be an exception, too. I'll see the doctor.

UNCLE CHRIS: *I* have seen doctor. I have told him you are not goot for Arne.

SIGRID: Not good for my own son. . . .

UNCLE CHRIS: Not goot at all. You cry over him. I go now. (*He starts to do so, but* JENNY *pushes* TRINA *forward.*)

TRINA (*with desperate courage*): Uncle Chris . . . Uncle Chris . . . I *must* speak to you.

UNCLE CHRIS: I have business.

TRINA: But, Uncle Chris . . . I want to get married.

UNCLE CHRIS: Well, then, *get* married. (*He starts off again.*)

TRINA: No, wait, I . . . I want to marry Mr. Thorkelson. Here. (*She produces him from behind her.*) Peter, this is Uncle Chris. Uncle Chris, this is Mr. Thorkelson.

UNCLE CHRIS (*staring at him*): So?

MR. THORKELSON: How are you, sir?

UNCLE CHRIS: Busy. (*He turns again.*)

TRINA: Please, Uncle Chris . . .

UNCLE CHRIS: What is? You want to marry him? All right, marry him. I have other things to think about.

TRINA (*eagerly*): Then . . . then you give your permission?

UNCLE CHRIS: Yes, I give my permission. If you want to be a fool, I cannot stop you.

TRINA (*gratefully*): Oh, thank you, Uncle Chris.

UNCLE CHRIS: So. Is all?

TRINA (*anxious to escape*): Yes, I think is all.

JENNY (*firmly*): No!!

UNCLE CHRIS: No? (MR. THORKELSON *is pushed forward again.*)

MR. THORKELSON: Well, there . . . there was a little something else. You see, Trina mentioned . . . well, in the old country it was always usual . . . and after all, we do all come from the old country. . . .

UNCLE CHRIS: What is it? What you want?

MR. THORKELSON: Well, it's a question of Trina's . . . well, not to mince matters . . . her dowry.

UNCLE CHRIS (*shouting*): Her what?

MR. THORKELSON (*very faintly*): Her dowry . . .

UNCLE CHRIS: Ah. Her dowry. Trina wants a dowry. She is forty-two years old. . . .

TRINA (*interrupting*): No, Uncle Chris. . . .

UNCLE CHRIS (*without pausing*): And it is not enough she gets husband. She must have dowry.

NURSE (*who has been trying to interrupt, now bangs on her desk and moves toward them.*): Please! Would you mind going and discussing your family matters somewhere else? This is a hospital, not a marriage bureau.

UNCLE CHRIS (*after glaring at the* NURSE, *turns to* MR. THORKELSON): You come into waiting room. I talk to you about dowry. (*He strides off into the darkness behind the* NURSE'S *desk.* MR. THORKELSON, *with an appealing look back at* TRINA, *follows him. The* AUNTS *now remember* MAMA, *sitting on the bench, and cross to her.*)

JENNY: Did you hear that, Marta?

MAMA (*out of a trance*): What?

JENNY: Uncle Chris.

MAMA: No, I do not hear. I wait for doctor. Is two hours since they take Dagmar to operating room. More.

SIGRID: Two hours? That's nothing! When Mrs. Bergman had her gall bladder removed she was *six* hours on the table.

MAMA: Sigrid, I do not want to hear about Mrs. Bergman. I do not want to hear about anything. I wait for doctor. Please, you go away now. You come this evening.

TRINA: But, Marta, you can't stay here all by yourself.

MAMA: I have Nels. Please, Trina . . . I wait for doctor . . . you go now.

JENNY: We go.

TRINA: Oh, but I must wait for Peter and Uncle Chris. . . .

JENNY: We'll go next door and have some coffee. Sigrid, do you have money?

SIGRID: Yes, I . . . I have a little.

JENNY: Good. Then I treat you. We'll be next door if you want us, Marta.

(MAMA *nods without looking at them, her eyes still fixed on the elevator door. The* AUNTS *leave, going down the steps from the stage as though they were the hospital steps, and for a moment the stage is quiet. Then a scrubwoman enters, carrying a mop and pail, which she puts into the closet, and then leaves. The elevator door opens and a doctor in white coat comes out, followed by an orderly, carrying a tray of dressings. They disappear behind the desk.* MAMA *rises, agitatedly, looking after them. Then* DR. JOHNSON *returns, carrying his hat and bag. He sees* MAMA *and crosses to her.*)

DOCTOR: Oh, Mrs. Hanson. . . .

MAMA: Doctor. . . .

DOCTOR: Well, Dagmar's fine. She came through it beautifully. She's back in bed now, sleeping off the anesthetic.

MAMA: Thank you, Doctor, (*She shakes hands with him.*)

DOCTOR: You're very welcome.

MAMA: Is good of you, Doctor. (*She shakes hands with him again.*) Where is she? I go to her now.

DOCTOR: Oh, I'm sorry, but I'm afraid that's against the rules. You shall see her tomorrow.

MAMA: Tomorrow? But, Doctor, she is so little. When she wakes she will be frightened.

DOCTOR: The nurse will take care of her. Excellent care. You needn't worry. You see, for the first twenty-four hours, clinic patients aren't allowed to see visitors. The wards must be kept quiet.

MAMA: I will not make a sound.

DOCTOR: I'm very sorry. Tomorrow. And now . . . (*He glances at his watch.*) Good afternoon. (*He puts on his hat and goes out, down the steps and off.* MAMA *stands still a moment, looking after him.*)

MAMA: Come, Nels. We go find Dagmar.

NELS: But, Mama, the doctor said . . .

MAMA: We find Dagmar. (*She looks vaguely around her. Then goes to the* NURSE's *desk.*) You tell me, please, where I can find my daughter?

NURSE: What name?

MAMA: Dagmar.

NELS: Dagmar Hanson.

NURSE (*looking at her record book*): Hanson, Ward A. Along there. (*She points upstage.* MAMA *starts to go up.*) Oh, just a moment. (MAMA *returns.*) When did she come in?

MAMA: This morning. They just finish operation.

NURSE: Oh, well, then, I'm afraid you can't see her today. No visitors for the first twenty-four hours.

MAMA: Am not visitor. I am her Mama.

NURSE: I'm sorry, but it's against the rules.

MAMA: Just for one minute. Please.

NURSE: I'm sorry, but it's against the rules.

(MAMA *stands staring.* NELS *touches her arm. She looks at him, nods, trying to smile, then turns and walks out with him.*)

MAMA: We must think of some way.

NELS: Mama, they'll let you see her tomorrow. They said so.

MAMA: If I don't see her today how will I know that all is well with her? What can I tell Papa when he comes home from work?

NELS: The nurses will look after her, Mama. Would you like to come next door for some coffee?

MAMA (*shaking her head*): We go home. We have coffee at home. But I must see Dagmar today. (*She plods off with* NELS.)

(*The travelers close. Spot goes up on turntable.* UNCLE CHRIS *and* MR. THORKELSON *are seated on a bench and chair, as in a waiting room. A table with a potted plant is between them. A clock on the wall points to 2:30.*)

UNCLE CHRIS (*on bench*): Well, it comes then to this. You love my niece, Trina? (MR. THORKELSON, *very scared, gulps and nods.*) You want to marry her? (MR. THORKELSON *nods again.*) You are in position to support her? (MR. THORKELSON *nods again.*) Why, then, you want dowry? (*No answer. He shouts.*) What for you want dowry?

MR. THORKELSON: Well . . . well, it would be a nice help. And it is customary.

UNCLE CHRIS: Is not customary. Who give dowries? Parents. Why? Because they are so glad they will not have to support their daughters any more, they pay money. I do not support Trina. I do not care if Trina gets married. Why then should I pay to have her married?

MR. THORKELSON: I never thought of it like that.

UNCLE CHRIS: Is insult to girl to pay dowry. If I do not give dowry, will you still marry Trina?

MR. THORKELSON: I . . . I don't know.

UNCLE CHRIS: You don't know? You don't know? You think I let Trina marry a man who will not take her without dowry?

MR. THORKELSON: No, I suppose you wouldn't.

UNCLE CHRIS: What kind of man would that be? I ask you, what kind of man would that be?

MR. THORKELSON (*fascinated—helpless*): Well, not a very nice kind of man.

UNCLE CHRIS: And are you that kind of man?

MR. THORKELSON: I . . . I don't think so.

UNCLE CHRIS (*conclusively*): Then you don't want dowry!!

MR. THORKELSON (*giving up*): No, I . . . I guess I don't.

UNCLE CHRIS (*slapping his back*): Goot. Goot. You are goot man. I like you. I give you my blessing. And I send you vedding present. I send you box of oranges!

43

(*While he is boisterously shaking* MR. THORKELSON's *hand,
blackout. Turntable revolves out. The curtain opens on the
kitchen. It is empty.* MAMA *and* NELS *come up the hill and
let themselves into the house. There is silence as they take
off their hats and coats.*)

MAMA (*after a moment*): Where are the girls?
NELS: I guess they're upstairs. (*Goes to back door and calls.*)
  Chris! Katrin!
GIRLS' VOICES: Coming!
NELS: Shall I make you some coffee? (MAMA *shakes her
  head.*) You said you'd have coffee when you got home.
MAMA: Later. First I must think.
NELS: Mama, please don't worry like that. Dagmar's all right.
  You know she's all right.

(*The* GIRLS *come in.*)

CHRISTINE (*trying to be casual*): Well, Mama, everything all
  right?
MAMA (*nodding*): Is all right. You have eaten?
KATRIN: Yes, Mama.
MAMA: You drink your milk?
CHRISTINE: Yes, Mama.
MAMA: Is good.
CHRISTINE (*seeing her face*): Mama, something's the matter.
KATRIN (*overdramatically*): Mama, Dagmar's not—? She isn't
  —? Mama!
MAMA: No, Dagmar is fine. The doctor say she is fine. (*She
  rises.*) What is time?
NELS: It's three o'clock.
MAMA: Three hours till Papa come home. (*She looks around
  and then goes slowly into the pantry.*)
KATRIN: Nels, what is it? There *is* something the matter.
NELS: They wouldn't let Mama see Dagmar. It's a rule of the
  hospital.

CHRISTINE: But Dagmar's all right?

NELS: Oh, yes, she's all right.

CHRISTINE (*impatiently*): Well, then . . . !

NELS: But Mama's very upset. She started talking to me in Norwegian in the street-car.

KATRIN (*emotionally*): What can we do?

CHRISTINE (*coldly*): You can't do anything. When *will* they let her see Dagmar?

NELS: Tomorrow.

CHRISTINE: Well, then, we'll just have to wait till tomorrow.

KATRIN: Chris, how can you be so callous? Can't you see that Mama's heart is breaking?

CHRISTINE: No. I can't. And you can't, either. People's hearts don't break.

KATRIN: They do, too.

CHRISTINE: Only in books. (MAMA *comes back, she wears an apron, and carries a scrub brush and a bucket of hot water.*) Why, Mama, what are you going to do?

MAMA (*coming down to table*): I scrub the floor. (*She gets down on her knees, facing front.*)

CHRISTINE: But you scrubbed it yesterday.

MAMA: I scrub it again. (*She starts to do so.*)

KATRIN: But, Mama . . .

MAMA (*bending low*): Comes a time when you've got to get down on your knees.

KATRIN (*to Christine*): Now do you believe me?

(CHRISTINE, *suddenly unendurably moved, turns and rushes from the room.*)

NELS: Mama, don't. Please don't. You must be tired.

KATRIN (*strangely*): Let her alone, Nels. (*They stand in silence watching* MAMA *scrub. Suddenly she stops.*) What is it, Mama? What is it?

MAMA (*sitting back on her haunches*): I tink of something! (*Slowly.*) I tink I tink of something!

45

(The lights dim and the curtains close on the kitchen. From the front UNCLE CHRIS' VOICE *singing. The lights slowly come up on the turntable, showing* ARNE *[a child of about nine] in a hospital bed, with* UNCLE CHRIS *beside him.)*

UNCLE CHRIS *(singing):*
    "Ten t'ousand Svedes vent t'rough de veeds
        At de battle of Coppen-hagen.
    Ten t'ousand Svedes vent t'rough de veeds
        Chasing vun Nor-ve-gan!"

ARNE: Uncle Chris!

UNCLE CHRIS: Yes, Arne?

ARNE: Uncle Chris, does it *have* to hurt like this?

UNCLE CHRIS: If you vant it to be vell, and not to valk alvays like Uncle Chris, it does . . . for a little. Is very bad?

ARNE: It is . . . kinda . . . Oo—oo . . . !

UNCLE CHRIS: Arne, don't you know any svear vords?

ARNE: W-what?

UNCLE CHRIS: Don't you know any svear vords?

ARNE: N-no, Uncle Chris. Not real ones.

UNCLE CHRIS: Then I tell you two fine vons to use when pain is bad. Are "Damn" and "Damittohell." You say them?

ARNE: N-now?

UNCLE CHRIS: No, not now. When pain comes again. You say them then. They help plenty. I know. I haf pain, too. I say them all the time. And if pain is *very* bad, you say, *God*damittohell. But only if is *very* bad. Is bad now?

ARNE: No, it's . . . it's a little better.

UNCLE CHRIS: You sleep some now, maybe?

ARNE: I'll try. Will . . . will you stay here, Uncle Chris?

UNCLE CHRIS: Sure. Sure. I stay here. You are not frightened of Uncle Chris?

ARNE: No. Not any more.

UNCLE CHRIS: Goot. Goot. You like I sing some more?

ARNE: If you wouldn't mind. But maybe something a little . . . well, quieter.

46

I Remember Mama

UNCLE CHRIS (*tenderly*): Sure. Sure. (*He begins quietly to sing a Norwegian lullaby, in the midst, ARNE cries out.*)

ARNE: Oo—oo . . . Oh, *damn.* Damn. Damittohell!

UNCLE CHRIS (*delighted*): Goot! It helps—eh?

ARNE (*with pleased surprise*): Yes—yes.

UNCLE CHRIS: Then you sleep some! (*He fixes ARNE's pillows for him, and resumes the lullaby, seated on his chair beside the bed. After another verse, he leans over, assuring himself that the child is asleep, and then very quietly, without interrupting his singing, takes a flask from his pocket and lifts it to his lips, as the light dims. The table revolves out.*)

(*The curtains part on the hospital corridor again. There is a different NURSE now at the reception desk, talking on the telephone as MAMA and KATRIN come in and go up the steps.*)

MAMA (*as they come up, in an undertone*): Is not the same nurse. Katrin, you take my hat and coat. (*She takes them off, revealing that she still wears her apron.*)

KATRIN: But, Mama, won't they . . .

MAMA (*interrupting, finger to lips*): Ssh! You let me go ahead. You wait on bench for me. (*She goes to the closet door above the bench and opens it. KATRIN stares after her in trepidation. MAMA takes out a damp mop and pail, and gets down on her knees by the nurse's desk, starting to clean the floor. The NURSE looks up. MAMA catches her eye, brightly.*) Very dirty floors.

NURSE: Yes, I'm glad they've finally decided to clean them. Aren't you working late?

MAMA (*quickly, lowering her head*): Floors need cleaning. (*She pushes her way, crawling on hands and knees, up behind the desk, and disappears up the corridor, still scrubbing. KATRIN steals to the bench, where she sits, still clutching MAMA's hat and coat, looking interestedly around her. The light dims, leaving her in a single spot, as she starts to talk to herself.*)

47

KATRIN (*to herself*): "The Hospital" . . . A poem by Katrin
Hanson. (*She starts to improvise.*)

> "She waited, fearful, in the hall,
> And held her bated breath."

Breath—yes, that'll rhyme with death. (*She repeats the
first two lines.*)

> "She waited fearful in the hall
> And held her bated breath.
> She trembled at the least footfall,
> And kept her mind on death."

(*She gets a piece of paper and pencil from her pocket and
begins to scribble, as a* NURSE *comes out of the elevator,
carrying some charts, which she takes to the desk, and then
goes out.* KATRIN *goes on with her poem.*)

> "Ah, God, 'twas agony to wait.
> To wait and watch and wonder. . . ."

Wonder—under—bunder—funder—sunder. Sunder! (*Nods
to herself and goes on again.*)

> "To wait and watch and wonder,
> About her infant sister's fate.
> If Death life's bonds would sunder."

(*Then to herself again, looking front.*) That's beautiful. Yes,
but it isn't true. Dagmar isn't dying. It's funny—I don't want
her to die—and yet when Mama said she was all right I
was almost—well, almost disappointed. It wasn't exciting
any more. Maybe Christine's right, and I haven't any heart.
How awful! "The girl without a heart." That'd be a nice
title for a story. "The girl without a heart sat in the hospital corridor. . . ."

(*The lights come up again as* UNCLE CHRIS *appears, behind the desk. He wears his hat and is more than a little drunk. He sees* KATRIN.)

UNCLE CHRIS: Katrinë! What you do here? (*He sits on the bench beside her.*)

KATRIN (*nervously*): I'm waiting for Mama.

UNCLE CHRIS: Where is she?

KATRIN (*scared*): I . . . I don't know.

UNCLE CHRIS: What you mean . . . you don't know?

KATRIN (*whispering*): I think . . . I think she's seeing Dagmar.

UNCLE CHRIS (*shaking his head*): Is first day. They do not allow visitors first day.

KATRIN (*trying to make him aware of the* NURSE): I know. But I think that's where she is.

UNCLE CHRIS: Where *is* Dagmar?

KATRIN: I don't know.

(UNCLE CHRIS *rises and goes to the* NURSE *at the desk.*)

UNCLE CHRIS: In what room is my great-niece, Dagmar Hanson?

NURSE (*looking at her book*): Hanson . . . Hanson . . . when did she come in?

UNCLE CHRIS: This morning.

NURSE: Oh, yes. Were you wanting to see her?

UNCLE CHRIS: What room is she in?

NURSE: I asked were you wanting to see her.

UNCLE CHRIS: And *I* ask what room she is in.

NURSE: We don't allow visitors the first day.

UNCLE CHRIS: Have I said I vant to visit her? I ask what room she is in.

NURSE: Are you by any chance, Mr. . . . (*looking at her book*) Halvorsen?

UNCLE CHRIS (*proudly, and correcting her pronunciation*): Christopher Halvorsen.

49

NURSE: Did you say you were her uncle?

UNCLE CHRIS: Her great-uncle.

NURSE: Well, then, I'm afraid I can't tell you anything about her.

UNCLE CHRIS: Why not?

NURSE: Orders.

UNCLE CHRIS: Whose orders?

NURSE: Dr. Johnson's. There's a special note here. Patient's uncle, Mr. Halvorsen, not to be admitted or given information under any circumstances.

UNCLE CHRIS (*after a moment's angry stupefaction*): Goddamittohell! (*He strides away, taking out his flask, and shaking it, only to find it empty.*)

(MAMA *returns, carrying the mop and pail, walking now and smiling triumphantly.*)

MAMA (*to the* NURSE): Thank you. (*She replaces the mop and pail in the closet, and then sees* UNCLE CHRIS. *Crossing to him.*) Uncle Chris, Dagmar is fine!

UNCLE CHRIS (*amazed*): You see her?

MAMA: Sure, Uncle Chris, I see her.

UNCLE CHRIS (*reiterating, incredulous*): You see Dagmar?

MAMA: Sure. (*She takes her hat from* KATRIN *and starts to put it on.*) Is fine hospital. But such floors! A mop is never good. Floors should be scrubbed with a brush. We go home. Uncle Chris, you come with us? I make coffee.

UNCLE CHRIS (*joining them in a little group on the steps*): Pah! Vot good is coffee? I go get drink.

MAMA (*reprovingly*): Uncle Chris!

UNCLE CHRIS: Marta, you are fine woman. Fine. But I go get drink. I get drunk.

MAMA (*quickly aside to* KATRIN): His leg hurts him.

UNCLE CHRIS: And you do not make excuses for me! I get drunk because I like it.

MAMA (*conciliating him*): Sure, Uncle Chris.

UNCLE CHRIS (*shouting*): I like it! (*Then, with a change.*)

No, is not true. You know is not true. I do not like to get drunk at all. But I do not like to come home with you, either. (*Growing slightly maudlin.*) You have family. Is fine thing. You do not know how fine. Katrinë, one day when you grow up, maybe you know what a fine thing family is. I haf no family.

KATRIN (*on the lower step*): But, Uncle Chris, Mama's always said you were the *head* of the family.

UNCLE CHRIS: Sure. Sure. I am head of the family, but I haf no family. So I go get drunk. You understand, Marta?

MAMA: Sure, Uncle Chris. You go get drunk. (*Sharply.*) But don't you feel sorry for yourself! (UNCLE CHRIS *glares at her a moment, then strides down the steps, boisterously singing his song of "Ten Thousand Swedes."* MAMA *watches him go, then takes her coat from* KATRIN.) Is fine man. Has fine ideas about family. (KATRIN *helps her on with her coat.*) I can tell Papa now that Dagmar is fine. She wake while I am with her. I explain rules to her. She will not expect us now until tomorrow afternoon.

KATRIN: You won't try and see her again before that?

MAMA (*gravely*): *No.* That would be against the rules! Come. We go home.

(*They go off.*)

ACT II

SCENE: *Opening, exactly as in Act I.* KATRIN *at her desk.*

KATRIN (*reading*): "It wasn't very often that I could get Mama to talk—about herself, or her life in the old country, or what she felt about things. You had to catch her unawares, or when she had nothing to do, which was very, very seldom. I don't think I can ever remember seeing Mama unoccupied." (*Laying down the manuscript and looking out front.*) I do remember one occasion, though. It was the day before Dagmar came home from the hospital. And as we left, Mama suggested treating me to an ice-cream soda. (*She rises, gets her hat from beside her—a schoolgirl hat—puts it on and crosses while she speaks the next lines.*) She had never done such a thing before, and I remember how proud it made me feel—just to sit and talk to her quietly like a grown-up person. It was a kind of special *treat*-moment in my life that I'll always remember—quite apart from the soda, which was *wonderful.* (MAMA *has come from between the curtains, and starts down the steps.*)

MAMA: Katrin, you like we go next door, and I treat you to an ice-cream soda?

KATRIN (*young now, and overcome*): Mama—do you mean it?

MAMA: Sure. We celebrate. We celebrate that Dagmar is well, and coming home again. (*They cross to the turntable, which represents a drugstore, with a table and two chairs at which they seat themselves.* MAMA *is at the left of table.*) What you like to have, Katrin?

52

KATRIN (*with desperate earnestness*): I think a chocolate . . .
no, a strawberry . . . no, a chocolate soda.

MAMA (*smiling*): You are sure?

KATRIN (*gravely*): I think so. But, Mama, can we *afford* it?

MAMA: I think this once we can afford it.

(*The* SODA CLERK *appears.*)

SODA CLERK: What's it going to be, ladies?

MAMA: A chocolate ice-cream soda, please—and a cup of
coffee.

(*The* SODA CLERK *goes.*)

KATRIN: Mama, he called us "ladies"! (MAMA *smiles.*) Why
aren't you having a soda, too?

MAMA: Better I like coffee.

KATRIN: When can I drink coffee?

MAMA: When you are grown up.

KATRIN: When I'm eighteen?

MAMA: Maybe before that.

KATRIN: When I graduate?

MAMA: Maybe. I don't know. Comes the day you are grown
up, Papa and I will know.

KATRIN: Is coffee really nicer than a soda?

MAMA: When you are grown up, it is.

KATRIN: Did you used to like sodas better . . . before you
were grown up?

MAMA: We didn't have sodas before I was grown up. It
was in the old country.

KATRIN (*incredulous*): You mean they don't have sodas in
Norway?

MAMA: Now, maybe. Now I think they have many things
from America. But not when I was little girl.

(*The* SODA CLERK *brings the soda and the coffee.*)

53

SODA CLERK: There you are, folks. (*He sets them down and departs.*)

KATRIN (*after a good pull at the soda*): Mama, do you ever want to go back to the old country?

MAMA: I like to go back once to look, maybe. To see the mountains and the fjords. I like to show them once to you all. When Dagmar is big, maybe we all go back once . . . one summer . . . like tourists. But that is how it would be. I would be tourist there now. There is no one I would know any more. And maybe we see the little house where Papa and I live when we first marry. And . . . (*her eyes grow misty and reminiscent*) something else I would look at.

KATRIN: What is that? (MAMA *does not answer.*) What would you look at, Mama?

MAMA: Katrin, you do not know you have brother? Besides Nels?

KATRIN: No! A brother? In Norway? Mama. . . .

MAMA: He is my first baby. I am eighteen when he is born.

KATRIN: Is he there now?

MAMA (*simply*): He is dead.

KATRIN (*disappointed*): Oh. I thought you meant . . . I thought you meant a real brother. A long-lost one, like in stories. When did he die?

MAMA: When he is two years old. It is his grave I would like to see again. (*She is suddenly near tears, biting her lip and stirring her coffee violently, spilling some. She gets her handkerchief from her pocketbook, dabs at her skirt, then briefly at her nose, then she returns the handkerchief and turns to* KATRIN *again. Matter-of-factly.*) Is good, your ice-cream soda?

KATRIN (*more interested now in* MAMA *than in it*): Yes. Mama . . . have you had a very *hard* life?

MAMA (*surprised*): Hard? No. No life is easy all the time. It is not meant to be. (*She pours the spilled coffee back from the saucer into her cup.*)

KATRIN: But . . . rich people . . . aren't *their* lives easy?

MAMA: I don't know, Katrin. I have never known rich people. But I see them sometimes in stores and in the streets, and they do not *look* as if they were easy.

KATRIN: Wouldn't you like to be rich?

MAMA: I would like to be rich the way I would like to be ten feet high. Would be good for some things—bad for others.

KATRIN: But didn't you come to America to *get* rich?

MAMA (*shocked*): No. We come to America because they are all here—all the others. Is good for families to be together.

KATRIN: And did you like it right away?

MAMA: Right away. When we get off the ferry boat and I see San Francisco and all the family, I say: "Is like Norway," only it is better than Norway. And then you are all born here, and I become American citizen. But not to get rich.

KATRIN: *I* want to be rich. Rich and famous. I'd buy you your warm coat. When are you going to get that coat, Mama?

MAMA: Soon now, maybe—when we pay doctor, and Mr. Hyde pay his rent. I think now I *must* ask him. I ask him tomorrow, after Dagmar comes home.

KATRIN: When I'm rich and famous, I'll buy you lovely clothes. White satin gowns with long trains to them. And jewelry. I'll buy you a pearl necklace.

MAMA: We talk too much! (*She signs to the* SODA CLERK.) Come, finish your soda. We must go home. (*The* SODA CLERK *comes.*) How much it is, please?

SODA CLERK: Fifteen cents.

MAMA: Here are two dimes. You keep the nickel. And thank you. Was good coffee. (*They start out and up the steps towards the curtains.*) Tomorrow Dagmar will be home again. And, Katrin, you see Uncle Elizabeth is there. This afternoon again she was asking for him. You keep Uncle Elizabeth in the house all day until she comes home.

(*They disappear behind the curtains. After a second, the howls of a cat in pain are heard from behind the curtains—*

low at first, then rising to a heart-rending volume, and then diminishing again as the curtains part on the kitchen once more. MAMA, PAPA, *and* DAGMAR *are entering the house.*)

DAGMAR (*standing on threshold, transfixed*): It's Uncle Elizabeth, welcoming me home! That's his song of welcome. Where is he, Mama? (*She looks around for the source of the howls.*)

MAMA: He is in the pantry . . . (*As* DAGMAR *starts to rush thither.*) But wait . . . wait a minute, Dagmar. I must tell you. Uncle Elizabeth is . . . sick.

DAGMAR: Sick? What's the matter with him?

PAPA: He has been in fight. Last night. He come home this morning very sick indeed.

(DAGMAR *starts for the pantry door, as* NELS *comes out.*)

MAMA: Nels, how is Uncle Elizabeth? Nels has been doctoring him.

NELS: He's pretty bad, Mama. I've dressed all his wounds again with boric acid, but . . . (*As* DAGMAR *tries to get past him.*) I wouldn't go and see him now, baby.

DAGMAR: I've got to. He's my cat. I haven't seen him in a whole month. More. (*She runs into the pantry and disappears.*)

MAMA: Nels, what you think?

NELS: I think we ought to have had him put away before she came home.

MAMA: But she would have been so unhappy if he was not here *at all.*

NELS: She'll be unhappier still if he dies.

(*Another howl is heard from the pantry, and then* DAGMAR *comes rushing back.*)

DAGMAR: Mama, what happened to him? What happened to him? Oh, Mama . . . when I tried to pick him up, his bandage slipped over his eye. It was bleeding. Oh, Mama, it looked awful. Oh . . . (*She starts to cry.*)

MAMA (*fondling her*): He looks like that all over. Nels, you go see to his eye again. (*Wearily, NELS returns to the pantry.*) Listen, Dagmar . . . *Lille Ven* . . . would it not be better for the poor thing to go quietly to sleep?

DAGMAR: You mean—go to sleep and never wake up again? (MAMA *nods gently.*) No.

PAPA: I think he die, anyway. Nels try to make him well. But I do not think he can.

DAGMAR: Mama can. Mama can do everything. (*Another howl from offstage. She clutches MAMA agonizedly.*) Make him live, Mama. Make him well again. *Please!*

MAMA: We see. Let us see how he gets through the night. And now, Dagmar, you must go to bed. I bring you your supper.

DAGMAR: But you will fix Uncle Elizabeth? You promise, Mama?

MAMA: I promise I try. Go now. (DAGMAR *goes out.*) I must fix her supper. (*She starts for the pantry. Howls again. She and PAPA stand and look at each other. NELS comes out.*)

NELS: Mama, it's just cruelty, keeping that cat alive.

MAMA: I know.

PAPA (*as another howl, the loudest yet, emerges*): You say we see how the cat get through the night. I ask you how do *we* get through the night? Is no use, Marta. We must put the cat to sleep. Nels, you go to the drugstore, and get something. Some chloroform, maybe. (*He gives him a coin.*)

NELS: How much shall I get?

PAPA: You ask the man. You tell him it is for a cat. He knows. (NELS *goes out and down the street. Looking at* MAMA's *face.*) Is best. Is the only thing.

MAMA: I know. But poor Dagmar. It is sad homecoming for her. And she has been so good in hospital. Never once she cry. (*She pulls herself together.*) I get her supper. (*Another howl from off stage.*) And I take the cat outside. Right outside, where we . . . where *Dagmar* cannot hear him. (*She goes into the pantry.* PAPA *takes a folded newspaper from his pocket, puts on his glasses and starts to read. The back door opens gently and* MR. HYDE *peeps out. He wears his hat and coat and carries his suitcase and a letter.* PAPA *has his back to him.* MR. HYDE *lays the letter on the dresser and then starts to tiptoe across to the door. Then* PAPA *sees him.*)

PAPA: You go out, Mr. Hyde?

MR. HYDE (*pretending surprise*): Oh. . . . Oh, I did not see you, Mr. Hanson. (*He puts down the suitcase.*) I did not know you were back. As a matter of fact, I . . . I was about to leave this letter for you. (*He fetches it.*) The fact is . . . I . . . I have been called away.

PAPA: So?

MR. HYDE: A letter I received this morning necessitates my departure. My immediate departure.

PAPA: I am sorry. (MAMA *returns with a tray, on which are milk, bread, butter, and jelly.*) Mama, Mr. Hyde says he goes away.

MAMA (*coming to the table with the tray*): Is true?

MR. HYDE: Alas, dear Madam, yes. 'Tis true, 'tis pity. And pity 'tis, 'tis true. You will find here . . . (*he presents the letter*) my check for all I owe you, and a note expressing my profoundest thanks for all your most kind hospitality. You will say good-by to the children for me? (*He bows, as* MAMA *takes the letter.*)

MAMA (*distressed*): Sure. Sure.

MR. HYDE (*bowing again*): Madam, my deepest gratitude. (*He kisses her hand.* MAMA *looks astonished. He bows to* PAPA.) Sir—my sincerest admiration! (*He opens the street door.*) It has been a privilege. Ave atque vale! Hail and farewell! (*He makes a gesture and goes.*)

MAMA: Was wonderful man! Is too bad. (*She opens the letter, takes out the check.*)

PAPA: How much is check for?

MAMA: Hundred ten dollar! Is four months.

PAPA: Good. Good.

MAMA: Is wonderful. Now we pay doctor everything.

PAPA: And you buy your warm coat. With fur now, maybe.

MAMA (*sadly*): But there will be no more reading. You take the check, Lars. You get the money?

PAPA (*taking it*): Sure. I get it. What does he say in his letter?

MAMA: You read it while I fix supper for Dagmar. (*She starts to butter the bread, and spread jelly, while* PAPA *reads.*)

PAPA (*reading*): "Dear Friends, I find myself compelled to take a somewhat hasty departure from this house of happiness. . . ."

MAMA: Is beautiful letter.

PAPA (*continuing*): "I am leaving you my library for the children. . . ."

MAMA: He leaves his books?

PAPA: He says so.

MAMA: But is wonderful. Go see, Lars. See if they are in his room.

(PAPA *lays down the letter and goes out.* NELS *and* CHRISTINE *appear, coming up to the house.* CHRISTINE *carries schoolbooks.*)

CHRISTINE: I'm sure it was him, Nels. Carrying his suitcase, and getting on the cable car. I'm sure he's going away.

NELS: Well, I hope he's paid Mama.

(*They open the street door.*)

CHRISTINE (*bursting in*): Mama, I saw Mr. Hyde getting on the cable car.

MAMA: I know. He leave.

CHRISTINE: Did he pay you?

MAMA: Sure, he pay me. Hundred ten dollar. . . .

NELS: Gee. . . .

MAMA (*smiling*): Is good.

CHRISTINE: Are you going to put it in the Bank?

MAMA: We need it right away. (PAPA *returns, staggering under an armload of books.*) Mr. Hyde leaves his books, too. For you.

NELS: Say! (PAPA *stacks them on the table.* NELS *and* CHRISTINE *rush to them, reading the titles.*) The Pickwick Papers, The Complete Shakespeare . . .

CHRISTINE: *Alice in Wonderland, The Oxford Book of Verse . . .*

NELS: *The Last of the Mohicans, Ivanhoe . . .*

CHRISTINE: We were right in the middle of that.

MAMA: Nels can finish it. He can read to us now in the evenings. He has fine voice, too, like Mr. Hyde. (NELS *flushes with pleasure.*) Is wonderful. So much we can learn. (*She finishes the supper-making.*) Christine, you take the butter back to the cooler for me, and the yelly, too. (CHRISTINE *does so.*) I go up to Dagmar now. (*She lifts the tray, then pauses.*) You get it, Nels?

NELS: What? . . . Oh. . . . (*Taking a druggist's small bottle from his pocket.*) Here.

MAMA: You put it down. After I come back, we do it. You know how?

NELS: Why, no, Mama, I . . .

MAMA: You do not ask?

NELS: No, I . . . I thought Papa . . .

MAMA: You know, Lars?

PAPA: No, I don't *know* . . . but it cannot be difficult. If you *hold* the cat . . .

MAMA: And watch him die? No! I think better you get rags . . . and a big sponge, to soak up the chloroform. You put it in the box with him, and cover him over. You get them ready out there.

NELS: Sure, Mama.

MAMA: I bring some blankets.

(NELS *goes off to the pantry, as* CHRISTINE *comes back. Again* MAMA *lifts the tray and starts for the door. But there is a knock on the street door from* AUNT JENNY, *who has come to the house in a state of some excitement.*)

MAMA (*agitated*): So much goes on! See who it is, Christine.

CHRISTINE (*peeping*): It's Aunt Jenny. (*She opens the door.*)

MAMA: Jenny. . . .

JENNY (*breathless*): Marta . . . has he gone?

MAMA (*above table*): Who?

JENNY (*near table*): Your boarder . . . Mr. Hyde. . . .

MAMA: Yes, he has gone. Why?

JENNY: Did he pay you?

MAMA: Sure he pay me.

JENNY: How?

MAMA: He give me a check. Lars has it right there.

JENNY (*with meaning*): A check!

MAMA: Jenny, what is it? Christine, you give Dagmar her supper. I come soon. (CHRISTINE *takes the tray from her and goes out.*) What is it, Jenny? How do you know that Mr. Hyde has gone?

JENNY: I was at Mr. Kruper's down the street . . . you know, the restaurant and bakery . . . and he told me Mr. Hyde was there today having his lunch, and when he left he asked if he would cash a check for him. For fifty dollars. (*She pauses.*)

PAPA: Well, go on.

JENNY: Your fine Mr. Hyde didn't expect Mr. Kruper to take it to the bank until tomorrow, but he did. And what do you think? Mr. Hyde hasn't even an *account* at that bank! (NELS *returns and stands in the pantry doorway.*)

MAMA: I don't understand.

PAPA (*taking the check from his pocket*): You mean the check is no good?

JENNY: No good at all. (*Triumphantly.*) Your Mr. Hyde was a crook, just as I always thought he was, for all his reading and fine ways. Mr. Kruper said he'd been cashing them all over the neighborhood. (MAMA *stands quite still, without answering.*) How much did he owe you? Plenty, I'll bet.

(*Still no answer.*) Eh? Marta, I said I bet he owed you plenty. Didn't he?

MAMA (*looks around, first at* NELS *and then down at the books on the table. She touches them*): No. No, he owed us nothing. (*She takes the check from* PAPA, *tearing it.*) Nothing.

JENNY (*persistently*): How much was that check for? (*She reaches her hand for it.*)

MAMA (*evading her*): It does not matter. He pay with better things than money. (*She goes to the stove, where she throws the check, watching it burn.*)

JENNY: I told you right in the beginning that you shouldn't trust him. But you were so sure . . . just like you always are. Mr. Hyde was a gentleman. A gentleman! I bet it must have been a hundred dollars that he rooked you of. Wasn't it?

MAMA (*returning to the table*): Jenny, I cannot talk now. Maybe you don't have things to do. I have.

JENNY (*sneeringly*): What? What have *you* got to do that's so important?

MAMA (*taking up the medicine bottle, fiercely*): I have to chloroform a cat!

(JENNY *steps back in momentary alarm, almost as though* MAMA *were referring to her, as she goes out into the pantry with the medicine bottle, not so very unlike Lady Macbeth with the daggers. Blackout and curtains close. After a moment, the curtains part again on the kitchen, the next morning. The books have been taken off the table, and* MAMA *is setting the breakfast dishes, with* PAPA *helping her.* DAGMAR *comes bursting into the room.*)

DAGMAR: Good morning, Mama. 'Morning, Papa. Is Uncle Elizabeth all better?

MAMA: Dagmar, there is something I must tell you.

DAGMAR: I want to see Uncle Elizabeth first. (*She runs into the pantry.* MAMA *turns helplessly to* PAPA.)

MAMA: Do something! Tell her!

PAPA: If we just let her think the cat die . . . by itself. . . .

MAMA: No. We cannot tell her lies.

(PAPA *goes to the pantry door, opening it.*)

DAGMAR (*heard in pantry, off*): What a funny, funny smell. Good morning, my darling, my darling Elizabeth. (MAMA *and* PAPA *stand stricken.* DAGMAR *comes in, carrying the cat, wrapped in an old shirt, with its head covered. She comes over to table.*) My goodness, you put enough blankets on him! Did you think he'd catch cold?

MAMA (*horror-stricken*): Dagmar, you must not. . . . (*She stops at the sight of the cat, whose tail is twitching, quite obviously alive.*) Dagmar, let me see . . . Let me see the cat! (*She goes over to her, below table front, and uncovers the cat's head.*)

DAGMAR (*overjoyed*): He's well. Oh, Mama, I *knew* you'd fix him.

MAMA (*appalled*): But, Dagmar, I didn't, I . . .

DAGMAR (*ignoring her*): I'm going to take him right up and show him to Nels. (*She runs off, calling.*) Nels! Nels! Uncle Elizabeth's well again!

MAMA (*turning to* PAPA): Is a miracle! (*She sits, dumfounded, on the bench in front of the table.*)

PAPA (*beside her, shrugging*): You cannot have used enough chloroform. You just give him good sleep, and that cures him. We rechristen the cat, Lazarus!

MAMA: But, Lars, we must tell her. Is not *good* to let her grow up believing I can fix *everything!*

PAPA: Is best thing in the world for her to believe. (*He chuckles.*) Besides, I know *exactly* how she feels. (*He lays his hand on hers.*)

MAMA (*turning with embarrassment from his demonstrativeness and slapping his hand*): We finish getting breakfast. (*She turns back to the table.*)

(The curtains close. Lights go up down front. KATRIN and CHRISTINE enter from the wings, in school clothes, wearing hats. CHRISTINE carries schoolbooks in a strap. KATRIN is reciting.)

KATRIN: "The quality of mercy is not strained,
        It droppeth as the gentle rain from heaven
        Upon the place beneath: it is twice blest;
        It blesseth him that gives, and him that takes. . . ."

(She dries up.) ". . . him that takes. It blesseth him that gives and him that takes. . . ." *(She turns to CHRISTINE.)* What comes after that?

CHRISTINE: I don't know. And I don't care.

KATRIN: Why, Chris!

CHRISTINE: I don't. It's all I've heard for weeks. The school play, and your graduation, and going on to High. And never a thought of what's happening at home.

KATRIN: What do you mean?

CHRISTINE: You see—you don't even know!

KATRIN: Oh, you mean the strike?

CHRISTINE: Yes, I mean the strike. Papa hasn't worked for four whole weeks, and a lot you care. Why, I don't believe you even know what they're striking *for*. Do you? All you and your friends can talk about is the presents you're going to get. You make me ashamed of being a girl.

(Two girls, MADELINE and DOROTHY, come through the curtains, talking.)

MADELINE *(to DOROTHY)*: Thyra Walsh's family's going to add seven pearls to the necklace they started for her when she was a baby. Oh, hello, Katrin! Did you hear about Thyra's graduation present?

KATRIN *(not very happily)*: Yes, I heard.

MADELINE: I'm getting an onyx ring, with a diamond in it.

KATRIN: A real diamond?

64

MADELINE: Yes, of course. A *small* diamond.

DOROTHY: What are *you* getting?

KATRIN: Well . . . well, they haven't actually told me, but I think . . . I think I'm going to get that pink celluloid dresser set in your father's drugstore.

DOROTHY: You mean that one in the window?

KATRIN (*to* MADELINE): It's got a brush and comb and mirror . . . and a hair-receiver. It's genuine celluloid!

DOROTHY: I wanted Father to give it to me, out of stock, but he said it was too expensive. Father's an awful tightwad. They're giving me a bangle.

MADELINE: Oh, there's the streetcar. We've got to fly. 'By, Katrin. 'By, Christine. See you tomorrow. Come on, Dorothy.

(*The* TWO GIRLS *rush off.*)

CHRISTINE: Who said you were going to get the dresser set?

KATRIN: Nobody's said so . . . for certain. But I've sort of hinted, and . . .

CHRISTINE (*going up the steps*): Well, you're not going to get it.

KATRIN: How do you know?

CHRISTINE (*turning up back. Still on steps*): Because I know what you *are* getting. I heard Mama tell Aunt Jenny. Aunt Jenny said you were too young to appreciate it.

KATRIN: What is it?

CHRISTINE: Mama's giving you her brooch. Her *solje*.

KATRIN: You mean that old silver thing she wears that belonged to Grandmother? What would I want an old thing like that for?

CHRISTINE: It's an heirloom. Mama thinks a lot of it.

KATRIN: Well, then, she ought to keep it. You don't really mean that's *all* they're going to give me?

CHRISTINE: What more do you want?

KATRIN: I want the dresser set. My goodness, if Mama

65

doesn't realize what's a suitable present . . . why, it's practically the most important time in a girl's life, when she graduates.

CHRISTINE: And you say you're not selfish!

KATRIN: It's not selfishness.

CHRISTINE: Well, I don't know what else you'd call it. With Papa not working, we need every penny we can lay our hands on. Even the Little Bank's empty. But you'll devil Mama into giving you the dresser set somehow. So why talk about it? I'm going home. (*She turns and goes through the curtains.*)

(KATRIN *stands alone with a set and stubborn mouth, and then sits on the steps.*)

KATRIN: Christine was right. I got the dresser set. They gave it to me just before supper on graduation night. Papa could not attend the exercises because there was a strike meeting to decide about going back to work. I was so excited that night I could hardly eat, and the present took the last remnants of my appetite clean away.

(*The curtains part on the kitchen.* PAPA, MAMA, *and* DAGMAR *at table, with coffee.* CHRISTINE *is clearing dishes.*)

CHRISTINE: I'll just stack the dishes now, Mama. We'll wash them when we come home. (*She carries them into the pantry.*)

PAPA (*at table. Holding up a cube of sugar*): Who wants coffee-sugar? (*He dips it in his coffee.*) Dagmar? (*He hands it to her.*) Katrin? (*She rises from the steps, coming into the scene for the sugar.*)

MAMA (*at other side of table*): You get your coat, Katrin; you need it.

(KATRIN *goes out.*)

DAGMAR (*behind table*): Aunt Jenny says if we drank black coffee like you do at our age, it would turn our complexions dark. I'd like to be a black Norwegian. Like Uncle Chris. Can I, Papa?

PAPA: I like you better blonde. Like Mama.

DAGMAR: When do you get old enough for your complexion *not* to turn dark? When can we drink coffee?

PAPA: One day, when you are grown up.

(JENNY *and* TRINA *have come to the door.* JENNY *knocks.*)

MAMA: There are Jenny and Trina. (*She goes to the door.*) Is good. We can start now. (*She opens the door.* JENNY *and* TRINA *come in.*)

JENNY: Well, are you all ready? Is Katrin very excited?

PAPA (*nodding*): She ate no supper.

(MAMA *has started to put on her hat, and to put on* DAGMAR'S *hat and coat for her.* CHRISTINE *comes back from the pantry.* PAPA *gives her a dipped cube of sugar.*)

JENNY: Is that *black* coffee you dipped that sugar in? Lars, you shouldn't. It's not good for them. It'll . . .

PAPA (*finishing for her*): Turn their complexions black. I know. Well, maybe it is all right if we have *one* colored daughter.

JENNY: Lars, really!

(KATRIN *returns with her coat.*)

KATRIN: Aunt Jenny, did you see my graduation present? (*She gets it from a chair.* CHRISTINE *gives her a disgusted look, and goes out.* KATRIN *displays the dresser set above the table.*) Look! It's got a hair-receiver.

JENNY (*at left of table*): But I thought . . . Marta, I thought you were going to give her . . .

MAMA: No, you were right, Jenny. She is too young to appreciate that. She like something more gay . . . more modern.

JENNY: H'm. Well, it's very pretty, I suppose, but . . . (*She looks up as* MAMA *puts on her coat.*) You're not wearing your *solje!*

MAMA (*quickly*): No. I do not wear it tonight. Come, Trina, we shall be late.

TRINA (*behind table*): Oh, but Peter isn't here yet.

MAMA: Katrin has her costume to put on. He can follow. Or do you like to wait for Peter?

TRINA: I think . . . if you don't mind . . .

MAMA: You can stay with Lars. He does not have to go yet.

JENNY: I hope Katrin knows her part.

PAPA: Sure she knows it. *I* know it, too.

TRINA: It's too bad he can't see Katrin's debut as an actress.

MAMA: You will be back before us, Lars?

PAPA (*nodding*): I think the meeting will not last long.

MAMA: Is good. We go now. (*She goes out with* JENNY *and* DAGMAR. CHRISTINE *and* NELS *return and follow, waiting outside for* KATRIN, *while the others go ahead.* KATRIN *puts on her hat and coat and picks up the dresser set.*)

PAPA (*to* TRINA): You like we play a game of checkers while we wait?

TRINA (*sitting at table*): Oh, I haven't played checkers in years.

PAPA: Then I beat you. (*He rises to get the checker set.* KATRIN *kisses him.*)

KATRIN: Good-by, Papa.

PAPA: Good-by, daughter. I think of you.

KATRIN: I'll see you there, Aunt Trina.

TRINA: Good luck!

PAPA: I get the checkers.

(KATRIN *goes out.* PAPA *gets the checker set from a cupboard under the dresser, brings it to the table and sets it up during the ensuing scene, which is played outside in the street.*)

CHRISTINE (*contemptuously*): Oh, bringing your cheap trash with you to show off?

KATRIN: It's not trash. It's beautiful. You're just jealous.

CHRISTINE: I told you you'd devil Mama into giving it to you.

KATRIN: I didn't. I didn't devil her at all. I just showed it to her in Mr. Schiller's window. . . .

CHRISTINE: And made her go and sell her brooch that her very own mother gave her.

KATRIN: What?

NELS: Chris . . . you weren't supposed to tell that!

CHRISTINE: I don't care. I think she ought to know.

KATRIN: Is that true? Did Mama—Nels—?

NELS: Well, yes, as a matter of fact, she did. Now, come on.

KATRIN: No, no, I don't believe it. I'm going to ask Papa.

NELS: You haven't time.

KATRIN: I don't care. (*She rushes back to the house and dashes into the kitchen. CHRISTINE goes off and NELS follows her.*) Papa—Papa—Christine says— Papa, did Mama sell her brooch to give me this?

PAPA (*above table*): Christine should not have told you that.

KATRIN: It's true, then?

PAPA: She did not sell it. She traded it to Mr. Schiller for your present.

KATRIN (*near tears*): Oh, but she shouldn't. . . . I never meant . . .

PAPA (*taking her by the shoulders*): Look, Katrin. You wanted the present. Mama wanted your happiness; she wanted it more than she wanted the brooch.

KATRIN: But I never meant her to do that. (*Crying.*) She *loved* it so. It was all she had of Grandmother's.

PAPA: She always meant it for you, Katrin. And you must not cry. You have your play to act.

KATRIN (*sobbing*): I don't want to act in it now.

PAPA: But you must. Your audience is waiting.

KATRIN (*as before*): I don't care.

PAPA: But you must care. Tonight you are not Katrin any

longer. You are an actress. And an actress must act, whatever she is feeling. There is a saying—what is it—

TRINA (*brightly*): The mails must go through!

PAPA: No, no. The show must go on. So stop your crying, and go and act your play. We talk of this later. Afterwards.

KATRIN (*pulling herself together*): All right, I'll go. (*Sniffing a good deal, she picks up the dresser set and goes back to the street and off.* PAPA *and* TRINA *exchange glances, and then settle down to their checkers.*)

PAPA: Now we play.

(*The lights fade and the curtains close. Spot up on turntable. The two girls from the earlier scene are dressing in costumes for* The Merchant of Venice *before a plank dressing table.*)

DOROTHY: I'm getting worried about Katrin. If anything's happened to *her* . . .

MADELINE (*pulling up her tights*): I'll forget my lines. I know I will. I'll look out and see Miss Forrester sitting there, and forget every single line. (KATRIN *rushes in. She carries the dresser set, places it on the dressing table.*) We thought you'd had an accident, or something. . . .

KATRIN: Dorothy, is your father here tonight?

DOROTHY: He's going to be. Why?

KATRIN: I want to speak to him. (*As she pulls off her hat and coat.*) Will you tell him . . . please . . . not to go away without speaking to me? After. After the exercises.

DOROTHY: What on earth do you want to speak to Father for?

KATRIN: I've got something to say to him. Something to ask him. It's important. *Very* important.

MADELINE: Is that the dresser set? (*Picking it up.*) Can I look at it a minute?

KATRIN (*snatching it from her, violently*): No!

MADELINE: Why, what's the matter? I only wanted to look at it.

KATRIN (*emotionally*): You can't. You're not to touch it. Dorothy, you take it and put it where I can't see it. (*She thrusts it at her.*) Go on . . . Take it! Take it! Take it!!

(*Blackout. Curtains part on the kitchen.* MAMA *and* PAPA *in conclave at the table with cups of coffee.*)

MAMA (*behind table*): I am worried about her, Lars. When it is over, I see her talking with Mr. Schiller—and then she goes to take off her costume and Nels tells me that he will bring her home. But it is long time, and is late for her to be out. And in the play, Lars, she was not good. I have heard her practice it here, and she was good, but tonight, no. It was as if . . . as if she was thinking of something else all the time.

PAPA (*at table*): I think maybe she was.

MAMA: But what? What can be worrying her?

PAPA: Marta . . . tonight, after you leave, Katrin found out about your brooch.

MAMA: My brooch? But how? Who told her?

PAPA: Christine.

MAMA (*angry*): Why?

PAPA: I do not know.

MAMA (*rising with a sternness we have not seen before, and calling*): Christine! Christine!

CHRISTINE (*emerging from the pantry, wiping a dish*): Were you calling me, Mama?

MAMA: Yes. Christine, did you tell Katrin tonight about my brooch?

CHRISTINE (*frightened, but firm*): Yes.

MAMA (*level with her*): Why did you?

CHRISTINE: Because I hated the smug way she was acting over that dresser set.

MAMA: Is no excuse. You make her unhappy. You make her not good in the play.

CHRISTINE: Well, she made *you* unhappy, giving up your brooch for her selfishness.

MAMA (*moving towards her, behind table*): Is not your

business. I choose to give my brooch. Is not for you to judge. And you know I do not want you to tell. I am angry with you, Christine.

CHRISTINE: I'm sorry. But I'm not sorry I told. (*She goes back to the pantry with a set, obstinate face.*)

PAPA: Christine is the stubborn one.

(*NELS and KATRIN have approached the house outside. They stop and look at each other in the lamplight. KATRIN looks scared. Then NELS pats her, and she goes in, NELS following. MAMA looks up inquiringly and searchingly into KATRIN'S face. KATRIN turns away, taking off her hat and coat, and taking something from her pocket.*)

NELS: What happened at the meeting, Papa?

PAPA: We go back to work tomorrow.

NELS: Gee, that's bully. Isn't it, Mama?

MAMA (*seated again, at table, absently*): Yes, is good.

KATRIN (*coming to MAMA*): Mama . . . here's your brooch. (*She gives it to her.*) I'm sorry I was so bad in the play. I'll go and help Christine with the dishes. (*She turns and goes into the pantry.*)

MAMA (*unwrapping the brooch from tissue paper*): Mr. Schiller give it back to her?

NELS (*behind table*): We went to his house to get it. He didn't want to. He was planning to give it to his wife for her birthday. But Katrin begged and begged him. She even offered to go and work in his store during her vacation if he'd give it back.

PAPA (*impressed*): So? So?

MAMA: And what did Mr. Schiller say?

NELS: He said that wasn't necessary. But he gave her a job all the same. She's going to work for him, afternoons, for three dollars a week.

MAMA: And the dresser set—she gave that back?

NELS: Yes. She was awful upset, Mama. It was kinda hard

for her to do. She's a good kid. Well, I'll say good night.
I've got to be up early.

PAPA: Good night, Nels.

NELS: Good night, Papa. (*He goes out back.*)

MAMA: Good night, Nels.

PAPA: Nels is the kind one. (*He starts to refill* MAMA's *coffee cup. She stops him, putting her hand over her cup.*) No?

MAMA (*rising and calling*): Katrin! Katrin!

KATRIN (*coming to the pantry door*): Yes, Mama?

MAMA (*sitting at table*): Come here. (KATRIN *comes to her.* MAMA *holds out the brooch.*) You put this on.

KATRIN: No . . . it's yours.

MAMA: It is your graduation present. I put it on for you. (*She pins the brooch on* KATRIN's *dress.*)

KATRIN (*near tears*): I'll wear it always. I'll keep it forever.

MAMA: Christine should not have told you.

KATRIN (*moving away*): I'm glad she did. Now.

PAPA: And I am glad, too. (*He dips a lump of sugar and holds it out to her.*) Katrin?

KATRIN (*tearful again, shakes her head*): I'm sorry, Papa. I . . . I don't feel like it. (*She crosses in front of the table and sits on the chest under the window, with her back to the room.*)

PAPA: So? So? (*He goes to the dresser.*)

MAMA: What you want, Lars? (*He does not answer, but takes a cup and saucer, comes to the table and pours a cup of coffee, indicating* KATRIN *with his head.* MAMA *nods, pleased, then checks his pouring and fills up the cup from the cream pitcher which she empties in so doing.* PAPA *puts in sugar and moves to* KATRIN.)

PAPA: Katrin. (*She turns. He holds out the cup.*)

KATRIN (*incredulous*): For me?

PAPA: For our grown-up daughter. (MAMA *nods, standing arm in arm with* PAPA. KATRIN *takes the cup, lifts it—then her emotion overcomes her. She thrusts it at* PAPA *and rushes from the room.*) Katrin is the dramatic one! Is too bad. Her first cup of coffee, and she does not drink it.

MAMA: It would not have been good for her, so late at night.

PAPA (*smiling*): And you, Marta, you are the practical one.

MAMA: You drink the coffee, Lars. We do not want to waste it. (*She pushes it across to him.*)

(*Lights dim. Curtains close. Light up on turntable, representing the parlor of JENNY's house. A telephone on a table, at which TRINA is discovered, talking.*)

TRINA (*into phone*): Yes, Peter. Yes, Peter. I know, Peter, but we don't know where he is. It's so long since we heard from him. He's sure to turn up soon. Yes, I know, Peter. I know, but . . . (*subsiding obediently*) Yes, Peter. Yes, Peter. (*sentimentally*) Oh, Peter, you know I do. Good-by, Peter. (*She hangs up, and turns, to see JENNY, who has come in behind her, eating a piece of toast and jam.*)

JENNY: What was all that about?

TRINA: Peter says we shouldn't wait any longer to hear from Uncle Chris. He says we should send the wedding invitations out right away. He was quite insistent about it. Peter can be very masterful sometimes . . . when he's alone with *me!*

(*The telephone rings again. JENNY answers it, putting down the toast, which TRINA takes up and nibbles at during the scene.*)

JENNY: This is Mrs. Stenborg's boardinghouse. Mrs. Stenborg speaking. Oh, yes, Marta . . . what is it? (*She listens.*)

(*Spot up on opposite turntable, disclosing MAMA standing at a wall telephone booth. She wears hat and coat, and has an opened telegram in her hand.*)

MAMA: Jenny, is Uncle Chris. I have a telegram. It says if we want to see him again we should come without delay.

JENNY: Where is he?

MAMA (*consulting the telegram*): It comes from a place called Ukiah. Nels says it is up north from San Francisco.

JENNY: Who is the telegram from?

MAMA: It does not say.

JENNY: That . . . woman?

MAMA: I don't know, Jenny. I think maybe.

JENNY: I won't go. (SIGRID *comes in through the curtains, dressed in hat and coat, carrying string marketing bags, full of vegetables.* JENNY *speaks to her, whisperingly, aside.*) It's Uncle Chris. Marta says he's dying. (*Then, back into phone.*) Why was the telegram sent to *you?* I'm the eldest.

MAMA: Jenny, is not the time to think of who is eldest. Uncle Chris is dying.

JENNY: *I* don't believe it. He's too mean to die. Ever. (NELS *comes to booth from wings and hands* MAMA *a slip of paper.*) I'm not going.

MAMA: Jenny, I cannot stop to argue. There is a train at eleven o'clock. It takes four hours. You call Sigrid.

JENNY: Sigrid is here now.

MAMA: Good. Then you tell her.

JENNY: What do you say the name of the place is?

MAMA: Ukiah. (*Spelling in Norwegian.*) U–K–I–A–H.

JENNY: I won't go.

MAMA: That *you* decide. (*She hangs up. Her spot goes out.*)

SIGRID: Uncle Chris dying!

JENNY: The wages of sin.

TRINA: Oh, he's old. Maybe it is time for him to go.

JENNY: Four hours by train, and maybe have to stay all night. All that expense to watch a wicked old man die of the D.T.'s.

SIGRID: I know, but . . . there is his will. . . .

JENNY: Huh, even supposing he's anything to leave—you know who he'd leave it *to,* don't you?

SIGRID: Yes. But all the same he's dying now, and blood is thicker than water. Especially when it's Norwegian. I'm going. I shall take Arne with me. Uncle Chris was always fond of children.

TRINA: I agree with Sigrid. I think we *should* go.

JENNY: Well, *you* can't go, anyway.

TRINA: Why not?

JENNY: Because of that woman. You can't meet a woman like that.

TRINA: Why not? If you two can . . .

SIGRID: We're married women.

TRINA: I'm engaged!

JENNY: That's not the same thing.

SIGRID: Not the same thing at all!

TRINA: Nonsense. I've never met a woman like that. Maybe I'll never get another chance. Besides, if he's going to change his will, there's still my dowry, remember. Do you think we should take Peter?

JENNY: Peter Thorkelson? Whatever for?

TRINA: Well, after all, I mean . . . I mean, his profession . . .

JENNY: Trina, you always were a fool. Anyone would know the last person a dying man wants to see is an undertaker!

(*Blackout. Turntable revolves out. Spot up on* KATRIN. *She wears her schoolgirl hat.*)

KATRIN: When Mama said I was to go with her, I was excited and I was frightened. It was exciting to take sandwiches for the train, almost as though we were going on a picnic. But I was scared at the idea of seeing death, though I told myself that if I was going to be a writer, I had to experience everything. But all the same, I hoped it would be all over when we got there. (*She starts to walk up the steps.*) It was afternoon when we arrived. We asked at the station for the Halvorsen ranch, and it seemed to me that the man looked at us strangely. Uncle Chris was obviously considered an odd character. The ranch was about three miles from the town: a derelict, rambling old place. There was long grass, and tall trees, and a smell of honeysuckle. We made quite a cavalcade, walking up from the gate. (*The procession comes in behind* KATRIN. MAMA, JENNY, TRINA, SIGRID *and* ARNE.) The woman came out on the steps to meet us.

(*The procession starts moving upwards. The* WOMAN *comes through the curtains, down one step. The* AUNTS *freeze in their tracks.* MAMA *goes forward to her.*)

MAMA: How is he? Is he—?

WOMAN (*with grave self-possession*): Come in, won't you? (*She holds the curtains slightly aside.* MAMA *goes in.* KATRIN *follows, looking curiously at the* WOMAN. *The* AUNTS *walk stiffly past her,* SIGRID *clutching* ARNE *and shielding him from contact with the* WOMAN. *They disappear behind the curtains. The* WOMAN *stands a moment, looking off into the distance. Then she goes in behind the curtains, too.*)

(*The curtains draw apart, revealing* UNCLE CHRIS' *bedroom. It is simple, and shabby. The door to the room is at the back. In the wall at left is a window, with curtains, drawn aside now. In front of it, a washstand. The afternoon sunlight comes through the window, falling onto the big double bed, in which* UNCLE CHRIS *is propped up on pillows. Beside him, on a small table, is a pitcher of water. He has a glass in his hand.* MAMA *stands to his right,* JENNY *to the left. The others are ranged below the window. The* WOMAN *is not present.*)

UNCLE CHRIS (*handing* MAMA *the empty glass*): I want more. You give me more. Is still some in the bottle.

MAMA: Uncle Chris, that will not help now.

UNCLE CHRIS: It always help. (*With a glance at* JENNY.) Now especially.

JENNY (*firmly*): Uncle Chris, I don't think you realize . . .

UNCLE CHRIS: What I don't realize? That I am dying? Why

else do I think you come here? Why else do I think you stand there, watching me? (*He sits upright.*) Get out. Get out. I don't want you here. Get out!

JENNY: Oh, very well. Very well. We'll be outside on the porch, if you want us. (*She starts toward the door.*)

UNCLE CHRIS: That is where I want you—on the porch! (JENNY *goes out.* TRINA *follows.* SIGRID *is about to go, too, when* UNCLE CHRIS *stops her.*) Wait. That is Arne. Come here, Arne. (ARNE, *propelled by* SIGRID, *advances toward the bed.*) How is your knee?

ARNE: It's fine, Uncle Chris.

UNCLE CHRIS: Not hurt any more? You don't use swear vords any more?

ARNE: N-no, Uncle Chris.

UNCLE CHRIS: You walk goot? Quite goot? Let me see you walk. Walk around the room. (ARNE *does so.*) Fast. Fast. Run! Run! (ARNE *does so.*) Is goot.

SIGRID (*encouraged and advancing*): Uncle Chris, Arne has always been so fond of you. . . .

UNCLE CHRIS (*shouting*): I tell you all to get out. Except Marta. (*As* KATRIN *edges with the* AUNTS *to the door.*) And Katrinë. Katrinë and I haf secret. You remember, Katrinë?

KATRIN: Yes, Uncle Chris.

MAMA: Uncle Chris, you must lie down again.

UNCLE CHRIS: Then you give me drink.

MAMA: No, Uncle Chris.

UNCLE CHRIS: We cannot waste what is left in the bottle. You do not drink it . . . who will drink it when I am gone? What harm can it do . . . now? I die, anyway. . . . You give it to me. (MAMA *goes to the washstand, pours him a drink of whisky and water, and takes it to him, sitting on the bed beside him. He drinks, then turns to her, leaning back against her arm and the pillows.*) Marta, I haf never made a will. Was never enough money. But you sell this ranch. It will not bring moch. I have not had it long enough. And there is mortgage. Big mortgage. But it leave

78

a little. Maybe two, three hundred dollars. You give to Yessie.

MAMA: Yessie?

UNCLE CHRIS: Yessie Brown. My housekeeper. No, why I call her that to you? You understand. She is my voman. Twelve years she has been my voman. My wife, only I cannot marry her. She has husband alive somewhere. She was trained nurse, but she get sick and I bring her to the country to get well again. There will be no money for *you,* Marta. Always I wanted there should be money to make Nils doctor. But there were other things . . . quick things. And now there is no time to make more. There is no money, but you make Nils doctor, all the same. You like?

MAMA: Sure, Uncle Chris. It is what Lars and I have always wanted for him. To help people who suffer. . . .

UNCLE CHRIS: Is the greatest thing in the world. It is to have a little of God in you. Always I wanted to be doctor myself. Is the only thing I have ever wanted. Nils must do it for me.

MAMA: He will, Uncle Chris.

UNCLE CHRIS: Is goot. (*He strokes her hand.*) You are the goot one. I am glad you come, *Lille Ven.* (*He moves his head restlessly.*) Where is Yessie?

MAMA: I think she wait outside.

UNCLE CHRIS: You do not mind if she is here?

MAMA: Of course not, Uncle Chris.

UNCLE CHRIS: You call her. I like you both be here. (MAMA *goes, with a quick glance at* KATRIN, *who has been standing, forgotten, listening intently.* UNCLE CHRIS *signs to* KATRIN *to come closer. She sits on the chair beside the bed.*) Katrinë, your Mama write me you drink coffee now? (*She nods. He looks at her affectionately.*) Katrinë, who will be writer. . . . You are not frightened of me now?

KATRIN: No, Uncle Chris.

UNCLE CHRIS: One day maybe you write story about Uncle Chris. If you remember.

KATRIN (*whispering*): I'll remember.

(MAMA *returns with the* WOMAN. *They come to his bed,
    standing on either side of it.*)

UNCLE CHRIS (*obviously exhausted and in pain*): I like you
    both stay with me . . . now. I think best now maybe
    Katrinë go away. Good-by, Katrinë (*Then he repeats it
    in Norwegian.*) Farvell, Katrinë.
KATRIN: Good-by, Uncle Chris.
UNCLE CHRIS: You say it in Norwegian, like I do.
KATRIN (*in Norwegian*): Farvell, Onkel Chris. (*She slips out,
    in tears.*)
UNCLE CHRIS: Yessie! Maybe I should introduce you to each
    other. Yessie, this is my niece, Marta. The only von of my
    nieces I can stand. Marta, this is Yessie, who have give me
    much happiness. . . .

(*The* TWO WOMEN *shake hands across the bed.*)

MAMA: I am very glad to meet you.
JESSIE: I am, too.
UNCLE CHRIS (*as they shake*): Is goot. And now you give me
    von more drink. You have drink with me . . . both of you.
    That way we finish the bottle. Yes?

(JESSIE *and* MAMA *look at each other.*)

MAMA: Sure, Uncle Chris.
UNCLE CHRIS: Goot. Yessie, you get best glasses. (*With a
    chuckle to* MAMA.) Yessie does not like to drink, but this
    is special occasion. (JESSIE *gets three glasses from a wall
    shelf.*) What is the time?
MAMA: It is about half-past four, Uncle Chris.
UNCLE CHRIS: The sun come around this side the house in
    afternoon. You draw the curtain a little maybe. Is strong
    for my eyes. (MAMA *goes over and draws the curtain over
    the window. The stage darkens.* JESSIE *pours three drinks,
    filling two of the glasses with water. She is about to put*

water in the third when UNCLE CHRIS *stops her.*) No, no, I take it now without water. Always the last drink without water. Is Norwegian custom. (*To* MAMA, *with a smile.*) True? (JESSIE *sits on the bed beside him, about to feed his drink to him, but he pushes her aside.*) No. No, I do not need you feed it to me. I can drink myself. (*He takes the glass from her.*) Give Marta her glass. (JESSIE *hands a glass to* MAMA. *The* TWO WOMEN *stand on either side of the bed, holding their glasses.*) So. . . . Skoal!

JESSIE (*clinking glasses with him*): Skoal.

MAMA (*doing likewise*): Skoal.

(*They all three drink. Slow dim to blackout. Curtains close. Spot up on turntable. A porch with a bench, and a chair, on which the three* AUNTS *are sitting.* JENNY *is dozing in the chair.*)

SIGRID (*flicking her handkerchief*): These gnats are awful. I'm being simply eaten alive.

TRINA: Gnats are always worse around sunset. (*She catches one.*)

JENNY (*rousing herself*): I should never have let you talk me into coming. To be insulted like that . . . turned out of his room . . . and then expected to sit here hour after hour without as much as a cup of coffee. . . .

SIGRID: I'd make coffee if I knew where the kitchen was.

JENNY: *Her* kitchen? It would poison me. (*Rising.*) No, I'm going home. Are you coming, Trina?

TRINA: Oh, I think we ought to wait a little longer. After all, you can't *hurry* these things. . . . I mean . . . (*She breaks off in confusion at what she has said.*)

JENNY (*to* SIGRID): And all your talk about his will. A lot of chance we got to say a word!

TRINA: Maybe Marta's been talking to him.

(MAMA *comes from between the curtains.*)

JENNY: Well?

MAMA: Uncle Chris has . . . gone.

(*There is a silence.*)

JENNY (*more gently than is her wont*): Did he . . . say anything about a will?

MAMA: There is no will.

JENNY: Well, then, that means . . . we're his nearest relatives. . . .

MAMA: There is no money, either.

SIGRID: How do you know?

MAMA: He told me. (*She brings out a small notebook that she is carrying.*)

JENNY: What's that?

MAMA: Is an account of how he spent the money.

JENNY: Bills from a liquor store.

MAMA: No, Jenny. No. I read it to you. (JENNY *sits again.*) You know how Uncle Chris was lame . . . how he walked always with limp. It was his one thought . . . lame people. He would have liked to be doctor and help them. Instead, he help them other ways. I read you the last page. . . . (*She reads from the notebook.*) "Joseph Spinelli. Four years old. Tubercular left leg. Three hundred thirty-seven dollars, eighteen cents." (*Pause.*) "Walks now. Esta Jensen. Nine years. Club-foot. Two hundred seventeen dollars, fifty cents. Walks now." (*Then, reading very slowly.*) "Arne Solfeldt. . . ."

SIGRID (*startled*): My Arne?

MAMA (*reading on*): "Nine years. Fractured kneecap. Four hundred forty-two dollars, sixteen cents."

(KATRIN *and* ARNE *come running in.*)

ARNE (*calling as he comes running across*): Mother . . . Mother . . . Are we going to eat soon? (*He stops, awed by the solemnity of the group, and by* MAMA, *who puts out*

her hand gently, to silence him.) What is it? Is Uncle
Chris . . . ?

MAMA (*to the* AUNTS): It does not tell the end about Arne. I
like to write "Walks now." Yes?

SIGRID (*very subdued*): Yes.

MAMA (*taking a pencil from the book*): Maybe even . . .
"runs"? (SIGRID *nods, moist-eyed.* TRINA *is crying.* MAMA
writes in the book, and then closes it.) So. Is finished. Is
all. (*She touches* JENNY *on the shoulder.*) It was good.

JENNY (*after a gulping movement*): I go and make some
coffee.

(*The woman,* JESSIE, *appears from between the curtains on
the steps.*)

JESSIE: You can go in and see him now if you want.
(JENNY *looks back, half-hesitant, at the others. Then she
nods and goes in.* TRINA *follows her, mopping her eyes.*
SIGRID *puts her arm suddenly around* ARNE *in a spasm
of maternal affection, and they, too, go in.* MAMA, KATRIN
and JESSIE *are left alone.* KATRIN *stands apart,* MAMA *and
JESSIE are in front of the curtains.*) I'm moving down to the
hotel for tonight . . . so that you can all stay. (*She is about
to go back, when* MAMA *stops her.*)

MAMA: Wait. What will you do now . . . after he is buried?
You have money? (JESSIE *shakes her head.*) Where you
live?

JESSIE: I'll find a room somewhere. I'll probably go back to
nursing.

MAMA: You like to come to San Francisco for a little? To
our house? We have room. Plenty room.

JESSIE (*touched, moving to* MAMA): That's very kind of you,
but . . .

MAMA: I like to have you. You come for a little as our guest.
When you get work you can be our boarder.

JESSIE (*awkwardly grateful*): I don't know why you should
bother. . . .

MAMA (*touching her*): You were good to Uncle Chris. (JESSIE *grasps her hand, deeply moved, then turns and goes quickly back through the curtains.* MAMA *turns to* KATRIN.) Katrin, you come and see him?

KATRIN (*scared*): See him? You mean . . .

MAMA: I like you see him. You need not be frightened. He looks . . . happy and at peace. I like you to know what death looks like. Then you are not frightened of it, ever.

KATRIN: Will you come with me?

MAMA: Sure. (*She stretches out her hand, puts her arm around her, and then leads her gently in through the curtains.*)

(*Spot up on turntable, representing a park bench against a hedge.* TRINA *and* MR. THORKELSON, *in outdoor clothes, are seated together.* TRINA *is cooing over a baby carriage.*)

TRINA: Who's the most beautiful Norwegian baby in San Francisco? Who's going to be three months old tomorrow? Little Christopher Thorkelson! (*To* MR. THORKELSON.) Do you know, Peter, I think he's even beginning to *look* a little like Uncle Chris! Quite apart from his black curls— and those, of course, he gets from *you*. (*To baby again.*) He's going to grow up to be a black Norwegian, isn't he, just like his daddy and his Uncle Chris? (*Settling down beside* MR. THORKELSON.) I think there's something about his mouth . . . a sort of . . . well . . . *firmness*. Of course, it's *your* mouth, too. But then I've always thought you had quite a lot of Uncle Chris about you. (*She looks back at the baby.*) Look—he's asleep!

MR. THORKELSON: Trina, do you know what next Thursday is?

TRINA (*nodding, smiling*): Our anniversary.

MR. THORKELSON: What would you think of our giving a little party?

TRINA: A party?

MR. THORKELSON: Oh, quite a modest one. Nothing showy or

ostentatious—but, after all, we have been married a year, and with your having been in mourning and the baby coming so soon and everything, we've not been able to entertain. I think it's time you . . . took your place in society.

TRINA (*scared*): What . . . sort of a party?

MR. THORKELSON: An evening party. (*Proudly.*) A soirée! I should say about ten people . . . some of the Norwegian colony . . . and Lars and Marta, of course. . . .

TRINA (*beginning to count on her fingers*): And Jenny and Sigrid. . . .

MR. THORKELSON: Oh . . . I . . . I hadn't thought of asking Jenny and Sigrid.

TRINA: Oh, we'd have to. We couldn't leave them out.

MR. THORKELSON: Trina, I hope you won't be offended if I say that I have never really felt . . . well, altogether comfortable with Jenny and Sigrid. They have always made me feel that they didn't think I was . . . well . . . *worthy* of you. Of course, I know I'm not, but . . . well . . . one doesn't like to be reminded of it . . . *all* the time.

TRINA (*taking his hand*): Oh, Peter.

MR. THORKELSON: But you're quite right. We must ask them. Now, as to the matter of refreshments . . . what would you suggest?

TRINA (*flustered*): Oh, I don't know. I . . . what would you say to . . . ice cream and cookies for the ladies . . . and coffee, of course . . . and . . . perhaps port wine for the gentlemen?

MR. THORKELSON (*anxiously*): Port wine?

TRINA: Just a little. You could bring it in already poured out, in *little* glasses. Jenny and Sigrid can help me serve the ice cream.

MR. THORKELSON (*firmly*): No. If Jenny and Sigrid come, they come as guests, like everyone else. You shall have someone in to help you in the kitchen.

TRINA: You mean a waitress? (MR. THORKELSON *nods, beaming.*) Oh, but none of us have *ever* . . . do you really think

. . . I mean . . . you did say we shouldn't be ostentatious. . . .

MR. THORKELSON (*nervously, rising and starting to pace up and down*): Trina, there's something I would like to say. I've never been very good at expressing myself or my . . . well . . . *deeper* feelings—but I want you to know that I'm not only very fond of you, but very . . . well . . . very *proud* of you as well, and I want you to have the best of everything, as far as it's in my power to give it to you. (*He sits again—then, as a climax.*) I want you to have a waitress!

TRINA (*overcome*): Yes, Peter. (*They hold hands.*)

(*The lights fade and the turntable revolves out. Curtains part on kitchen, slightly changed, smartened and refurnished now. MAMA and PAPA seated as usual. MAMA is darning. DAGMAR, looking a little older, is seated on the chest, reading a solid-looking book. NELS enters from back door, carrying a newspaper. He wears long trousers now, and looks about seventeen.*)

NELS (*hitting PAPA playfully on the head with the paper*): Hello! Here's your evening paper, Papa.

(*PAPA puts down the morning paper he is reading and takes the evening one from NELS.*)

PAPA (*at table*): Is there any news?

NELS: No. (*He takes out a package of cigarettes with elaborate unconcern. MAMA watches with disapproval. Then, as he is about to light his cigarette, he stops, remembering something.*) Oh, I forgot. There's a letter for Katrin. I picked it up on the mat as I came in. (*Going to back door and calling.*) Katrin! Katrin! There's a letter for you.

KATRIN (*answering from off stage*): Coming!

MAMA (*at table*): Nels, you know who the letter is from?

NELS: Why, no, Mama. (*Hands it to her.*) It looks like her own handwriting.

MAMA (*gravely inspecting it*): Is bad.

PAPA: Why is bad?

MAMA: She get too many like that. I think they are stories she send to the magazines.

DAGMAR (*closing her book loudly, rising*): Well, I'll go and see if I have any puppies yet. (*Crosses below the table and then turns.*) Mama, I've just decided something.

MAMA: What have you decided?

DAGMAR: If Nels is going to be a doctor, when I grow up, I'm going to be a—(*looking at the book title, and stumbling over the word*)—vet-vet-veterinarian.

MAMA: And what is that?

DAGMAR: A doctor for animals.

MAMA: Is good. Is good.

DAGMAR: There are far more animals in the world than there are human beings, and far more human doctors than animal ones. It isn't fair. (*She goes to the pantry door.*) I suppose we couldn't have a horse, could we? (*This only produces a concerted laugh from the family. She turns, sadly.*) No. . . . I was afraid we couldn't. (*She goes into the pantry.*)

(KATRIN *comes in. She wears a slightly more adult dress than before. Her hair is up and she looks about eighteen.*)

KATRIN: Where's the letter?

MAMA (*handing it to her*): Here.

(KATRIN *takes it, nervously. She looks at the envelope, and her face falls. She opens it, pulls out a manuscript and a rejection slip, looks at it a moment, and then replaces both in the envelope. The others watch her covertly. Then she looks up, with determination.*)

KATRIN (*above table*): Mama . . . Papa . . . I want to say something.

PAPA: What is it?

KATRIN: I'm not going to go to college.

PAPA: Why not?

KATRIN: Because it would be a waste of time and money. The only point in my going to college was to be a writer. Well, I'm not going to be one, so . . .

MAMA: Katrin, is it your letter that makes you say this? It is a story come back again?

KATRIN: Again is right. This is the tenth time. I made this one a test. It's the best I've ever written, or ever shall write. I know that. Well, it's no good.

NELS: What kind of a story is it?

KATRIN: Oh . . . it's a story about a painter, who's a genius, and he goes blind.

NELS: Sounds like *The Light That Failed*.

KATRIN: Well, what's wrong with that?

NELS (*quickly*): Nothing. Nothing!

KATRIN (*moving down*): Besides, it's not like that. My painter gets better. He has an operation and recovers his sight, and paints better than ever before.

MAMA: Is good.

KATRIN (*bitterly unhappy*): No, it isn't. It's rotten. But it's the best I can do.

MAMA: You have asked your teachers about this?

KATRIN: Teachers don't know anything about writing. They just know about literature.

MAMA: If there was someone we could ask . . . for advice . . . to tell us . . . tell us if your stories are good.

KATRIN: Yes. Well, there isn't. And they're *not*.

PAPA (*looking at the evening paper*): There is something here in the paper about a lady writer. I just noticed the headline. Wait. (*He looks back for it and reads.*) "Woman writer tells key to literary success."

KATRIN: Who?

88

PAPA: A lady called Florence Dana Moorhead. It gives her picture. A fat lady. You have heard of her?

KATRIN: Yes, of course. Everyone has. She's terribly successful. She's here on a lecture tour.

MAMA: What does she say is the secret?

PAPA: You read it, Katrin. (*He hands her the paper.*)

KATRIN (*grabbing the first part*): "Florence Dana Moorhead, celebrated novelist and short story writer . . . blah-blah-blah . . . interviewed today in her suite at the Fairmont . . . blah-blah-blah . . . pronounced sincerity the essential quality for success as a writer." (*Throwing aside the paper.*) A lot of help that is.

MAMA: Katrin, this lady . . . maybe if you sent her your stories, *she* could tell you what is wrong with them?

KATRIN (*wearily*): Oh, Mama, don't be silly.

MAMA: Why is silly?

KATRIN (*behind table*): Well, in the first place because she's a very important person . . . a celebrity . . . and she'd never read them. And in the second, because . . . you seem to think writing's like . . . well, like cooking, or something. That all you have to have is the recipe. It takes a lot more than that. You have to have a gift for it.

MAMA: You have to have a gift for cooking, too. But there are things you can learn, if you have the gift.

KATRIN: Well, that's the whole point. I haven't. I *know* . . . now. So, if you've finished with the morning paper, Papa, I'll take the want ad section, and see if I can find myself a job. (*She takes the morning paper and goes out.*)

MAMA: Is bad. Nels, what you think?

NELS: I don't know, Mama. Her stories seem all right to me, but I don't know.

MAMA: It would be good to know. Nels, this lady in the paper . . . what else does she say?

NELS (*taking up the paper*): Not much. The rest seems to be about *her* and her home. Let's see. . . . (*He reads—walking down.*) "Apart from literature, Mrs. Moorhead's main interest in life is gastronomy."

MAMA: The stars?

NELS: No—eating. "A brilliant cook herself, she says that she would as soon turn out a good soufflé as a short story, or find a new recipe as she would a first edition."

MAMA (*reaching for the paper*): I see her picture? (*She looks at it.*) Is kind face. (*Pause while she reads a moment. Then she looks up and asks.*) What is first edition?

(*Blackout. Lights up on turntable, representing the lobby of the Fairmont Hotel. A couch against a column with a palm behind it. An orchestra plays softly in the background. MAMA is discovered seated on the couch, waiting patiently. She wears a hat and a suit, and clutches a newspaper and a bundle of manuscripts. A couple of guests come through the curtains and cross, disappearing into the wings. MAMA watches them. Then FLORENCE DANA MOORHEAD enters through the curtains. She is a stout, dressy, good-natured, middle-aged woman. A BELLBOY comes from the right, paging her.*)

BELLBOY: Miss Moorhead?

F. D. MOORHEAD: Yes?

BELLBOY: Telegram.

F. D. MOORHEAD: Oh, . . . Thank you. (*She tips him, and he goes. MAMA rises and moves towards her.*)

MAMA: Please . . . Please . . . Miss Moorhead . . . Miss Moorhead.

F. D. MOORHEAD (*looking up from her telegram, on the steps*): Were you calling me?

MAMA: Yes. You are . . . Miss Florence Dana Moorhead?

F. D. MOORHEAD: Yes.

MAMA: Please . . . might I speak to you for a moment?

F. D. MOORHEAD: Yes—what's it about?

MAMA: I read in the paper what you say about writing.

F. D. MOORHEAD (*with a vague social smile*): Oh, yes?

MAMA: My daughter, Katrin, wants to be writer.

F. D. Moorhead (*who has heard that one before*): Oh, really? (*She glances at her watch on her bosom.*)

Mama: I bring her stories.

F. D. Moorhead: Look, I'm afraid I'm in rather a hurry. I'm leaving San Francisco this evening. . . .

Mama: I wait two hours here for you to come in. Please, if I may talk to you for one, two minutes. That is all.

F. D. Moorhead (*kindly*): Of course, but I think I'd better tell you that if you want me to read your daughter's stories, it's no use. I'm very sorry, but I've had to make a rule never to read anyone's unpublished material.

Mama (*nods—then after a pause*): It said in the paper you like to collect recipes . . . for eating.

F. D. Moorhead: Yes, I do. I've written several books on cooking.

Mama: I, too, am interested in gastronomy. I am good cook. Norwegian. I make good Norwegian dishes. Lutefisk. And Kjötboller. That is meat balls with cream sauce.

F. D. Moorhead: Yes, I know. I've eaten them in Christiania.

Mama: I have a special recipe for Kjötboller . . . my mother give me. She was best cook I ever knew. Never have I told this recipe, not even to my own sisters, because they are not good cooks.

F. D. Moorhead (*amused*): Oh?

Mama: But . . . if you let me talk to you . . . I give it to you. I promise it is good recipe.

F. D. Moorhead (*vastly tickled now*): Well, that seems fair enough. Let's sit down. (*They move to the couch and sit.*) Now, your daughter wants to write, you say? How old is she?

Mama: She is eighteen. Just.

F. D. Moorhead: *Does* she write, or does she just . . . *want* to write?

Mama: Oh, she write all the time. Maybe she should not be author, but it is hard to give up something that has meant so much.

F. D. Moorhead: I agree, but . . .

MAMA: I bring her stories. I bring twelve.

F. D. MOORHEAD (*aghast*): Twelve!

MAMA: But if you could read maybe just one . . . To know if someone is good cook, you do not need to eat a whole dinner.

F. D. MOORHEAD: You're very persuasive. How is it your daughter did not come herself?

MAMA: She was too unhappy. And too scared . . . of you. Because you are celebrity. But I see your picture in the paper. . . .

F. D. MOORHEAD: That frightful picture!

MAMA: Is the picture of woman who like to eat good. . . .

F. D. MOORHEAD (*with a rueful smile*): It certainly is. Now, tell me about the Kjötboller.

MAMA: When you make the meat balls you drop them in boiling stock. Not water. That is one of the secrets.

F. D. MOORHEAD: Ah!

MAMA: And the cream sauce. That is another secret. It is half *sour* cream, added at the last.

F. D. MOORHEAD: That sounds marvelous.

MAMA: You must grind the meat six times. I could write it out for you. And . . . (*tentatively*) while I write, you could read?

F. D. MOORHEAD (*with a laugh*): All right. You win. Come upstairs to my apartment. (*She rises.*)

MAMA: Is kind of you. (*They start out.*) Maybe if you would read *two* stories, I could write the recipe for Lutefisk as well. You know Lutefisk . . . ?

(*They have disappeared into the wings, and the turntable revolves out. KATRIN is at her desk.*)

KATRIN: When Mama came back, I was sitting with my diary, which I called my Journal now, writing a Tragic Farewell to my Art. It was very seldom that Mama came to the attic, thinking that a writer needed privacy, and I was surprised to see her standing in the doorway. (*She looks up.* MAMA *is standing on the steps.*) Mama!

MAMA: You are busy, Katrin?

KATRIN (*jumping up*): No, of course not. Come in.

MAMA (*coming down*): I like to talk to you.

KATRIN: Yes, of course.

MAMA (*seating herself at the desk*): You are writing?

KATRIN (*on the steps*): No. I told you, that's all over.

MAMA: That is what I want to talk to you about.

KATRIN: It's all right, Mama. Really, it's all right. I was planning to tear up all my stories this afternoon, only I couldn't find half of them.

MAMA: They are here.

KATRIN: Did *you* take them? What for?

MAMA: Katrin, I have been to see Miss Moorhead.

KATRIN: Who's Miss . . . ? You don't mean Florence Dana Moorhead? (MAMA *nods.*) You don't mean . . . (*She comes down to her.*) Mama, you don't mean you took her my stories?

MAMA: She read five of them. I was two hours with her. We have glass of sherry. Two glass of sherry.

KATRIN: What . . . did she say about them?

MAMA (*quietly*): She say they are not good.

KATRIN (*turning away*): Well, I knew that. It was hardly worth your going to all that trouble just to be told that.

MAMA: She say more. Will you listen, Katrin?

KATRIN (*trying to be gracious*): Sure. Sure. I'll listen.

MAMA: I will try and remember. She say you write now only because of what you have read in other books, and that no one can write good until they have felt what they write about. That for years she write bad stories about people in the olden times, until one day she remember something that happen in her own town . . . something that only she could know and understand . . . and she feels she must tell it . . . and that is how she write her first good story. She say you must write more of things you know. . . .

KATRIN: That's what my teacher always told me at school.

93

MAMA: Maybe your teacher was right. I do not know if I explain good what Miss Moorhead means, but while she talks I think I understand. Your story about the painter who is blind . . . that is because . . . forgive me if I speak plain, my Katrin, but it is important to you . . . because you are the dramatic one, as Papa has said . . . and you think it would feel good to be a painter and be blind and not complain. But never have you imagined how it would really be. Is true?

KATRIN (*subdued*): Yes, I . . . guess it's true.

MAMA: But she say you are to go on writing. That you have the gift. (KATRIN *turns back to her, suddenly aglow.*) And that when you have written story that is real and true . . . then you send it to someone whose name she give me. (*She fumbles for a piece of paper.*) It is her . . . agent . . . and say she recommend you. Here. No, that is recipe she give me for goulash as her grandmother make it . . . here . . . (*She hands over the paper.*) It helps, Katrin, what I have told you?

KATRIN (*subdued again*): Yes, I . . . I guess it helps. Some. But what have *I* got to write about? I haven't seen anything, or been anywhere.

MAMA: Could you write about San Francisco, maybe? Is fine city. Miss Moorhead write about her home town.

KATRIN: Yes, I know. But you've got to have a central character or something. She writes about her grandfather . . . he was a wonderful old man.

MAMA: Could you maybe write about Papa?

KATRIN: Papa?

MAMA: Papa is fine man. Is wonderful man.

KATRIN: Yes, I know, but . . .

MAMA (*rising*): I must go fix supper. Is late. Papa will be home. (*She goes up the steps to the curtains, and then turns back.*) I like you should write about Papa. (*She goes inside.*)

KATRIN (*going back to her seat behind the desk*): Papa. Yes, but what's he ever done? What's ever happened to him? What's ever happened to *any* of us? Except always being poor and having illness, like the time when Dagmar went to hospital and Mama . . . (*The idea hits her like a flash.*) Oh. . . . Oh. . . . (*Pause—then she becomes the* KATRIN *of today.*) And that was how it was born . . . suddenly in a flash . . . the story of "Mama and the Hospital" . . . the first of all the stories. I wrote it . . . oh, quite soon after that. I didn't tell Mama or any of them. But I sent it to Miss Moorhead's agent. It was a long time before I heard anything . . . and then one evening the letter came. (*She takes an envelope from the desk in front of her.*) For a moment I couldn't believe it. Then I went rushing into the kitchen, shouting. . . . (*She rises from the desk, taking some papers with her, and rushes upstage, crying, "Mama, Mama." The curtains have parted on the kitchen—and the family tableau—*MAMA, PAPA, CHRISTINE, *and* NELS. DAGMAR *is not present.* KATRIN *comes rushing in, up the steps. The turntable revolves out as soon as she has left it.*) Mama . . . Mama . . . I've sold a story!

MAMA (*at table*): A story?

KATRIN: Yes, I got a letter from the agent . . . with a check for . . . (*gasping*) five hundred dollars!

NELS (*on the chest*): No kidding? (*He rises.*)

MAMA: Katrin . . . is true?

KATRIN: Here it is. Here's the letter. Maybe I haven't read it right. (*She hands the letter.* PAPA *and* MAMA *huddle and gloat over it.*)

CHRISTINE (*behind* MAMA's *chair*): What will you *do* with five hundred dollars?

KATRIN: I don't know. I'll buy Mama her warm coat, I know that.

CHRISTINE: Coats don't cost five hundred dollars.

KATRIN: I know. We'll put the rest in the Bank.

NELS (*kidding*): Quick. Before they change their mind, and stop the check.

KATRIN: Will you, Mama? Will you take it to the Bank downtown tomorrow? (*MAMA looks vague.*) What is it?

MAMA: I do not know how.

NELS: Just give it to the man and tell him to put it in your account, like you always do.

(MAMA *looks up at* PAPA.)

PAPA: You tell them . . . now.

CHRISTINE: Tell us what?

MAMA (*desperately*): Is no bank account! (*She rises, feeling hemmed in by them—sits on bench.*) Never in my life have I been inside a bank.

CHRISTINE: But you always told us . . .

KATRIN: Mama, you've always said . . .

MAMA: I know. But was not true. I tell a lie.

KATRIN: But why, Mama? Why did you pretend?

MAMA: Is not good for little ones to be afraid . . . to not feel secure. (*Rising again.*) But now . . . with five hundred dollar . . . I think I can tell.

KATRIN (*going to her, emotionally*): Mama!

MAMA (*stopping her, quickly*): You read us the story. You have it there?

KATRIN: Yes.

MAMA: Then read.

KATRIN: Now?

MAMA: Yes. No—wait. Dagmar must hear. (*She opens pantry door and calls.*) Dagmar.

DAGMAR (*off*): Yes, Mama?

MAMA (*calling*): Come here, I want you.

DAGMAR (*off*): What is it?

MAMA: I want you. No, you leave the rabbits! (*She comes back.*) What is it called . . . the story?

KATRIN (*seating herself in the chair that* MR. HYDE *took in the opening scene.*) It's called "Mama and the Hospital."

PAPA (*delighted*): You write about Mama?

KATRIN: Yes.

MAMA: But I thought . . . I thought you say . . . I tell you . . . (*She gestures at* PAPA, *behind his back.*)

KATRIN: I know, Mama, but . . . well, that's how it came out.

(DAGMAR *comes in.*)

DAGMAR: What is it? What do you want?

MAMA: Katrin write story for magazine. They pay her five hundred dollar to print it.

DAGMAR (*completely uninterested*): Oh. (*She starts back for the pantry.*)

MAMA (*stopping her*): She read it to us. I want you should listen. (DAGMAR *sits on the floor at* MAMA's *feet.*) You are ready, Katrin?

KATRIN: Sure.

MAMA: Then read.

(*The group around the table is now a duplicate of the grouping around* MR. HYDE *in the first scene, with* KATRIN *in his place.* CHRISTINE *is in* TRINA's *chair.*)

KATRIN (*reading*): "For as long as I could remember, the house on Steiner Street had been home. All of us were born there. Nels, the oldest and the only boy . . ." (NELS *looks up, astonished to be in a story*) "my sister, Christine . . ." (CHRISTINE *does likewise*) "and the littlest sister, Dagmar. . . ."

DAGMAR: Am I in the story?

MAMA: Hush, Dagmar. We are all in the story.

KATRIN: "But first and foremost, I remember Mama." (*The lights begin to dim and the curtain slowly to fall. As it descends, we hear her voice continuing.*) "I remember that every Saturday night Mama would sit down by the kitchen table and count out the money Papa had brought home in the little envelope. . . ."

(*By now, the curtain is down.*)

LIFE WITH FATHER

INTRODUCTION

What makes a play run on Broadway for 3,224 performances, and establish the all-time record? Such was the record
of *Life with Father*, which opened at the Empire Theatre,
in New York, on November 8, 1939, and closed on July 12,
1947. What history was made while the Day family portrayed
life on Madison Avenue in the 1880's! World War II was
begun and ended. The first atomic bomb was dropped on
Hiroshima. World leaders met at Casablanca, Yalta, Potsdam
—history-making conferences that are still affecting the fate of
the world. New nations were born and old nations disappeared. The Days kept marching on night after night, de-
lighting thousands of theatregoers who came to forget the
troubles of the times, to escape into a happier past and to
identify themselves with the tightly knit family on Madison
Avenue in the days of the horsecars and elevated trains.

The origin of the play has more than usual interest. Three
books of sketches by Clarence Day had attracted the attention of playwrights even before Mr. Day died, in 1935. However, both he and later his widow were reluctant to give permission to have these sketches of rather intimate family life
dramatized. After consent had been obtained, Howard Lindsay and Russel Crouse collaborated for two years before the
script was finally acceptable to them, to Mrs. Katherine P.
Day and other members of the family and to the producer,
Oscar Serlin.

Howard Lindsay, the coauthor, played Father Day and

Dorothy Stickney, his wife in real life, played Mother Day. As the years went by, other distinguished actresses played Mother Day, including Lily Cahill, Nydia Westman, Margalo Gilmore, Dorothy Gish and Lillian Gish. The play opened in London on June 5, 1947.

What made what had once been a collection of sketches in *The New Yorker* such a successful play? It was not the plot, which admittedly is pretty thin. The antics of a successful businessman of the 1880's, as he tries to avoid being baptized while his wife uses a whole gamut of feminine wiles to get him to accede, are hardly the stuff of a well-made play. Rather we are interested in the play because we enjoy being in the "house with Father. It is exciting living with Clarence Day, Sr., not for what he does, but for what he is." [1]

It is a cliché, but still valid, that what makes a play memorable after its original brief run is its characters. To thousands of playgoers Father Day was real. He may have reminded them of Father Days in their own households or in those of their friends and relatives. Mother Day represented to them the feminine head of the household, whose devotion to her husband and children was equaled by her ignorance of finance. This was long before the days of the working mother, who does not have to account to her husband for every penny she spends for the household.

Nostalgic as it was throughout those dark years of World War II, *Life with Father* has some of those verities that belonged to ages before the 1880's and to the decades after. Clarence and Mary's idyl is the tale of adolescent affection from time immemorial. Father Day is not unique in his attitude toward visiting relatives who stay longer than they should. Thus, by using sharply delineated characters who are real enough to make you recall your own family counterparts, the dramatists fashioned this amusing, and at times tender, vehicle. As John Mason Brown wrote the day after it opened, "Merely as a play it may be unimportant, but, as a

---

[1] Kenneth Thorpe Rowe, *A Theatre in Your Head*, p. 122.

biography of everyone's family, except Caspar Milquetoast's, it is as shrewdly drawn as it is ingratiating." [2]

In time it became as necessary to see *Life with Father* as to have seen Niagara Falls, the Statue of Liberty or the Metropolitan Museum of Art. [3]

THE MAN OF 3,224 NIGHTS

Some of Howard Lindsay's experiences as Father Day for more than 3,000 performances were related in his article "Confessions of Father Day," in *The New York Times* of January 16, 1949. [4] Here we have the unique reflections of a dramatist upon his own performance of a part he had written. One quotation is particularly revealing, because it gets at the heart of Father Day's character:

> For example, during most of the moments of Father's frequent indignations, there should be uppermost his sense of incredulity that these things could be happening to him. It was very easy for me to lose this edge of astonishment and become merely exasperated.
>
> Also, there would creep into my explosions an acerbity that was most unattractive. I still recall with deep gratitude a remark Dorothy made to me as we were driving home after a performance. "You know, Howard, I don't think Father is so much bad-tempered as hot-tempered." [5]

THE PLAYWRIGHTS

Howard Lindsay was born March 29, 1889, in Waterford, New York. He likes to relate the story that he developed an interest in elocution because a penniless elocution teacher paid for an advertisement in his uncle's newspaper by giving

---

[2] *Broadway in Review*, p. 99.
[3] Charles Angoff, in his review in the *North American Review*. Quoted by Barnard Hewitt, *Theatre U.S.A.*, p. 419.
[4] Reprinted in entirety in Edward A. Wright, *A Primer for Playgoers*, pp. 189–192.
[5] Wright, *op. cit.*, p. 192.

lessons to young Howard. He has always believed that those four years of speech training determined him to be an actor. After a year at Harvard, he took a course at the American Academy of Dramatic Arts and joined a touring company of *Polly of the Circus* for three years. In addition to acting, he has staged such plays as *Dulcy* and *To the Ladies,* by George S. Kaufman and Marc Connelly, and *The Poor Nut,* by J. C. Nugent and Elliott Nugent. A third career in the theatre was that of writing, which he began in the 1920's with Bertrand Robinson as collaborator. His successes include *She Loves Me Not* (1934) and *A Slight Case of Murder* (1935), written with Damon Runyon. With Russel Crouse as coauthor, he has written *Anything Goes* (1934), *Red, Hot, and Blue* (1936), *Hooray for What?* (1937), *Strip for Action* (1942), *State of the Union* (1945), which won the Pulitzer Prize, *Life with Mother* (1948), *Call Me Madam* (1950), with music by Irving Berlin, and *Remains to Be Seen* (1951). As coproducer with Russel Crouse, he has scored with *Arsenic and Old Lace* (1941), *The Hasty Heart* (1945) and *Detective Story* (1949).

Russel Crouse was born in Findlay, Ohio, February 20, 1893. At seventeen he began to write as a reporter for the Cincinnati *Commercial-Tribune.* Among his other newspaper assignments, he was news and sports reporter for the Kansas City, Missouri, *Star,* reporter and columnist for the New York *Globe, Evening Mail* and *Evening Post.* He wrote several books that revealed his different interests: *Mr. Currier and Mr. Ives* (1930), *It Seems Like Yesterday* (1931) and *Murder Won't Out* (1932), a collection of essays about unsolved New York murders.

In 1934 he began his collaboration with Howard Lindsay with the writing of *Anything Goes,* a collaboration that has been described by one critic as "the most successful team of dramaturgists since Gilbert and Sullivan." They are close personal friends as well as coauthors, and their work has enlivened many a Broadway season in the past quarter century. "We don't complement each other," Lindsay has said. "We supplement each other. If any two people can be said to think alike, we do."

ADDITIONAL READING

Brown, John Mason. *Broadway in Review,* pp. 96–101. New York: Norton, 1940.

Gagey, Edmond M. *Revolution in American Drama,* pp. 183–184. New York: Columbia, 1947.

Hewitt, Barnard. *Theatre U.S.A., 1668 to 1957,* pp. 419–420. New York: McGraw-Hill, 1959.

Kunitz, Stanley J. *Twentieth Century Authors.* First Supplement. New York: Wilson, 1955. See page 584 for a discussion of Howard Lindsay and pages 248–249 for Russel Crouse.

Mantle, Burns. *The Best Plays of 1939–40.* New York: Dodd, Mead, 1940. Contains an extract of the play.

Rowe, Kenneth Thorpe. *A Theatre in Your Head,* pp. 122–123. New York: Funk & Wagnalls, 1960.

Shipley, Joseph T. *Guide to Great Plays,* pp. 404–405. Washington, D.C.: Public Affairs Press, 1956.

Wright, Edward A. *A Primer for Playgoers,* pp. 189–192. New York: Prentice-Hall, 1958.

LIFE WITH FATHER

BY HOWARD LINDSAY AND RUSSEL CROUSE

ACT I

SCENE 1

SCENE: *The morning room in the Day home at 420 Madison Avenue, New York City, which served both as a breakfast room and a living room for the family.*

In the center of the stage is a wide archway, dividing the room from the hall. The archway can be closed by the use of sliding doors. It is usually open, however, and through it can be seen the stairs leading to the second floor, going up left, and below them the rail of the stair well leading to the basement. The front door, which we often hear slam, is to the right.

The room is furnished with the massive furniture of the period—which is the late eighties. The drapes and upholstery of most of the furniture are green.

The window, at the right, fronts on Madison Avenue. In front of the window is a large comfortable chair, upholstered in gold color, where Father generally sits to read his paper. Farther to the right is the table, which serves as a living-room table, with its proper table cover and bowl of fruit, but at mealtimes it is expanded by extra leaves, and becomes a dining table. A sofa is at left.

In left wall is a fine fireplace and mantel, over which is a very large mirror. There is a drape on the mantel and a clock, two vases and two candelabras.

Against the back wall, left and right are large console or side tables, which the maid uses as serving tables. There is a drawer in each of these.

A stand and large lamp are at one side of the left console table.

To the right of Father's chair is a tabouret used as a smoking stand, on which there are a silver-topped glass jar of cigars, a match stand and ash tray, a small vase of flowers and two beautifully bound books.

Toward the back there is an upholstered bench, which is put below the table when the room is not used as a dining room.

At the moment, there is a large fancy tablecloth folded on this bench, which during the action of the first scene is put on the dining table.

In the upper right and left corners of the room are stands upon which are large palms in handsome jardinieres.

Just behind the right corner of the sofa is an occasional table, on which there is a lamp, two framed photographs and an imposing ornament.

To the left of the sofa is a small end table, which in Scene 2 is moved to the front of the right end of the sofa and used as a tea table. At the moment, this table has on it a vase of flowers, three books and an ornament.

Just before the fireplace is an ornament stand, properly dressed. And in front of it is a small armchair.

Just above the fireplace is a bell pull.

Above the window right is a small stand on which is a tall rubber plant in a handsome jardiniere.

There are a number of very fine paintings, beautifully framed, on the walls.

On the console table at left are a large vase of flowers and

*two smaller vases. Also, at the moment, there are four
coffee cups and saucers; a tray, on which are four plates
holding half an orange each and two small plates; cereal
bowls of cereal and a silver toast rack with toast.*

*On a console table up right there are a large vase of flowers,
two smaller vases and two small framed photographs. Also,
at the moment, there is a tray on which there are six
napkins in silver rings.*

*The dining table is set for breakfast. Six plates, six knives and
forks, six teaspoons, four fruit spoons, six pats of butter, four
silver salt and pepper shakers, a silver sugar bowl and
spoon, a silver cream pitcher. A bowl of fruit is in the
center of the table.*

*A handsome five-light gas chandelier hangs from the ceiling.
Two handsome five-candle sconces are on the curved walls.*

The clock on mantel says eight-thirty.

The morning Times is on Father's armchair.

As the curtain rises, ANNIE, *the new maid, is finishing setting the table. After an uncertain look at the result, she
crosses over to her tray on the side of console table at left.
Gets toast rack—takes it to the breakfast table—then again
returns to the console table.*

VINNIE *comes down the stairs and into the room. She has red
hair.*

VINNIE: Good morning, Annie.

ANNIE: Good morning, ma'am.

VINNIE: How are you getting along?

ANNIE: All right, ma'am, I hope.

VINNIE: Now don't be nervous, just because this is your first
day. Everything's going to be all right—but I do hope
nothing goes wrong. (*She goes to back of table—then to
right of it.*) Now, let's see, is the table all set? (*Surveys table
and indicates the cream pitcher and sugar bowl.* ANNIE
follows to above table.) The cream and the sugar go down
at this end. (*Pointing to place near where Father's coffee
cup will be placed.*)

ANNIE (*placing them where indicated*): I thought in the center, ma'am; everyone could reach them easier.

VINNIE: Mr. Day sits here.

ANNIE (*getting tray of napkins from side table*): I didn't know where to place the napkins, ma'am.

VINNIE: You can tell which go where by the rings. (*She takes one from tray.*) This one belongs to Whitney—it has his initial on it—"W." (*She goes to below table and puts it at lower right. She picks up another. ANNIE follows her.*) This one with the little dog on it is Harlan's, of course. He's the baby. (*She puts it at lower left side of table. She picks up another and crosses left of table to above it; ANNIE follows.*) This "J" is for John. (*Puts it at upper left side of table. Then picks up another.*) The "C" is for Clarence— he sits here. (*Puts it at upper right side of table. Picks up another; ANNIE is at the left of VINNIE's chair.*) This plain one is mine. (*Puts it at left end of table. Picking up last one.*) And this one is Mr. Day's. It's just like mine—except that it got bent—one morning. (*Puts it at right end of table.*) And that reminds me, Annie—always be sure Mr. Day's coffee is piping hot.

ANNIE: Ah, your man has coffee instead of tea of a morning?

VINNIE (*right*): We all have coffee except the two youngest boys. They have their milk. And, Annie, always speak of my husband as Mr. Day.

ANNIE: I will that.

VINNIE (*correcting*): "Yes, ma'am," Annie.

ANNIE: Yes, ma'am.

VINNIE: And if Mr. Day should speak to you just say "yes, sir." (*Crosses in front of table.*) Don't be nervous—you'll get used to him.

(ANNIE *puts tray on side table, moving at same time that* VINNIE *does.* CLARENCE, *the eldest son, about seventeen, comes down the stairs and into the room. He is a manly, serious, good-looking boy. Because he is starting in Yale next year he thinks he is grown up. He is redheaded. The*

*left pocket of his coat shows where it had been torn and
mended.*)

CLARENCE: Good morning, Mother. (*He kisses her.*)

VINNIE: Good morning, Clarence. (ANNIE *crosses to side
table.*)

CLARENCE: Did you sleep well, Mother?

VINNIE: Yes, dear.

CLARENCE: Good. (CLARENCE *crosses and picks up morning
paper.*)

VINNIE (*to* ANNIE): We always start with fruit, except the
two young boys who have porridge. (ANNIE *takes tray of
four fruit and two cereals to table and places them from
right upper and left upper corners of table.*)

CLARENCE (*looking at newspaper*): Jimminy! Another wreck
on the New Haven! That always disturbs the stock market.
Father won't like that.

VINNIE: I do wish that New Haven would stop having wrecks.
If they knew how it upset your father— (*She indicates*
CLARENCE'S *torn and mended coat. Crosses to him.*) Mercy!
Clarence, what's happened to your coat?

CLARENCE: I tore it. Margaret mended it for me.

VINNIE: It looks terrible. Why don't you wear your blue suit?

CLARENCE: That looks worse than this one. You know, I
burnt that hole in it.

VINNIE: You can't go around looking like that. (JOHN, *who is
about fifteen, starts downstairs and into room.* JOHN *is redheaded.*) I'll have to speak to your father. Oh, dear!
(VINNIE *crosses to center.*)

JOHN (*meeting* VINNIE): Good morning, Mother. (*He kisses
her.*)

VINNIE: Good morning, John. (VINNIE *goes to upper left
corner of table;* ANNIE *has finished at table and stands
awaiting orders.*)

JOHN (*crossing to* CLARENCE): Who won?

CLARENCE: I haven't looked yet.

JOHN: Let me see. (*He tries to take paper away from* CLARENCE.)

CLARENCE: Be careful.

VINNIE: Boys—don't wrinkle that paper before your father's looked at it.

CLARENCE (*to* JOHN): Yes! (VINNIE *turns to* ANNIE.)

VINNIE: Annie, you'd better get things started. We want everything ready when Mr. Day comes down. (ANNIE *exits—taking tray with her;* VINNIE *suddenly remembers something.*) Oh! Clarence, right after breakfast, I want you and John to move the small dresser from my room into yours.

CLARENCE: What for? Is somebody coming to visit us?

JOHN (*moves a few steps left*): Who's coming?

VINNIE (*innocently*): I haven't said anyone was coming. (*Crosses between boys with sudden thought.*) And don't you say anything about it. I want it to be a surprise.

CLARENCE (*knowingly*): Oh! Father doesn't know yet!

VINNIE: No—and I'd better speak to him about a new suit for you before he finds out he's being surprised by visitors.

(WHITNEY *comes running downstairs and rushes into room. He is about ten. Suiting his age, he is a lively, active boy. He is redheaded.*)

WHITNEY (*meets* VINNIE): Good morning, Mother. (*He kisses his mother quickly, then runs to* CLARENCE *and* JOHN.)

VINNIE: Good morning, dear.

(ANNIE *enters with two glasses of milk on a tray just as* WHITNEY *arrives at foot of stairs. She lets* WHITNEY *pass her. She places milk at* HARLAN'S *and* WHITNEY'S *places. She then puts tray on side table;* VINNIE *goes to corner of table—a last look to be sure everything is in order.*)

WHITNEY: Who won?

JOHN: The Giants, seven to three. Buck Ewing hit a home run.

(HARLAN *comes sliding down bannister. He enters room. He runs to his mother and kisses her.* HARLAN *is a lovable, good-natured youngster of six. He is redheaded. He has a small removable finger bandage on first finger of right hand.*)

WHITNEY: Let me see.

HARLAN: Good morning, Mother.

VINNIE: Good morning, darling. How's your finger?

HARLAN: It itches.

VINNIE (*kissing finger*): That's a sign it's getting better. Now don't scratch it. Sit down, boys. (To HARLAN.) Get in your chair, darling. (BOYS *move to table and take their places.* CLARENCE *puts newspaper to left of Father's place at table;* JOHN *stands behind chair, ready to place* VINNIE's *chair when she sits;* WHITNEY *gets his oatmeal ready, with cream and sugar.* VINNIE *goes up to* ANNIE.) Now, Annie, watch Mr. Day; as soon as he has finished his fruit— (*there is a bellow from* FATHER *upstairs.*)

FATHER'S VOICE: Vinnie! Vinnie! (*All eyes turn toward staircase;* VINNIE *crosses to foot of stairs.*)

VINNIE: What's the matter, Clare?

FATHER'S VOICE: Where's my necktie?

VINNIE: Which necktie?

FATHER'S VOICE: The one I gave you yesterday.

VINNIE: It isn't pressed yet. I forgot to give it to Margaret.

FATHER'S VOICE: I told you distinctly I wanted to wear that tie today.

VINNIE: You've got plenty of neckties. Put on another one right away, (*she starts toward her chair*) and come down to breakfast. (JOHN *moves to back of her chair.*)

FATHER'S VOICE: Oh, damn!—damnation! (*All react to* FATHER's *"damn."* WHITNEY *starts to eat;* JOHN *helps* VINNIE *into her chair.*)

CLARENCE: Whitney!

VINNIE: Wait for your father, Whitney.

WHITNEY: But I'm in a hurry. John, can I borrow your baseball today? I'm going to pitch.

JOHN (*sits*): If I don't play myself.

WHITNEY: Look, if you need it, we're playing at the corner of Fifty-seventh Street.

VINNIE: Way up there!

WHITNEY: They're building a house on that vacant lot on Fiftieth.

VINNIE: (*putting napkin on her lap*): My! My! My! Here we move to Forty-eighth Street just to get out of the city! (JOHN *and* CLARENCE *take their napkins.*)

WHITNEY: Can't I start breakfast, Mother? I promised to be there by eight o'clock.

VINNIE: After breakfast, Whitney, you have to study your catechism.

WHITNEY: Aw, Mother! Can't I do that this afternoon?

VINNIE: Whitney, you know you have to learn five questions every morning before you leave the house.

WHITNEY: Aw, Mother—

VINNIE: You weren't very sure of yourself when I heard you last evening.

WHITNEY: I know them now.

VINNIE: Let's see. (WHITNEY *rises—stands at right of his chair, faces* VINNIE.) "What is your name?"

WHITNEY: Whitney Benjamin.

VINNIE: "Who gave you this name?"

WHITNEY: "My sponsors in baptism, wherein I was made a member of Christ, the child of God and an inheritor of the Kingdom of Heaven." Mother, if I hadn't been baptized wouldn't I have a *name*?

VINNIE: Not in the sight of the church. "What did your sponsors then for you?"

WHITNEY: "They did promise and vow three things in my name—"

(FATHER *makes his appearance on stairway.* FATHER *is about fifty, distinguished in appearance, with great charm and vitality, extremely well-dressed in a conservative way. He is redheaded.*)

FATHER (*heartily interrupting* WHITNEY): Good morning, boys. (*They rise and answer him;* FATHER *enters the room.*) Good morning, Vinnie.

VINNIE: Good morning, Clare.

FATHER (*he goes to her and kisses her*): Did you have a good night?

VINNIE: Yes, thank you, Clare.

FATHER: Good. (*Postman's whistle is blown twice, then doorbell rings.*) Sit down, boys. (FATHER *crosses to right of table.*)

VINNIE: That's the doorbell, Annie. (ANNIE *exits.*) Clare, that new suit looks very nice.

FATHER: Too damn tight! (*He sits.*) What's the matter with those fellows over in London? I wrote them a year ago they were making my clothes too tight! (Boys *dive into their breakfasts.* WHITNEY *passes cream and sugar to* HARLAN—*after he uses them,* WHITNEY *replaces them near* FATHER.)

VINNIE: You've put on a little weight, Clare.

FATHER (*putting his napkin on his knee*): I weigh just the same as I always have. (ANNIE *enters with mail on silver salver, starts to take it to* VINNIE. *There are three letters: a blue envelope and letter addressed to* VINNIE, *a business letter from the "Gem Home Popper" addressed to* CLARENCE DAY, JR., *and an unimportant envelope of notepaper size addressed to* CLARENCE DAY, ESQ. *To* ANNIE.) What's that? The mail? That goes to me. (ANNIE *gives mail to* FATHER *and exits with her tray. She returns salver, then crosses hall to left.*)

VINNIE: Clarence has just managed to tear the only decent suit of clothes he has.

FATHER (*looking through mail*): Here's one for you, Vinnie.

John, hand that to your mother. (*He passes letter on to* VINNIE—*puts other two letters right of his place, then starts on his breakfast.*)

VINNIE: I'm sorry, Clare dear; but I'm afraid Clarence is going to have to have a new suit of clothes.

FATHER: Clarence has to learn not to be so hard on his clothes.

CLARENCE: Father, I thought—

FATHER: Clarence, when you start in Yale in the Fall, I'll set aside a thousand dollars just to outfit you—but you'll get no new clothes this summer.

CLARENCE: Can't I have one of your old suits made over for me?

FATHER: Every suit I own still has plenty of wear in it. I wear my clothes until they're worn out.

VINNIE: Well, if you want your clothes worn out, Clarence can wear them out much faster than you can.

CLARENCE: Yes, and Father, you don't get a chance to wear them out. (ANNIE *enters with tray on which is a pot of coffee and a platter of scrambled eggs and bacon. She puts tray down on side table, then crosses to breakfast table, gets* VINNIE's *and* JOHN's *fruit cup, puts them on tray on side table.*) Every time you get a new batch of clothes, Mother sends the old ones to the Missionary barrel. I guess I'm just as good as any old missionary.

VINNIE: Clarence, before you compare yourself to a missionary, remember the sacrifices they make. (VINNIE *opens her letter and glances through it.* CLARENCE *has finished his fruit.*)

FATHER (*finished with his orange, chuckling*): I don't know, Vinnie. I think my clothes would look better on Clarence than on some Hottentot. (*To* CLARENCE.) Clarence, have that black suit of mine made over to fit you before your mother gets her hands on it. (VINNIE *takes piece of toast;* ANNIE *takes* FATHER's *fruit plate.*)

CLARENCE: Thank you, Father. (*To* JOHN.) Gee, one of Father's suits. Thank you, sir! (WHITNEY *is eating very rapidly.* ANNIE *takes Clarence's fruit plate and places them on tray. Then takes tray and fruit plates to side table. She then pours two cups of coffee and prepares to serve bacon and eggs.* VINNIE *is reading her letter.*)

FATHER: Whitney, don't eat so fast.

WHITNEY: But, Father, I'm going to pitch today and I promised to get there early, but before I go I have to study my catechism.

FATHER: What do you bother with that for?

VINNIE (*shocked—looks up from letter suddenly*): If he doesn't know his catechism he can't be confirmed.

WHITNEY: (*pleading to mother*): But I'm going to pitch today.

FATHER: Vinnie, Whitney's going to pitch today and he can be confirmed any old time. (ANNIE *starts with platter of bacon and eggs to breakfast table.*)

VINNIE: Clare, sometimes it seems to me that you don't care whether your children get to heaven or not.

FATHER: Oh, Whitney'll get to heaven all right. (*To* WHITNEY.) I'll be there before you are, Whitney, I'll see that you get in. (ANNIE *has reached Father's side—she leans over so that the platter of bacon and eggs is very close to* FATHER'S *plate.* FATHER *takes serving fork and spoon from platter.*)

VINNIE: What makes you so sure they'll let you in?

FATHER (*with good-humored gusto*): Well, if they don't, I'll certainly make a devil of a row. (ANNIE, *a very religious girl, is shocked, and draws back, raising platter.*)

VINNIE (*with shocked awe*): Clare, dear, I do hope you'll behave yourself when you get to heaven. (FATHER *turns to serve himself from platter, but* ANNIE *is holding it too high for him.*)

FATHER (*storming*): Vinnie, how many times have I asked you not to engage a maid who doesn't even know how to serve properly?

VINNIE (*trying to quiet* FATHER): Clare, can't you see she's new and doing her best?

FATHER: How can I serve myself when she's holding that platter over my head?

VINNIE: Annie, why don't you hold it lower? (ANNIE *lowers platter. She is frightened.* VINNIE *reads her letter again.* FATHER *serves himself but goes on talking.*)

FATHER: Where'd she come from anyway? What became of the one we had yesterday? (ANNIE *goes to* CLARENCE *and* JOHN *and serves them. She begins to sniffle.*) I don't see why you can't keep a maid.

VINNIE (*looks up from letter*): Oh, you don't!

FATHER: All I want is service. (FATHER *eats one bite of egg—then turns to* WHITNEY, *coming back to his genial tone.*) Whitney, when we get to heaven we'll organize a baseball team of our own. (BOYS *laugh.*)

VINNIE (*laughingly, putting letter down*): It would be just like you to try to run things up there. (ANNIE *serves* VINNIE.)

FATHER: Well, from all I've heard about heaven, it seems to be a very unbusinesslike place. They could probably use a good man like me. (FATHER, *after tasting bacon, swings his chair front and stamps on floor three times. After* FATHER's *first stamp* ANNIE *goes toward back. She puts bacon and egg platter on tray with fruit.*)

VINNIE (*anxiously*): What are you stamping for Margaret for? What's wrong? (ANNIE *has reached side table and is sniffling audibly.* FATHER *hears her but doesn't recognize the source.*)

FATHER (*looking to right*): What's that damn noise? (ANNIE *sniffling again. The four* BOYS *look at* ANNIE.)

VINNIE: Shhh—it's Annie.

FATHER: Annie? Who's Annie?

VINNIE: The maid. (VINNIE *looks towards* ANNIE. ANNIE, *seeing that she has attracted attention, cries loudly and hurries out into hall, taking tray of fruit and platter of bacon and eggs. After* ANNIE *exits,* VINNIE *turns her head slowly toward* FATHER. *The heads of the four* BOYS *turn*

118

at same time. All are looking at FATHER.) Clare, aren't
you ashamed of yourself?

FATHER (surprised): What have I done now?

VINNIE: You made her cry—speaking to her the way you did.

FATHER: I never said a word to her—I was addressing myself
to you. (*He eats again.*)

VINNIE: I do wish you'd be careful. It's hard enough to keep
a maid—and the uniforms just fit this one.

(MARGARET, *the cook, a small Irishwoman of about fifty,
comes into room. She is a little worried.* VINNIE *starts to
read her letter again, while eating.*)

MARGARET: What's wanting?

FATHER: Margaret, this bacon is *good*. (MARGARET *beams
and gestures deprecatingly.* ANNIE *enters, drying her eyes—
and goes to left—pours two more cups of coffee.*) It's good.
It's done just right!

MARGARET: Yes, sir! (*She smiles very pleased, and exits. As*
MARGARET *exits—*WHITNEY *passes rack of toast to* FATHER,
who takes a slice. WHITNEY *takes one and passes it to*
CLARENCE *who helps himself and passes it to* JOHN. *He
serves himself and puts rack behind bowl of fruit on table.*)

VINNIE: Clare, this letter gives me a good idea. I've decided
that next winter I won't give a series of dinners. (ANNIE
starts to table with two cups of coffee.)

FATHER: I should hope not.

VINNIE: I'll give a big musicale instead.

FATHER: You'll give a what?

VINNIE: A musicale.

FATHER (*peremptorily*): Vinnie, I will not have my peaceful
home turned into a Roman arena with a lot of hairy fiddlers
prancing about.

VINNIE: I didn't say a word about hairy fiddlers. (ANNIE
places cup by FATHER. *She is still afraid of him.* ANNIE
serves CLARENCE, *then gets two other cups.*) Mrs. Spiller

has written me about this lovely young girl who will come for very little.

FATHER: What instrument does this inexpensive paragon play? (FATHER *uses cream and sugar.* ANNIE *serves coffee to* JOHN *and* VINNIE. *After* FATHER *has used cream and sugar* CLARENCE *uses them and passes them to* JOHN, *who uses them after* MOTHER *has served herself. Then they are returned to near* FATHER's *place.*)

VINNIE: She doesn't play, Clare, she whistles.

FATHER (*astonished*): Whistles!!

VINNIE: She whistles sixteen different pieces. All for twenty-five dollars.

FATHER: I won't pay twenty-five dollars to any human peanut stand! (*He tastes his coffee, grimaces, and stamps on the floor three times.*)

VINNIE (*using cream and sugar. Speaking after* FATHER's *third stamp*): Clare, I can arrange this so it won't cost you a penny. If I invite fifty people and charge them fifty cents apiece, there's the twenty-five dollars right there!

FATHER: You can't invite people to your own house and then charge them admission.

VINNIE: I can, if the money's for the missionary fund.

FATHER: Then where are you going to get the twenty-five dollars for her whistling?

VINNIE (*thinks it over for a second*): Now, Clare, let's cross that bridge when we come to it. (*Puts letter in envelope.*)

FATHER: And if we do cross it—it will cost me twenty-five dollars—Vinnie, I'm going to be firm about this musicale—just as I had to be firm about keeping this house full of visiting relatives. Why can't we live here by ourselves in peace and comfort?

(MARGARET *comes into room.*)

MARGARET (*smiling*): What's wanting?

FATHER (*sternly*): Margaret, what is this? (*He holds his coffee cup out.*)

MARGARET (*very concerned. Crosses to above table*): It's coffee, sir.

FATHER: It is not coffee! You couldn't possibly take water and coffee beans and arrive at that! (*Pointing at cup.*) It's slops, that's what it is—slops! Take it away! Take it away, I tell you! (*Passes cup and saucer to left hand and extends it to her.* MARGARET *takes* FATHER's *cup and dashes out.* ANNIE *hurriedly starts to take* VINNIE's *cup.*)

VINNIE: Leave my coffee there, Annie! It's perfectly all right! (ANNIE *exits after getting tray and coffeepot.*)

FATHER (*angrily*): It is not. I swear I can't imagine how she concocts such an atrocity. I come down to this table every morning hungry—(*The heads of the four* BOYS *turn in unison towards* FATHER *as he speaks and towards* MOTHER *as she speaks. All are at a tension until* FATHER *breaks it.*)

VINNIE: Well, if you're hungry, Clare, why aren't you eating your breakfast?

FATHER: What?

VINNIE: If you're hungry, why aren't you eating your breakfast?

FATHER (*thrown out of bounds*): I am. (*He takes a mouthful of bacon, munches it happily and smiles, the tension is relieved and* EVERYONE *starts eating again.* FATHER's *eyes fall on* HARLAN.) Harlan, how's that finger? (HARLAN *holds up finger.*) Come over here and let me see it. (HARLAN *goes to* FATHER's *side, taking off finger cap. Shows his finger.* FATHER *puts on his glasses.*) Well, that's healing nicely. Now don't pick that scab or it will leave a scar and we don't want scars on your fingers, do we? (*He chuckles;* HARLAN *laughs.*) I guess you'll know the next time that cats don't like to be hugged. It's all right to stroke them, but don't squeeze them. Now go back and finish your oatmeal. (WHITNEY *has finished his breakfast, so folds napkin and puts in ring.*)

HARLAN (*crosses toward center*): I don't like oatmeal.

FATHER (*kindly*): Go back and eat it. It's good for you.

HARLAN (*turns, faces* FATHER): But I don't like it.

FATHER (*quietly, but firmly*): I'll tell you what you like and what you don't like. You're not old enough to know about such things. You've no business not to like oatmeal. It's good.

HARLAN (*almost yelling*): I hate it.

FATHER (*sharply*): That's enough! We won't discuss it! Finish that oatmeal at once! (HARLAN *stares at* FATHER *defiantly for a second—then goes slowly to his chair, sits and starts to eat slowly.*)

WHITNEY (*not speaking until* HARLAN *is seated*): I've finished my oatmeal. May I be excused?

FATHER: Yes, Whitney, you may go.

WHITNEY: Thank you, sir. (*He gets up quickly—pushes his chair under table and runs around table.*)

FATHER (*opening a letter, putting envelope to his right*): Pitch a good game.

(WHITNEY *has arrived in left of arch, where he pauses just long enough to bow towards his parents—good manners in those days. He starts to exit hurriedly, but is stopped short by his* MOTHER's *voice.*)

VINNIE: Whitney!

WHITNEY (*quickly turning and starting to stairs*): I'm going upstairs, to study my catechism.

VINNIE: Oh, that's all right, dear. Run along. (WHITNEY *bolts upstairs.*)

WHITNEY (*stopping on way up*): Harlan, you'd better hurry up and finish your oatmeal if you want to go with me. (*Exits.* HARLAN *begins to eat faster.*)

FATHER (*letter bewilders* FATHER): I don't know why I'm always getting damn fool letters like this!

VINNIE: What is it, Clare?

FATHER: "Dear Friend Day: We are assigning you the exclusive rights for Staten Island, to make a house-to-house canvas selling the Gem Home Popper for popcorn."

CLARENCE: I think that's for me, Father.

FATHER (*loudly, annoyed*): Then why didn't they address it to Clarence Day, Jr.? (*He looks at envelope.*) Oh, they did. (MARGARET *slips in hurriedly and puts a cup of coffee beside* FATHER, *and exits.*) I'm sorry, Clarence. I didn't mean to open your mail. (FATHER *hands letter and envelope to* CLARENCE. *Puts cream in his coffee, then picks up newspaper.* CLARENCE *puts letter in his pocket.*)

VINNIE: I wouldn't get mixed up in that, Clarence. People like popcorn but they won't go all the way to Staten Island to buy it.

FATHER (*reading newspaper*): Chauncey Depew's having another birthday.

VINNIE: How nice. (CLARENCE *puts napkin in ring.*)

FATHER: He's always having birthdays. Two or three a year. (*Exploding.*) Damn! Another wreck on the New Haven!

VINNIE: Yes. Oh, that reminds me. Mrs. Bailey dropped in last evening.

FATHER (*looking at her*): Was she in the wreck? (JOHN *puts napkin in ring.*)

VINNIE: No. She was born in New Haven. (FATHER *goes back to his paper.*) Clarence, you're having tea Thursday afternoon with Edith Bailey. (*She puts napkin in ring.*)

CLARENCE: Oh, Mother, do I have to?

JOHN (*singing. The tune is the verse of "Ta-ra-ra boom-de-aye"*): "I like coffee, I like tea. I like the girls and the girls like me." (FATHER *drinks his fresh coffee.* HARLAN *finishes oatmeal—folds and puts napkin in ring.*)

CLARENCE: Well, the girls don't like me and I don't like them.

VINNIE: Edith Bailey's a very nice girl, isn't she, Clare?

FATHER: Edith Bailey? Don't like her. I don't blame Clarence.

(FATHER *rises and goes to his chair by window and settles down to his newspaper and cigar, which he takes from cigar holder on smoking table. Others rise.* HARLAN *pushes his chair under table and exits upstairs.* ANNIE *enters with large tray, crosses behind* Boys *to right of table and starts clearing that half.*)

VINNIE (*in a guarded tone*): Clarence, you and John go upstairs and—do what I asked you to.

CLARENCE: You said the small bureau, Mother?

VINNIE: Sh! Run along! (JOHN *and* CLARENCE *exit upstairs. We hear* HARLAN *yelling—"Whitney."* VINNIE *looks at* FATHER, *hoping he hadn't heard* CLARENCE. MARGARET *enters.*)

MARGARET: If you please, ma'am, there's a package been delivered with a dollar due on it. Some kitchen knives.

VINNIE: Oh, yes, those knives from Lewis and Conger's. (VINNIE *puts letter in drawer of side table and takes out her purse opening it, giving* MARGARET *a dollar.*) Here, give this dollar to the man, Margaret. (MARGARET *exits.*)

FATHER (*getting cigar ready—a formal rite with him*): Make a memorandum of that, Vinnie. One dollar and whatever it was for.

VINNIE (*crossing to him and looking into purse*): Clare, dear, I'm afraid I'm going to need some more money.

FATHER: What for?

VINNIE: You were complaining of the coffee this morning. Well, that nice French drip coffeepot is broken—and you know how it got broken. (VINNIE *crosses to* FATHER. ANNIE *has finished right side of table and exits with loaded tray.*)

FATHER (*putting cigar down, taking out wallet*): Never mind that. As I remember, that coffeepot cost five dollars and something. I'll give you six dollars. (*He gives her a five-dollar bill and a one-dollar bill.*) And when you get it, enter the exact amount in the ledger downstairs.

VINNIE (*puts money in purse*): Thank you, Clare.

FATHER (*putting wallet in pocket*): We can't go on month after month having the household accounts in such a mess.

VINNIE (*sits on arm of* FATHER's *chair*): No—and Clare

dear, I've thought of a system that will make my book-keeping perfect.

FATHER: I'm certainly relieved to hear that. What is it?

VINNIE: Well, Clare, you never make half the fuss over how much I've spent as you do over my not being able to remember what I've spent it for.

FATHER: Exactly. This house must be run on a business basis. That's why I insist on your keeping books.

VINNIE: That's the whole point, Clare. All we have to do is open charge accounts everywhere and the stores will do my bookkeeping for me.

FATHER: Wait a minute, Vinnie.

VINNIE: Then when the bills came in you'd know exactly where your money had gone.

FATHER: I certainly would. Vinnie, I get enough bills as it is.

VINNIE: Yes, and those bills always help. They show you where I spent the money. Now, if we had charge accounts everywhere—

FATHER: Now, Vinnie, I'm not so sure that—

VINNIE (*sweetly—putting her cheek on* FATHER's *head*): Clare, dear, don't you hate those arguments we have every month. I certainly do. Not to have those I should think would be worth something to you.

FATHER (*pleasantly*): Well, I'll open an account at Lewis and Conger's—and one at McCreery's to begin with—we'll see how it works out.

VINNIE: Thank you, Clare. (*Kisses his cheek, then starts up and puts purse in drawer of side table. The smile fades from* FATHER's *face and he shakes his head doubtfully, then picks up his paper.* VINNIE *to back of table.*) Oh—the rector's coming to tea this afternoon.

FATHER: The rector? Well, I'm glad you warned me. I'll go to the Club. Don't expect me home until dinner time.

VINNIE (*crossing to back of* FATHER's *chair—a little to right of it*): I wish you'd take a little more interest in the church, Clare.

FATHER: Getting me into heaven's your job, Vinnie. (*Lov-*

ingly to her.) If there's anything wrong with my ticket when I get there, you can fix it up. Everybody loves you so much—I'm sure God must, too.

VINNIE: I'll do my best, Clare. It wouldn't be heaven without you.

FATHER (*with gusto*): If you're there, Vinnie, I'll manage to get in some way—even if I have to climb the fence. (*Picks up his cigar again.*)

JOHN (*from upstairs*): Mother! Mother, we've moved it. Is there anything else? (VINNIE *crosses in front of table.*)

FATHER (*about to light his cigar*): What's being moved?

VINNIE: Never mind, Clare. I'll come right up, John. (*She goes up a few steps and stops. She suddenly remembers that* CORA *may arrive very soon, and she wants* FATHER *out of the house before* CORA *comes. She glances towards clock on mantel. Looks back at* FATHER, *who is lighting his cigar.*) Oh, Clare, dear, it's eight-thirty. You don't want to be late at the office.

FATHER: Plenty of time. (VINNIE *looks nervously toward front door, then goes upstairs.* FATHER *returns to his newspaper.* VINNIE *has barely disappeared when something in paper makes* FATHER *yell.*) Oh, God! (VINNIE *comes tearing downstairs and into room.*)

VINNIE: What's the matter, Clare? What's wrong?

FATHER: Why did God make so many damn fools and Democrats?

VINNIE (*relieved*): Oh, politics. (*She turns and goes upstairs.*)

FATHER (*shouting after her*): Yes, but it's taking the bread out of our mouths. (*Looks at paper again.*) It's robbery, that's what it is, highway robbery! Honest Hugh Grant! Honest! Bah! A fine Mayor you've turned out to be. (FATHER *looks left, as if the Mayor was in the room and he was talking directly to him.*) If you can't run this city without raising our taxes every five minutes you'd better get out and let someone who can. Let me tell you, sir, the real estate owners of New York City are not going to tolerate these conditions any longer. Tell me this—are these increased taxes going into public improvements or are they going into graft—answer me that, honestly, if you can, Mr. Honest Hugh Grant! You can't! I thought so. Bah!

(ANNIE *enters hearing* FATHER *talking, she goes into hall but seeing* VINNIE *coming downstairs she stops.* ANNIE *must be sure not to look toward left side of room.* VINNIE *comes downstairs during the next speech.*)

If you don't stop your plundering of the pocketbooks of the good citizens of New York we're going to throw you and your boodle Board of Aldermen out of office. (*Reads paper again.*)

VINNIE (*in arch*): Annie, why aren't you clearing the table?

ANNIE: Mr. Day's got a visitor.

FATHER (*looking up, still talking to Mayor*): I'm warning you for the last time.

VINNIE: Nonsense, Annie, he's just reading his paper. Clear the table. (VINNIE *goes off.* ANNIE *comes in timidly and starts to clear table at lower corner of it.*)

FATHER (*speaks as* ANNIE *gets to table—still lecturing Mayor*): We pay you a good round sum to watch after our interests and all we get is inefficiency! (ANNIE *looks around sheepishly and is surprised to find there is no one in room.* FATHER *seems to be directing next speech to her.*) I know you're a nincompoop and I strongly suspect you of being a scalawag. (ANNIE *stands there petrified.* WHITNEY *comes running downstairs.*) It's graft—that's what it is—Tammany graft—and if you're not getting it, somebody else is.

WHITNEY: Where's John? Do you know where John is? (*He looks from* FATHER *to* ANNIE, *who is frightened and hurries to get all the rest of dishes on tray.* HARLAN *runs downstairs.*)

FATHER (*looking right through* WHITNEY—*still talking to Mayor*): Dick Croker's running this town and you're just his cat's-paw.

(VINNIE *comes in from downstairs.* FATHER *goes right on*

talking. OTHERS *carry on their conversation right through his speech.*)

HARLAN: Mother, where's John?

VINNIE: He's upstairs, dear. (*Then she crosses above sofa to mantel—just looking things over. Then crosses below sofa for her next line.* WHITNEY *runs up to stairway and up two steps.*)

FATHER: And, as for you, Richard Croker—don't think that just because you're hiding behind these minions you've put in public office, you're going to escape your legal responsibilities.

WHITNEY (*during* FATHER's *speech, calling upstairs*): John, John, I'm going to take your baseball.

JOHN (*off stage*): Don't you lose it! And don't forget to bring it back either!

WHITNEY: I won't. (HARLAN *and* WHITNEY *exit.*)

VINNIE: Annie, you should have cleared the table long ago. (ANNIE *works fast from now on.* VINNIE *goes out in hall as she is talking.*)

FATHER (*rises*): Legal responsibilities—by gad, sir, I mean *criminal* responsibilities! (*Slams paper on chair. Crosses behind table up towards arch, taking off his glasses as he goes.*)

VINNIE (*starting upstairs*): Now you watch Harlan, Whitney. Don't let him be anywhere the ball can hit him. Do what Whitney says, Harlan. And don't be late for lunch. (VINNIE *exits.*)

WHITNEY (*off*): We won't. (*Door slams.*)

FATHER (*at right corner of table—still talking to Mayor*): Don't forget what happened to William Marcy Tweed— (*Crosses to arch.* ANNIE *is again petrified*)—and if you put our taxes up once more, we'll put you in jail! (*He goes out of arch to left. A few seconds later he is seen passing arch toward outer door, wearing his hat and carrying his stick, puffing his cigar. Door is heard to slam loudly.*

ANNIE *has everything on tray, except fruit bowl. She seizes tray and runs out of arch toward basement stairs. A second later, a scream and a tremendous crash is heard.* JOHN *and* CLARENCE *come running downstairs and look over rail of stairs below.* VINNIE *follows them almost immediately.*)

VINNIE (*on upper stairs*): What is it? What happened?

CLARENCE: The maid fell downstairs.

VINNIE (*coming down*): I don't wonder with your father getting her so upset. (*Coming into room.*) Why couldn't she have finished with the table before she fell downstairs? (CLARENCE *crosses behind* VINNIE, *toward window.*)

JOHN (*coming to* VINNIE): I don't think she hurt herself.

VINNIE: Boys, will you finish the table! (*She starts out.* JOHN *crosses to table.*) Don't leave the house, Clarence, until I talk to you. (*She exits to left.*)

JOHN (*taking dish of fruit from table, puts it on side table*): What do you suppose Mother wants to talk to you about?

CLARENCE (*pushing* FATHER's *chair away from table*): Oh, probably about Edith Bailey.

JOHN (*to left of table—pushes* VINNIE's *chair out of way*): What do you talk about when you have tea alone with a girl?

(*During following speeches,* JOHN *and* CLARENCE *fold tablecloth and silencer as if it were one object—*JOHN *throws his end to* CLARENCE *to finish folding. Fold is really not the correct word, for they are very careless about it.* JOHN *puts his chair at right of arch—then opens drawer in side table.* CLARENCE *brings tablecloth up to him—he takes it and stuffs it in drawer as* CLARENCE *goes to right of table.* JOHN *goes to left of table and they pull table apart.* JOHN *takes one leaf—leans it against left end of side table.* CLARENCE *has taken other leaf and goes back with it.* JOHN *takes it from him, puts it with other one. Then* JOHN *goes to left of table and* CLARENCE *to right—they push table together. Then* CLARENCE *gets fancy tablecloth from bench*

at right and puts it on table, JOHN *helping him.* JOHN
places VINNIE'S *chair back near table—facing it front.*)

CLARENCE: We don't talk about anything. I say "Isn't it a
nice day?" And she says "Yes" and I say "I think it's a
little warmer than yesterday," and she says, "Yes, I like
warm weather, don't you?" And I say, "Yes" and then we
wait for tea to come in. (*It is at this point that* JOHN *stuffs
tablecloth in drawer as described above.*) And then she
says "How many lumps," and I say "Two, thank you," and
she says "You must have a sweet tooth" and I can't say
"Yes" and I can't say "No," so we just sit there and look
at each other for a half an hour. Then I say "Well, it's
time I was going," and she says "Must you?" and I say
"I've enjoyed seeing you very much" and she says "You
must come again" and I say "I will" and get out.

JOHN: Some fellows like girls.

CLARENCE: I don't.

JOHN: And did you ever notice fellows, when they get sweet
on a girl—the silly things a girl can make them do? And
they don't even seem to know they are acting silly. (*He
puts* CLARENCE'S *chair at right.*)

CLARENCE: Well, not for Yours Truly! (VINNIE *returns
from downstairs.* CLARENCE *crosses to back of table.*)

VINNIE: I declare I don't see how anyone could be so clumsy.

CLARENCE: Did she hurt herself?

VINNIE: No, she's not hurt—she's just hysterical, she doesn't
even make sense. Your father may have raised his voice a
little; and if she doesn't know how to hold a platter properly, she deserved it—but I know he didn't threaten to put
her in jail. (VINNIE *crosses to back of table. Then* JOHN
comes down right of table—placing FATHER'S *chair at table,
facing it front.*) Oh, well! Clarence, I want you to move
your things into the front room. You'll have to sleep with
the other boys for a night or two.

CLARENCE: You haven't told us who's coming.

VINNIE (*happily*): Cousin Cora. Isn't that nice?

CLARENCE: It's not nice for me. I can't get any sleep in there with those children.

JOHN. Wait'll Father finds out she's here! There'll be a rumpus.

VINNIE: John, don't criticize your father. He's very hospitable (*she smooths the tablecloth*)—after he gets used to the idea. (*Doorbell rings.* CLARENCE *moves up to side table.*)

JOHN (*goes to lower side of window;* VINNIE *goes to window, too.* CLARENCE *gets bowl of fruit from side table—puts it center of table*): Yes, it's Cousin Cora. Look, there's somebody with her.

VINNIE (*looking out*): She wrote me she was bringing a friend of hers. They're both going to stay here. (*A limping* ANNIE *passes through hall.*) Finish with the room, boys. (*Crosses front of table.*)

CLARENCE: Mother, do I have to sleep with the other boys and have tea with Edith Bailey all in the same week?

VINNIE: Yes, and you'd better take your father's suit to the tailor's right away so it will be ready by Thursday.

(VINNIE *goes down hall to right to greet* CORA *and* MARY. CLARENCE *goes quickly to table, gets* HARLAN's *chair and puts it left of arch, then gets table leaves and exits.* JOHN *takes* WHITNEY's *chair to left corner of room, then comes down to front of sofa.*)

VINNIE (*off stage*): Cora dear—

CORA: Cousin Vinnie, I'm so glad to see you. This is Mary Skinner.

VINNIE: Ed Skinner's daughter? How do you do. Leave your bags right in the hall. Come right upstairs. (VINNIE *enters —going toward stairs.* CORA *follows her but seeing* JOHN, *she enters room and goes to him.* MARY *enters as* VINNIE *goes toward center.* CORA *is an attractive woman of thirty.* MARY *is a very pretty, wide-eyed girl of seventeen.*)

CORA: Well, Clarence, it's so good to see you!

VINNIE (*comes down*): Oh, no, that's John. (ANNIE *crosses right to left in hall.*)

CORA: John! Why, how you've grown. You'll be a man before your mother. (*She laughs at her own wit then turns toward center to* MARY.) John, this is Mary Skinner.

MARY (*crossing to* JOHN): How do you do. (JOHN *bows.*)

CORA: This is Mary's first trip to New York. (CORA *crosses to* VINNIE.) Oh, Vinnie, I have so much to tell you. We wrote you Aunt Carrie broke her hip. That was the night Robert Ingersoll lectured. Of course she couldn't get there; and it was a good thing for Mr. Ingersoll she didn't. (CLARENCE *enters.*) And Grandpa Ebbetts hasn't been at all well. (VINNIE *indicates* CLARENCE's *presence—* CORA *turns to him.*)

CLARENCE: How do you do, Cousin Cora. I'm glad to see you.

CORA (*at his right*): This can't be Clarence.

VINNIE: Yes, it is.

CORA (*shakes his hand*): My goodness, every time I see you boys you've grown another foot. Let's see—you're going to St. Paul's now, aren't you?

CLARENCE (*with pained dignity*): St. Paul's. I was through with St. Paul's long ago. (*Facing front; proudly.*) I'm starting in Yale this fall.

MARY (*moves quickly to* CLARENCE—*very interested*): Yale!

CORA: Oh, Mary, this is Clarence—Mary Skinner. (CLARENCE *nods.* MARY *smiles and says "How do you do."*) This is Mary's first trip to New York. (CLARENCE *smiles but abruptly turns and crosses back of table toward window. He doesn't like girls.* VINNIE *crosses to* MARY *to cover up his seeming rudeness.*) She was so excited when she saw a horse car.

VINNIE: We'll have to show Mary around. I'll tell you—I'll have Mr. Day take us all to Delmonico's to dinner tonight.

MARY (*delighted*): Delmonico's!

CORA: Oh, that's marvelous. Think of that, Mary—Delmonico's! And Cousin Clare's such a wonderful host.

VINNIE (*starting out*): I know you girls want to freshen up. So come upstairs. (CORA *starts up.*)

CORA: Is it straight up?

VINNIE: The same little room.

CORA (*going upstairs*): Oh, yes, I know the way. (*The above three lines are in the nature of an ad lib and are not given any importance.* VINNIE *is now at right in arch.* MARY *follows up slowly until she is left of newel post.*)

VINNIE: Clarence, I'll let the girls use your room now and when they've finished you can move. And, bring up their bags. They're out in the hall. (VINNIE *starts upstairs, following* CORA *who has disappeared.*) I've given you girls Clarence's room but he didn't know about it until this morning and he hasn't moved out yet. (VINNIE *has disappeared upstairs.*)

CORA (*off stage*): It's a shame to put him out. (MARY *follows more slowly, and when she is up two steps she turns and leans toward* CLARENCE. CLARENCE *has gone into hall with his back toward* MARY.)

CLARENCE (*speaking during last part of* VINNIE's *speech*): John, get their old bags. (JOHN *runs—exits toward front door.* CLARENCE *moves to right of newel post. Voices of* VINNIE *and* CORA *have trailed off into the upper reaches of the house.* CLARENCE *turns to scowl in their direction and finds himself looking full into the face of* MARY.)

MARY: Cora didn't tell me about you. I never met a Yale man before. (*She gives him a smile, then turns and goes quickly upstairs with an excited girlish whinny.* CLARENCE *follows her up a step and stares after her a second, then turns toward audience with a look of "What happened to me just then?" and then a broad grin comes over his face.*)

SCENE 2

The same day. Teatime. The clock says six-ten. There is an upholstered bench in front of night table.

The tea service is on VINNIE's *right.* VINNIE *and the* RECTOR *are having tea. The* REV. DR. LLOYD *is a plump, bustling man, very good-hearted and pleasant.* VINNIE *and* DR. LLOYD *have one strong point in common: their devotion to the church and its rituals.* VINNIE's *devotion comes from her natural piety;* DR. LLOYD's *is a little more professional.*

As the curtain rises DR. LLOYD *is seated in armchair at left— with cup of tea.* VINNIE *is seated on right end of sofa.* WHITNEY *is standing near* DR. LLOYD, *stiffly erect in the manner of a boy reciting.* HARLAN *is seated on sofa, beside his mother, leaning against her and watching* WHITNEY's *performance.*

WHITNEY (*reciting*): ". . . to worship Him; to give Him thanks; to put my whole trust in Him, to call upon Him . . ." (*He hesitates.*)

VINNIE (*prompting*): "To honor—"

WHITNEY: "To honor His Holy Name and His Word—and to serve Him truly all the days of my life." (*He bows to* DR. LLOYD, *then turns toward his mother, hoping that is the end.*)

DR. LLOYD: "What is thy duty toward thy neighbor?" (WHITNEY *knows this is a tough one, shakes his head and goes "whew." Then he pulls himself together and makes a brave start.*)

WHITNEY: "My duty toward my neighbor is to love him as myself, and to do to all men as I would they should do unto me; to love, honor and succor my father and mother; to honor and obey . . .

VINNIE: "—civil authorities!"

WHITNEY (*very quickly*): "civil authorities. To—to—" (*When Whitney says first "to" he is smiling because he is confident that he knows the rest. Suddenly the smile fades from his face as he realizes he doesn't remember; the second "to" is said very uncertainly.*)

VINNIE (*to* DR. LLOYD): He really knows it.

WHITNEY: I know most of the others.

DR. LLOYD: He's done very well for so young a boy. I'm sure
if he applies himself between now and Sunday, I could
hear him again—with the others.

VINNIE: There, Whitney, you'll have to study very hard if
you want Dr. Lloyd to send your name in to Bishop Potter
next Sunday.

WHITNEY: Yes, Mother.

VINNIE: I must confess to you, Dr. Lloyd, it's really my fault.
Instead of hearing Whitney say his catechism this morning,
I let him play baseball.

WHITNEY (*excitedly to* DR. LLOYD): We won, too; thirty-
five to twenty-seven.

DR. LLOYD: That's splendid, my child. I'm glad your side
won. But winning over your catechism is a richer and fuller
victory.

WHITNEY (*to his mother, almost pleadingly*): May I go now?

VINNIE: Yes, darling. Thank Dr. Lloyd for hearing you and
run along.

WHITNEY: Thank you, Dr. Lloyd.

DR. LLOYD: Not at all, my little man.

(WHITNEY *bows to* DR. LLOYD, *then starts out quickly but
sees the cake on teatray, so he slyly but quickly turns back,
grabs a piece and runs out, hesitating at arch to give a very
quick bow. He exits right and we hear front door slam.
During above business,* VINNIE *and* DR. LLOYD *are drinking their tea.*)

VINNIE: Little Harlan is very apt at learning things by heart.

HARLAN (*rises—to* DR. LLOYD): I can spell Constantinople.
Want to hear me?

DR. LLOYD: Constantinople?

HARLAN: Yes, sir. C-o-ennaconny—annaconny—sissaconny—
tan-tan-tee-and-anople and a pople and a Constantinople!
(HARLAN *laughs.*)

DR. LLOYD (*laughingly*): Very well done, my child.

VINNIE (*putting her teacup on tray and handing* HARLAN *a*

cake from teatray): That's nice, darling. This is what you get for saying it so well.

HARLAN (*quickly taking cake*): Oh! (*Then to* DR. LLOYD.) Want me to say it again for you?

VINNIE: No, darling. One cake is enough. You run along and play with Whitney.

HARLAN (*to* DR. LLOYD): I can spell huckleberry pie.

VINNIE: Run along, dear. (HARLAN *goes out, skipping in rhythm to his recitation.*)

HARLAN: H-a-huckle—b-a-buckle—h-a-huckle—high. H-a-huckle—b-a-buckle huckleberry-pie! (*We hear door slam as he joins* WHITNEY.)

DR. LLOYD (*rises, crosses to* VINNIE—*amused*): You and Mr. Day must be very proud of your children.

VINNIE (*beaming*): Yes, we are.

DR. LLOYD (*he sits on sofa beside her, hands his cup and saucer to her*): Thank you. I was hoping I'd find Mr. Day at home this afternoon.

VINNIE (*evasively*): Well, he's usually home from the office by this time.

DR. LLOYD: Perhaps he's gone for a gallop in the park—it's such a fine day. He's very fond of horseback riding, I believe.

VINNIE: Oh, yes.

DR. LLOYD: Tell me—has Mr. Day ever been thrown from a horse?

VINNIE: Oh, no—no horse would throw Mr. Day.

DR. LLOYD: I've wondered. I thought he might have had an accident. I notice he never kneels in church.

VINNIE: Oh, that's no accident. But I don't want you to think Mr. Day doesn't pray. He does. Why, sometimes, you can hear him pray all over the house. But he never kneels.

DR. LLOYD: Never kneels! Dear me! (*He rises, crosses to his chair and sits.*) I was hoping to have the opportunity to tell you and Mr. Day about our plans for the New Edifice.

VINNIE: I'm so glad we're going to have a new church.

DR. LLOYD: I'm happy to announce that we're now ready to proceed. The only thing left to do is raise the money.

VINNIE: No one should hesitate about contributing to that! (*Front door slams.*)

DR. LLOYD: Perhaps that's Mr. Day now.

VINNIE (*sure that it isn't*): Oh, no, I hardly think so.

(FATHER *appears in arch. He sees* RECTOR—*stops suddenly.*)

FATHER: Oh, damn. I forgot.

VINNIE (*very flustered—rises, crosses to arch*): Clare dear. Dr. Lloyd's here for tea.

FATHER (*trying to smile*): I'll be right in. (*He disappears almost dejectedly to left.* VINNIE *goes to bellpull, pulls it—then to back of sofa.*)

VINNIE: I'll order some fresh tea.

DR. LLOYD: Now we can tell Mr. Day about our plans for the New Edifice.

VINNIE (*knowing her man*): Yes—after he's had his tea. (*Crosses back to sofa—up to arch.* FATHER *enters room and walks front of sofa to greet the Rector.* DR. LLOYD *rises.* VINNIE *follows* FATHER *to front of sofa.*)

FATHER (*speaking as he enters*): How are you, Dr. Lloyd? (CLARENCE *enters downstairs.*)

CLARENCE: Oh, it was Father.

DR. LLOYD: Very well, thank you. (*They shake hands.*)

CLARENCE (*to* VINNIE): They're not back yet?

VINNIE (*waving her hand to him to go*): No! Clarence, no! (CLARENCE *turns, disappointed, and goes back upstairs.*)

DR. LLOYD: It's a great pleasure to have a visit with you, Mr. Day. Except for a fleeting glimpse on the Sabbath, I don't see much of you. (FATHER *indicates to* DR. LLOYD *to sit down.* DR. LLOYD *sits.* DELIA, *the new maid, appears in arch and comes down.*)

DELIA: Yes, ma'am.

VINNIE (*sits right end of sofa*): Some fresh tea for Mr. Day. (DELIA *takes teapot from table and exits.* FATHER *sits left end of sofa, not noticing* DELIA. VINNIE *hurriedly starts conversation.*) Well, Clare, did you have a busy day at the office?

FATHER: Damn busy.

VINNIE (*in a whisper, touching his arm*): Clare!

FATHER (*smiling, to* DR. LLOYD): Very busy day. Tired out.

VINNIE: I've ordered some fresh tea. (*To* DR. LLOYD.) Poor Clare, he must work very hard. He always comes home tired. Although, how a man can get tired just sitting at his desk all day, I don't know. (FATHER *gives her a quiet, astonished look.*) I suppose Wall Street is just as much a mystery to you as it is to me, Dr. Lloyd.

DR. LLOYD: No, no, it's all very clear to me. My mind often goes to the businessman. The picture I'm most fond of is when I envisage him at the close of the day's work. There he sits—this hard-headed man of affairs, surrounded by the ledgers that he has been studying closely and harshly for hours. (FATHER, *bored, looks away.*) I see him pausing in his toil—and by chance he raises his eyes and looks out of the window at the light in God's sky, and it comes over him that money and ledgers are dross. (FATHER *stares at* DR. LLOYD *with some amazement.*) He realizes that all those figures of profit and loss are without importance or consequence—(VINNIE *looks toward arch—hoping that* DELIA *will interrupt*)—vanity and dust. And I see this troubled man bow his head and with streaming eyes resolve to devote his life to far higher things.

FATHER (*staring at him amazed*): Well, I'll be damned!

(DR. LLOYD, *wrapped up in his little sermon, doesn't hear* FATHER. DELIA *enters with fresh tea for* FATHER. *She puts pot on table and stops to arrange cups, etc. She is right of teatable.*)

VINNIE (*pouring tea*): Here's your tea, Clare. (FATHER *notices new maid.*)

FATHER: Who's this?

VINNIE (*quietly—handing tea, on saucer of which is a piece of cake—to* FATHER): The new maid.

FATHER: Where's the one we had this morning? (DELIA *picks up cake plate—extends it towards* FATHER *and* VINNIE.)

VINNIE: Never mind, Clare.

FATHER: The one we had this morning was prettier. (DELIA *puts plate down—tosses her head and hurriedly exits.* FATHER *attacks cake with relish.*) Vinnie, these cakes are good.

DR. LLOYD: Delicious!

VINNIE (*again trying to start conversation*): Dr. Lloyd wants to tell us about the plans for the New Edifice.

FATHER: The new what?

VINNIE: The new church—Clare, you know that we were planning to build a new church?

DR. LLOYD: Of course, we're going to have to raise a large sum of money.

FATHER (*alive to the danger*): Well, personally, I'm against the church hop-skipping and jumping all over town. And it so happens that during the last year I've suffered heavy losses in the market—damned heavy losses—

VINNIE (*again in whisper, touches his arm*): Clare!

FATHER: So any contribution I make will have to be a small one.

VINNIE: But, Clare, for so worthy a cause!

FATHER: —And if your finance committee thinks it's too small they can blame the rascals that are running the New Haven Railroad.

DR. LLOYD: The amount each one is to subscribe has already been decided.

FATHER (*bristling*): Who decided it?

DR. LLOYD: After considerable thought, we've found a formula which we believe is fair and equitable. It apportions the burden lightly on those least able to carry it, and justly on those whose shoulders we know are stronger. We've voted that our supporting members shall each contribute a sum equal to the cost of his pew.

FATHER (*indignantly*): I paid five thousand dollars for my pew.

VINNIE: Yes, Clare. That makes our contribution five thousand dollars.

FATHER: That's robbery! Do you know what that pew is worth today? Three thousand dollars. (*To* DR. LLOYD.) That's what the last one sold for. I've taken a dead loss of two thousand dollars on that pew already. (*Starts to lift cup but next thought stops him.*) Old Frank Baggs sold me his pew when the market was at the peak. He knew when to get out. (*Stares at* DR. LLOYD *a second, then turns to* VINNIE.) And I'm warning you now, Vinnie, if the market ever goes up, I'm going to unload that pew. (*He drinks his tea.*)

VINNIE: Clarence Day, how can you speak of the temple of the Lord as though it was something to be bought and sold on Wall Street!

FATHER: Vinnie, this is a matter of dollars and cents and that's something you don't know anything about!

VINNIE: You talking of religion in terms of dollars and cents seems to me pretty close to blasphemy.

DR. LLOYD (*soothingly*): Now, Mrs. Day, your husband is a businessman and he has a practical approach toward this problem. We've had to be practical about it, too—we have all the facts and figures.

FATHER: Oh! Well. (*Giving teacup to* VINNIE.) What's the new piece of property going to cost you?

DR. LLOYD: I think the figure I've heard mentioned is $85,000 —or was it $185,000?

FATHER: What's the property worth where we are now?

DR. LLOYD: Well, there's quite a difference of opinion about that.

FATHER (*becoming a little annoyed at* DR. LLOYD'S *vagueness*): How much do you have to raise to build the new church?

DR. LLOYD: Now, I've seen those figures—let me see—I know it depends somewhat upon the amount of the mortgage.

FATHER: Mortgage? What are the terms of the amortization?

DR. LLOYD: Amortization? That's not a word I'm familiar with.

FATHER: It all seems very vague and unsound to me. (*Doorbell rings.*) I certainly wouldn't let any customer of mine invest on what I've heard.

DR. LLOYD: We've given it a great deal of thought. I don't see how you can call it vague. (DELIA *crosses hall left to right.*)

FATHER (*after a moment, speaking rather kindly*): Dr. Lloyd, you preach that some day we'll all have to answer to God.

DR. LLOYD: We shall indeed!

FATHER (*speaking firmly*): Well, I hope God doesn't ask you any questions with figures in them.

(*We hear front door close.* CORA's *voice is heard in hall, thanking* DELIA. VINNIE *goes to arch just in time to meet* CORA *and* MARY *as they enter.* CORA *carries a corset box and* MARY *has two small bonnet boxes.* MARY *puts bonnet boxes on side table and goes around to front of bench.* FATHER *rises.*)

CORA: Oh, Vinnie, what a day. We've been to every shop in town and—

FATHER (*crossing*): Cora!

CORA: Cousin Clare! (*Crosses to right.* DR. LLOYD *rises as* LADIES *enter.*)

FATHER (*cordially*): What are you doing in New York?

(DELIA *enters, carrying about six packages of different sizes—she puts them with bonnet boxes on side table—then waits there arranging flowers, etc.*)

CORA: We're just passing through on our way to Springfield.

FATHER: We? (CLARENCE *comes downstairs into room; crosses above table to right.*)

VINNIE (*crosses left—between* FATHER *and* DR. LLOYD):

Oh, Dr. Lloyd, this is my favorite cousin, Miss Cartwright, and her friend, Mary Skinner. (*Mutual how-do-you-do's.*)

DR. LLOYD: This seems to be a family reunion. I'll just run along.

FATHER (*promptly*): Good-by, Dr. Lloyd.

DR. LLOYD: Good-by, Miss Cartwright, good-by, Miss—er— (CLARENCE *has been standing to one side with his eyes on* MARY.)

VINNIE: Clarence, you haven't said how-do-you-do to Dr. Lloyd.

CLARENCE (*so intent on* MARY, *he doesn't realize what he is saying*): Good-by, Dr. Lloyd.

VINNIE: I'll go to the door with you. (FATHER *bows to* DR. LLOYD. DR. LLOYD *and* VINNIE *go out talking.* DELIA *crosses down to tea table—ready for orders.*)

FATHER: Cora, this is certainly a pleasant surprise. Have some tea with us. (*To* DELIA.) Bring some fresh tea—and some more of those cakes.

CORA: Oh, we've had tea! (FATHER *indicates to* DELIA *to leave. She picks up tea table—puts it behind sofa—then takes tray and exits.*) We were so tired shopping, we had tea downtown.

MARY (*a great treat to a country girl*): At the Fifth Avenue Hotel.

FATHER: At the Fifth Avenue Hotel, eh? (*Crosses to* MARY.) Who'd you say this pretty little girl is?

CORA: She's Ed Skinner's daughter. (FATHER *shakes her hand. She curtsies.*) Well, Mary, at last you've met Mr. Day. I've told Mary so much about you, Cousin Clare, that she's just been dying to meet you.

FATHER (*indicating bench to* MARY *and sofa to* CORA, *who crosses to it;* FATHER *is center*): Well, sit down. Sit down. (MARY *sits on bench.*) Even if you have had tea you can stop and visit for a while. (*To* MARY) As a matter of fact, why don't you both stay to dinner? (VINNIE *enters just in time to hear this, and cuts in quickly.*)

VINNIE (*crossing down between* FATHER *and* CORA): That's

all arranged, Clare. Cora and Mary are going to have dinner with us.

FATHER: That's fine. That's fine.

CORA (*sitting on sofa*): Cousin Clare, I don't know how to thank you and Vinnie for your hospitality.

MARY: Yes, Mr. Day.

FATHER (*To* MARY): Well, you'll have to take pot luck.

CORA: No, I mean—

VINNIE (*close to* FATHER—*quickly interrupting*): Clare, dear, did you know the girls are going to visit Aunt Judith in Springfield for a whole month?

FATHER: A whole month. (*Crossing* VINNIE—*towards sofa.*) How long are you going to be in New York, Cora?

CORA: All week.

FATHER: Splendid. We'll hope to see something of you.

CORA: Why—we—are—

VINNIE (*crossing to* CORA—*quickly*): Did you find anything you wanted in the shops?

CORA: Just everything.

VINNIE (*trying to get* CORA *out of room*): I want to see what you got.

CORA: I just can't wait to show you. (*Rises. Crosses before* VINNIE—*stops at left of* FATHER. *Coyly to* FATHER, *indicating package in her hand, half hiding it.*) Oh! I'm afraid some of the packages can't be opened in front of Cousin Clare.

FATHER: Shall I leave the room? (FATHER *laughs first, then they all join in. All but* VINNIE.)

CORA (*on* FATHER's *left*): Clarence, do you mind taking the packages up to our room, or should I say your room? (CLARENCE *goes up to side table. To* FATHER.) Wasn't it nice of Clarence to give up his room to us for a whole week? (MARY *rises.* FATHER *has a sudden drop in temperature.*)

VINNIE (*more anxious to get* CORA *out*): Come on, Cora, I just can't wait to see what's in those packages. (CORA, MARY *and* VINNIE *start upstairs.* CORA *first—*MARY *second.* CLARENCE *is gathering up packages.*)

FATHER (*crosses to right—ominously*): Vinnie, I wish to speak to you before you go upstairs.

VINNIE: I'll be down in just a minute, Clare. (*She starts upstairs.*)

FATHER (*firmly*): I wish to speak to you now! (CORA *and* MARY *have disappeared upstairs.*)

VINNIE (*stops short on stairs*): I'll be up in just a minute, Cora. (*We hear a faint "all right" from upstairs.* VINNIE *moves slowly toward* FATHER. *As* VINNIE *comes in room.*)

FATHER (*his voice is low but incredulous*): Are those two women encamped in this house?

VINNIE: Now, Clare!

FATHER (*louder*): Answer me, Vinnie!

VINNIE (*very hurriedly—starting toward center*): Just a minute—

FATHER (*much louder*): Answer me!

VINNIE: Control yourself, Clare. (VINNIE, *scenting coming storm, hurries to sliding doors.* CLARENCE *has reached hall with his packages and he too has recognized the danger signal, and as* VINNIE *closes one door, he closes other, closing himself out into the hall. As door closes* VINNIE *turns and smiles shyly at* FATHER. *Persuasively. Coming down towards him.*) Now, Clare, you know you've always been fond of Cora.

FATHER: What has that to do with her planking herself down in my house and bringing hordes of strangers with her?

VINNIE (*sweetly reproachful*): How can you call that sweet little girl a horde of strangers?

FATHER: Why don't they go to a hotel? New York is full of hotels built for the express purpose of housing such nuisances.

VINNIE: Clare! Two girls alone in a hotel. Who knows what might happen to them?

FATHER (*crosses to center—exploding*): All right. Then put 'em on the next train. (*Turns to* VINNIE.) If they want to roam—the damned gypsies—(*crosses to left*)—lend 'em a hand. Keep 'em roaming!

VINNIE (*following him to his left*): What have we got a home for if we can't show a little hospitality?

FATHER: I didn't buy this home to show hospitality—I bought it for my own comfort!

VINNIE (*pleading*): How much are they going to interfere with your comfort living in that little room of Clarence's?

FATHER: The trouble is, damn it, they don't live there! They live in the bathroom. (*Crosses to back of table.* VINNIE *moves to sofa.*) Every time I want to take my bath it's full of giggling females washing their hair. From the time they take, you'd think it was the Seven Sutherland Sisters. (*Crosses to table.*) Get them out of here. Send 'em to a hotel. I'll pay the bill, gladly, but get them out of here. (CLARENCE *looks in through sliding doors.*)

CLARENCE: Father, I'm afraid they can hear you upstairs.

FATHER (*very matter-of-fact*): Then keep these doors closed! (CLARENCE *starts to close them.*)

VINNIE (*with spirit, but quietly*): Clarence!—you open those doors—open them all the way. (CLARENCE *does so and stands at arch.* VINNIE, *lowering her voice, crossing to center table but maintaining her spirit.*) Now, Clare, you behave yourself! They're here and they're going to stay here.

FATHER (*with great dignity*): That's enough, Vinnie! I want no more of this argument. (*With a nod of decision he goes to his armchair below window, muttering.*) Damnation! (*He sits.*)

CLARENCE: Mother, Cousin Cora's waiting for you.

FATHER: What I don't understand is why this swarm of locusts always descends on us without any warning. (VINNIE *is convinced of her victory, so starts upstairs.*) Damn! Damnation! (*He looks toward stairs.*) Damn! ! ! (VINNIE *disappears upstairs. Helplessly.*) Vinnie. (*He remembers that he loves her and chuckles.*) Dear Vinnie. (*He remembers that he is angry with her.*) Damn!

CLARENCE (*crosses to front of table*): Father, can't I go along with the rest of you to Delmonico's tonight?

FATHER: What's that? Delmonico's?

CLARENCE: You're taking Mother, Cora and Mary to Delmonico's for dinner.

FATHER (*explodes*): Oh, God! (*Rises and crosses to center. At this sound from* FATHER, VINNIE *comes flying downstairs again.* CLARENCE *quickly gets out of way by going to right of table.*) I won't have it. I won't have it. (*He crosses left.*)

VINNIE (*on the way down*): Clarence! The doors! (VINNIE *and* CLARENCE *rush and close sliding doors again.* CLARENCE *stays at arch.*)

FATHER: I won't stand it, by God! I won't stand it! I won't submit myself . . . (*After doors are closed* VINNIE *goes down and faces* FATHER.)

VINNIE (*very simply and sweetly*): What's the matter now, dear?

FATHER (*quietly intense*): Do I understand that I am not to be allowed to have dinner in my own home?

VINNIE (*lovingly—crossing to him*): It'll do us both good to get out of this house. You need a little change. It'll make you feel better.

FATHER (*still quiet*): I have a home to have dinner in. Any time I can't have dinner at home, this house is for sale!

VINNIE (*quietly stating a fact*): Well, you can't have dinner here tonight, because it isn't ordered.

FATHER (*exploding*): I'm ready to sell this place this very minute if I can't live here in peace. (*Turns, facing* VINNIE.) Then we can all go and sit under a palm tree and live on breadfruit and pickles.

VINNIE (*crossing to sofa*): But, Clare, Cora and Mary want to see something of New York.

FATHER: Oh, that's it! (*Crossing to doors.*) Well, that's no affair of mine. (*Faces* VINNIE.) I am not a guide to China-town and the Bowery.

(*He throws open sliding doors, first left, then right.* MARY *comes tripping downstairs as he opens first door. She is wearing a charming party dress.* FATHER *is at right of arch.*)

MARY (*in center of arch*): Oh, Mr. Day, I just love your
house. I could live here forever. (FATHER *draws himself
up and continues on upstairs.* MARY *looks after* FATHER,
then comes into room, a little wide-eyed.) Cora's waiting
for you, Mrs. Day.

VINNIE: Oh, yes, I'll run right up. (*She goes upstairs. There
is a slight pause—*MARY *moves down after a glance over
her shoulder at* CLARENCE.)

CLARENCE: I'm glad you like our house.

MARY: Oh, yes, I like it very much. (*Stops front of sofa and
touches green sofa cushion.*) I like green.

CLARENCE (*crossing to her*): I like green myself.

MARY (*looks up at his red hair rather shyly*): Red's my
favorite color.

CLARENCE (*abashed, he can't look at her*): It's an interesting
thing about colors. Red's a nice color in a house, too, but
outside, too much red would be bad. I mean, for instance,
if all the trees and the grass were red—(*now he has control
of himself and turns to her*)—outside, green is the best
color.

MARY (*impressed*): That's right! I've never thought of it that
way—but when you do think of it, it's quite a thought. I'll
bet you'll make your mark at Yale.

CLARENCE (*pleased, but modest*): Oh!

MARY: My mother wants *me* to go to college. Do you believe
in girls going to college?

CLARENCE: I guess it's all right if they want to waste that
much time—before they get married, I mean.

(*Door slams and* JOHN *comes in, bringing the* Youth's Companion. *He stops in center of arch long enough to throw
his hat off, as if he threw it on hat rack.* HE *makes a
whistling sound as he throws it.*)

JOHN: Oh, hello! (*They say "Hello" to him*) Look! A new
Youth's Companion! (JOHN *hurriedly crosses front of table
to armchair.*)

CLARENCE (*to* MARY—*from a mature height*): John enjoys the *Youth's Companion*. (JOHN *sits right down in* FATHER's *armchair and starts to read.* CLARENCE *is worried by this.*) JOHN! (JOHN *looks at him nonplused.* CLARENCE *gestures for him to get up.* JOHN *remembers his manners and stands. Formally to* MARY.) Won't you sit down?

MARY: Oh, thank you. (*She sits.* JOHN *sits down again quickly and dives back in* Youth's Companion. CLARENCE *turns as if to tell* JOHN *he may sit now, but* JOHN *has beaten him to it.* CLARENCE *sits beside* MARY.)

CLARENCE: As I was saying—I think it's all right for a girl to go to college if she goes to a girls' college.

MARY: Well, mother wants me to go to Ohio Wesleyan because it's Methodist. (*Then almost as a confession.*) You see, we're Methodists.

CLARENCE: Oh, that's too bad. (*Quickly correcting himself.*) I don't mean it's too bad that you're a Methodist. Anybody's got a right to be anything they want. But what I mean is—(*Unhappily.*) We're Episcopalians.

MARY: Yes, I know. I've known ever since I saw your minister—and his collar— (*She looks pretty sad for a moment, and then her face brightens.*) Oh, I just remembered—my father was an Episcopalian. He was baptized an Episcopalian. He was an Episcopalian right up to the time he married my mother. (*Almost bitterly.*) She was the Methodist.

CLARENCE (*enthusiastically*): I'll bet your father's a nice man.

MARY (*brightening*): Yes, he is. He owns the livery stable.

CLARENCE: He does? Then you must like horses. (FATHER *starts downstairs.*)

MARY: Oh, I love horses!

CLARENCE (*very manly*): They're my favorite animal. Father and I both think there's nothing like a horse! (FATHER *comes into room.* CHILDREN *all stand.*)

MARY (*crossing toward him*): Oh, Mr. Day, I'm having such a lovely time here.

FATHER: Clarence is keeping you entertained, eh?

MARY: Oh, yes, sir. (*She crosses quickly back to* CLARENCE, *then faces* FATHER.) We've been talking about everything—colors—and horses—and religion—

FATHER: Hm-m. (*He turns to* JOHN.) Has the evening *Sun* come yet?

JOHN: No, sir.

FATHER (*crosses to back of table*): What are you reading? (CLARENCE *invites* MARY *to go up left.* CLARENCE *shows her the stereoscope and pictures which are on console table. We hear front door slam.*)

JOHN: The *Youth's Companion,* sir. (WHITNEY *and* HARLAN *run in from hall.* HARLAN *goes to lower left corner of table;* WHITNEY *carries a box of tiddlywinks.*)

WHITNEY (*to corner of table*): Look what we've got!

FATHER: What is it?

WHITNEY (*opening box*): Tiddlywinks. We put our money together and bought it.

FATHER: That's a nice game. Do you know how to play it?

WHITNEY (*taking cup and tiddlywinks out of box*): I've played it lots of times.

HARLAN: Show me how to play it.

FATHER (*takes cup and tiddlywinks from* WHITNEY'S *hand*): Here, I'll show you, Harlan. (FATHER *arranges the things.* WHITNEY *goes below table—leans on table.* HARLAN *left of table.*)

MARY: Are you going out to dinner with us tonight?

CLARENCE (*looking at* FATHER): I don't know yet—but it's beginning to look as though I might.

FATHER: It's easy, Harlan. You press down like this and snap the little fellow into the glass. Now watch me—(*He snaps it and it goes off table, toward center.* FATHER *is as surprised as the boys.*) The table isn't quite large enough. You boys better play on the floor. (FATHER *points to tiddlywink on the floor—*HARLAN *gets it.* CLARENCE *puts stereoscope away.* MARY *crosses to below sofa—*CLARENCE *joins her there.*)

WHITNEY (*to floor front of table. They take box of tiddly-winks with them and start to play*): Come on, Harlan, I'll take the reds and you take the yellows. (JOHN *crosses back of table as if to leave room.*)

FATHER: John.

JOHN (*stops near arch*): Yes, sir.

FATHER: Have you practiced your piano today?

JOHN: I was going to practice this evening.

FATHER: Better do it now. (VINNIE *and* CORA *start downstairs, quickly, talking as they come.*)

CORA: Don't say anything to Cousin Clare.

VINNIE: I will, too.

CORA: Please, Cousin Vinnie. (*Above three lines are in the nature of an ad lib and do not interfere with* FATHER'S *line.*)

FATHER (*to* MARY): Music is a delight in the home. (CORA *and* VINNIE *enter room.* JOHN *waits for* VINNIE *and* CORA *to enter—then exits.* CORA *stays up a little.*)

VINNIE: Clare, what do you think Cora has just told me? (*She brings* CORA *down to* FATHER. CORA *is between* FATHER *and* VINNIE.) She and Clyde are going to be married this Fall.

FATHER: So, you finally landed him, eh? (*Everybody laughs.* VINNIE *crosses and sits on bench.*) Well, Cora, he's a very lucky man. Being married, Cora, is the only way to live.

(*From next room we hear* JOHN *playing "The Happy Farmer."*)

CORA: Well, if we can be half as happy as you and Cousin Vinnie. (*Sits at table.* FATHER *listens a moment to* JOHN'S *piano-playing—then goes to sofa.*)

VINNIE (*on bench*): Boys, shouldn't you be playing that on the table?

WHITNEY: The table isn't big enough. Father told us to play on the floor.

VINNIE: My soul and body, look at your hands! (*They do so.*)

And your supper almost ready. Go wash your hands right away and come back and show Mother they're clean. (*Boys pick up tiddlywinks saying "Yes, Mother," and depart quickly.*)

FATHER (*sitting down on sofa, indicating to* MARY *to join him, which she does*): Vinnie, this young lady looks about the same age you were when I came out to Pleasantville to rescue you.

VINNIE: Rescue me! You came out there to talk me into marrying you.

FATHER: It worked out just the same. I saved you from spending the rest of your life in that one-horse town.

VINNIE (*rises*): Cora, the other day I came across a tintype taken of Clare in Pleasantville. I want to show it to you. You'll see who needed rescuing. (*She goes to console table, at right of arch and starts to rummage around in drawer.*)

FATHER: There isn't time for that, Vinnie—hadn't we all better be getting dressed—if we're going to Delmonico's for dinner? (*He includes* CLARENCE *and* MARY *with a look —looks at his watch.* MARY *and* CLARENCE *exchange pleased looks.*) It's after six now!

CORA (*rises*): Gracious! I'll have to start. (*FATHER and* MARY *rise.*) If I'm going to dine in public with a prominent citizen like you, Cousin Clare—I'll have to look my best. (*She crosses to arch.*)

MARY: I'm changed already.

CORA: Yes, I know, Mary, but I'm afraid I'll have to ask you to come along and hook me up. (CORA *goes to foot of stairs.*)

MARY (*crossing—front of* FATHER): Of course. (*FATHER moves a little to right, ready to bow to* LADIES *as they leave room.*)

CORA: Won't take a minute, then you can come right back. (*Going up a step or two.* MARY *turns and looks back at* FATHER. CLARENCE *has gone up behind sofa to left of arch.*)

MARY (*a little afraid to ask, but it is so important to her*):
Mr. Day—were you always an Episcopalian?

FATHER: What?

MARY: Were you always an Episcopalian?

FATHER: I've always gone to the Episcopal church, yes.

MARY: But you weren't baptized a Methodist or anything,
were you? You were baptized an Episcopalian?

FATHER: Come to think of it, I don't believe I was ever baptized at all. (MARY, *a little shocked, joins* CORA *on stairs.*)

VINNIE: Clare, that's not very funny, joking about a subject
like that.

FATHER: I'm not joking—I remember now—(*to* MARY)—I
never was baptized.

VINNIE: Clare, that's ridiculous, everyone's baptized.

FATHER (*sits on sofa*): Well, I'm not.

VINNIE: Why, no one would keep a little baby from being
baptized.

FATHER: You know Father and Mother—Free Thinkers, both
of them—believed their children should decide those things
for themselves.

VINNIE: But, Clare—

FATHER: I remember when I was ten or twelve years old,
Mother said I ought to give some thought to it. (JOHN
finishes playing piano.) I suppose I thought about it, but
I never got around to having it done to me.

(VINNIE *walks slowly down toward* FATHER, *staring at him in
horror.* FATHER *is quite happily curling his moustache.
There is a decided pause.*)

VINNIE (*quietly*): Clare, do you know what you're saying?

FATHER: I'm saying I've never been baptized.

VINNIE (*excitedly*): Then something has to be done about
it right away!

FATHER: Now, Vinnie: don't get excited over nothing.

VINNIE: Nothing? I've never heard of anyone who wasn't
baptized. Even the savages in darkest Africa—

FATHER (*matter-of-factly*): It's all right for savages—and children. But if an oversight was made in my case it's too late to correct it now.

VINNIE: Clare, why haven't you ever told me?

FATHER (*getting a little annoyed*): What difference does it make?

VINNIE: But you're not a Christian, if you're not baptized.

FATHER (*rises—exploding*): Why, confound it, of course I'm a Christian. A damn good Christian, too. (CLARENCE *rushes to sliding doors and quickly closes them—shutting himself*, MARY *and* CORA *out*.) A lot better Christian than those psalm-singing donkeys in church. (*He crosses back to* VINNIE.)

VINNIE: You can't be if you won't be baptized.

FATHER: I won't be baptized and I will be a Christian. I'll be a Christian in my own way.

VINNIE: Clare, don't you want to meet us all in heaven?

FATHER: Of course, and I'm going to.

VINNIE: You can't, unless you're baptized.

FATHER (*crosses to right*): That's a lot of folderol.

VINNIE (*following him to front of bench*): Clarence Day, don't you blaspheme like that. You're coming to church with me before you go to the office in the morning and be baptized then and there.

FATHER: Vinnie, don't be ridiculous! If you think I'm going to stand there and have some minister splash water on me at my age—you're mistaken.

VINNIE: But, Clare—

FATHER (*firmly*): That's enough, Vinnie. (*He thinks for a second.*) I'm hungry. (*Crosses center.*) I'm dressing for dinner.

(FATHER *goes to doors and opens them.* WHITNEY *and* HARLAN *are there, leaning over as if listening at keyhole. They straighten up quickly.* FATHER's *attention is on door he had opened, so he passes boys and starts upstairs*

153

*before he notices them. He hesitates only a moment, then
stalks upstairs. The two* BOYS *look after* FATHER *and then
come down into room, staring at their mother.*)

WHITNEY (*awed—remembering what Mother had told him
at breakfast—not speaking until they are center*): Mother,
if Father hasn't been baptized he hasn't any name. In the
sight of the church he hasn't any name.

VINNIE: That's right! (*She sinks on bench. To herself.*) Maybe we're not even married! (*This awful thought takes
possession of* VINNIE. *Her eyes turn slowly toward children,
and she suddenly realizes their doubtful status. Her hand
goes to her mouth to cover a quick gasp of horror as*
CURTAIN FALLS.)

Act II

Scene 1

SCENE: *The same. The following Sunday, after church. A stool is left of* FATHER's *armchair. The tea table is again at left of sofa, with its ornaments on it. The clock says twelve-thirty. The stage is empty as curtain rises.*

VINNIE *comes into arch from street door, dressed in her Sunday best, carrying her prayer book, and a cold indignation. She looks over her shoulder—toward front door—then comes down to front of chair at left of table—turns her back on audience, and watches as* FATHER *passes across hall, in his Sunday cutaway, gloves and cane, and wearing his silk hat.*

As FATHER *disappears,* VINNIE *drops her prayer book rather heavily on table, and starts to take off her gloves—still facing toward arch.*

HARLAN, CORA *and* WHITNEY *come into room.* JOHN *follows them on, and goes off to hang up his hat.*

HARLAN (*pulling* CORA *to back of sofa and indicating tiddly-winks box which is on mantel*): Cousin Cora, will you play a game of tiddlywinks with me before you go?

CORA: I'm going to be busy packing until it's time to leave.

WHITNEY: We can't play games on Sunday.

CORA (*as* JOHN *enters from left and starts upstairs*): John, where are Clarence and Mary?

JOHN: They dropped behind—way behind! (JOHN *goes upstairs.* CORA *crosses to window.* WHITNEY *takes* HARLAN's *hat from him and starts toward arch.*)

VINNIE: Whitney, don't hang up your hat. I want you to go to Sherry's for the ice cream for dinner. (HARLAN *goes to* WHITNEY.) Tell Mr. Sherry strawberry—if he has it. And take Harlan with you.

WHITNEY: Yes, Mother. (WHITNEY *hands* HARLAN *his hat; then they bow to their mother—then put on their hats, turn and exit,* HARLAN *following* WHITNEY. *We hear door slam.*)

CORA (*crosses to right of table*): Oh, Vinnie, I hate to leave! We've had such a lovely week.

VINNIE (*taking off her hat—puts it on table. Sits left of table*): Cora, what must you think of Clare, making such a scene on the way out of church?

CORA: Cousin Clare probably thinks that you put the Rector up to preaching that sermon.

VINNIE: Well—I had to go to Dr. Lloyd to find out whether we were really married. The sermon on baptism was his own idea. If Clare just hadn't shouted so—now the whole congregation knows he's never been baptized. But he's going to be, Cora—you mark my words—he's going to be. I just couldn't go to heaven without Clare. Why, I get lonesome for him when I go to Ohio.

(FATHER *enters, his watch in his hand.*)

FATHER (*at center*): Vinnie, I went to the dining room and the table isn't even set for dinner yet.

VINNIE: We're having dinner late today.

FATHER: Why can't I have my meals on time?

VINNIE: The girls' train leaves at half-past one. Their cab's coming for them at one o'clock.

FATHER (*crosses back of sofa—to mantel*): Cab? The horse cars go right past our door.

VINNIE: They have those heavy bags.

FATHER (*sets clock by his watch*): Clarence and John could have gone along to carry their bags. Cabs are just a waste of money. Why didn't we have an early dinner? (FATHER *crosses to front of sofa.*)

VINNIE: There wasn't time for an early dinner and church, too.

FATHER: As far as I'm concerned this would have been a a very good day to miss church.

VINNIE (*rises—spiritedly*): I wish we had.

FATHER (*flaring*): I'll bet you put him up to preaching that sermon. (CORA *moves to get out of the seeming quarrel.*)

VINNIE (*crossing to left*): I've never been so mortified in all my life. You stamping out of church, roaring your head off at the top of your voice.

FATHER (*crossing right*): That Lloyd needn't preach at me as though I were some damn criminal. I wanted him to know it, (*turns to center*) and as far as I'm concerned, the whole congregation can know it, too.

VINNIE: They certainly know it now.

FATHER: That suits me.

VINNIE (*crossing to him, pleading*): Clare, you don't seem to understand what the church is for.

FATHER: Vinnie, if there is one place the church should leave alone, it's a man's soul. (*Crosses to left.*)

VINNIE (*moves toward him*): Clare, dear, don't you believe what it says in the Bible?

FATHER (*smilingly*): A man has to use his common sense about the Bible, Vinnie, if he has any! For instance, you'd be in a pretty fix if I gave all my money to the poor.

VINNIE (*after a moment's thought*): Oh—that's just silly. (*Crosses to left of table.*)

FATHER: Speaking of money—where are this month's household bills?

VINNIE (*turning quickly*): Now, Clare—it isn't fair to go over the household accounts while you're hungry.

FATHER: Where are those bills, Vinnie?

VINNIE: They're downstairs on your desk. (FATHER *exits.*) Of all times! (VINNIE *sits at left end of bench. To* CORA.)

It's awfully hard on a woman to love a man like Clare so much.

CORA (*moves down and sits on bench beside her*): Yes, men can be aggravating. Clyde gets me so provoked. We kept company for six years, but the minute he proposed, that is, from the moment I said "Yes," he began to take me for granted.

VINNIE: You have to expect that, Cora. I don't believe Clare has come right out and told me he loves me since we've been married. Of course I know he does, because I keep reminding him of it. You have to keep reminding them, Cora. (*Door slams.*)

CORA: There's Mary and Clarence. (*There is a moment's pause, then the two WOMEN look towards hall—then at each other with a knowing sort of smile. CORA rises, goes up to left side of arch—peeks out—then faces front and says innocently.*) Is that you, Mary?

MARY (*dashes in—very flustered*): Yes. (*CLARENCE crosses arch, with great dignity, wearing black suit and a straw hat. He exits to hang up hat.*)

CORA: Well! We have to change our clothes and finish our packing.

(*CORA goes upstairs. MARY follows her. CLARENCE enters. VINNIE takes up hat, etc.—starts up center as if to follow MARY upstairs.*)

MARY (*on first step. To CLARENCE*): It won't take me long.

CLARENCE: Can I help you pack?

VINNIE (*shocked*): Clarence! (*MARY runs upstairs. CLARENCE turns into living room, somewhat abashed. VINNIE puts her hat and gloves back on table, looks at CLARENCE.*) Clarence, why didn't you kneel in church today?

CLARENCE: What, Mother?

VINNIE: Why didn't you kneel in church today?

CLARENCE: I just couldn't.

VINNIE (*crosses to him*): Has it anything to do with Mary? I know she's a Methodist.

CLARENCE: Oh, no, Mother. Methodists kneel. Mary told me. They don't get up and down so much, but they stay down longer.

VINNIE: If it's because your Father doesn't kneel—you must remember he wasn't brought up to kneel in church. But you were—you always have—and, Clarence, you want to, don't you?

CLARENCE: Oh, yes. I wanted to today. I started to—you saw me start—but I just couldn't.

VINNIE: Is that suit of your Father's too tight for you?

CLARENCE (*crosses to right*): No, it's not too tight. It fits fine. (*Stops, turns to* VINNIE.) But it is the suit. Very peculiar things have happened to me since I started to wear it. I haven't been myself since I put it on.

VINNIE (*crossing to* CLARENCE): What do you mean, Clarence? What do you mean? (CLARENCE *pauses, then blurts out his problem.*)

CLARENCE: Mother, I can't make these clothes do anything Father wouldn't do.

VINNIE: That's nonsense—(CLARENCE *moves to right*)—and not to kneel in church is a sacrilege.

CLARENCE (*coming back to* VINNIE): But making Father's trousers kneel is more of a sacrilege.

VINNIE: Clarence!

CLARENCE: No! Remember the first night I wore this? It was at Dora Wakefield's party for Mary. Do you know what happened? We were playing Musical Chairs and Dora Wakefield sat down suddenly right in my lap. I jumped up so fast she almost got hurt.

VINNIE: But it was all perfectly innocent.

CLARENCE: It wasn't that Dora was sitting on my lap—she was sitting on Father's trousers. Mother, I've got to have a suit of my own. (*Moves right a little.*)

VINNIE: My soul and body! Well, Clarence, you have a talk with your Father. (VINNIE *follows him to right.* MARY *hurries downstairs.*) I'm sure if you approach him the right way—you know—tactfully—he'll see—

(MARY *comes into room.*)

MARY: Oh—excuse me.

VINNIE (*turning to* MARY): Gracious, have you finished your packing already?

MARY: Practically. I never put my comb and brush in until I'm ready to close my bag.

VINNIE (*she pats her son's arm, then crosses around left of table to back of it—to get hat, etc.*): I must see Margaret about your box lunch for the train. (MARY *moves to back of chair left of table, looking starry-eyed at* CLARENCE.) I'll leave you two together. (VINNIE *crosses up to arch.*) Remember—it's Sunday. (*Exits. After a short embarrassed pause,* MARY *moves center.*)

CLARENCE: I was hoping we could have a few minutes together before you left.

MARY (*not to admit her eagerness—crosses to left front of sofa*): Cora had so much to do I wanted to get out of her way.

CLARENCE (*following her*): Didn't you want to see *me?*

MARY (*self-consciously*): I did want to tell you how much I have enjoyed our—friendship. (*"Friendship" almost sounds like "love."*)

CLARENCE: You're going to write me when you get to Springfield, aren't you?

MARY: Of course, if you write first.

CLARENCE: But you'll have something to write about—your trip and Aunt Judith—and how things are in Springfield. You write to me as soon as you get there.

MARY (*rather coyly—sits*): Maybe I'll be too busy. Maybe I won't have time.

CLARENCE (*sounding like his father*): You find the time! Let's not have any nonsense about that! (MARY *at first is very surprised at his tone—then she smiles happily—im-*

pressed by his manliness. He sits.) You'll write me first—
and you'll do it right away, the first day!

MARY (*egging him on*): How do you know I'll take orders
from you?

CLARENCE: I'll show you. (*Takes quick glance toward the
hall—then holds out his left hand.*) Give me your hand!

MARY: Why should I?

CLARENCE (*very much like* FATHER): Give me your hand,
confound it!

MARY (*innocently*): What do you want with my hand? (*She
lifts her hand so it's near his, but doesn't give it to him.*)

CLARENCE (*takes her hand, sharply*): I just—(*holding her
hand, he melts*)—wanted it.

CLARENCE (*their hands, clasped together, rest on* CLARENCE's
knee and they relax happily—after a moment MARY *looks
away*): What are you thinking about?

MARY: I was just—thinking.

CLARENCE: About what?

MARY: Well, when we were talking about writing each
other, I was hoping you would write me first because that
would mean that you liked me.

CLARENCE: What's writing first got to do with my liking
you?

MARY (*turns to him*): Oh, you do like me?

CLARENCE: Of course I do. I like you better than any girl I
ever met.

MARY (*rather triumphantly*): But you don't like me well
enough to write first?

CLARENCE: I don't see how one thing's got anything to do
with the other.

MARY (*a little flustered*): But a girl can't write first because—
she's a girl.

CLARENCE (*thinks that over for a second*): That doesn't make
sense. If a girl has something to write about and a fellow
hasn't, there's no reason why she shouldn't write first.

MARY (*taking a different tack—being a little hurt*): You
know, the first few days I was here you'd do anything for

me, and then you changed. You used to be a lot of fun—
and then all of a sudden you turned into an old sober-sides.

CLARENCE: When did I?

MARY: The first time I noticed it was when we walked home
from Dora Wakefield's party. My, you were on your
dignity. You've been that way ever since. You even dress
like an old sober-sides. (CLARENCE's *face changes as*
FATHER's *pants rise to haunt him. Then he notices that
their clasped hands are resting on these very pants, and he
lifts them off, and lets go of her hand. Agony obviously is
setting in.* MARY *sees the expression on his face.*) What's
the matter?

CLARENCE (*so tense his voice is husky*): I just happened to
remember something.

MARY: What? (CLARENCE *doesn't answer.*) Oh, I know.
This is the last time we'll be together. (MARY *puts hand
on his shoulder.*)

CLARENCE (*afraid to have her even touch* FATHER's *coat*):
Mary, please.

MARY: But, Clarence—we'll see each other in a month. And
we'll be writing each other, too. I hope we will. (*She gets
up, facing him, leaving her handkerchief on sofa.*) Oh,
Clarence, please write me first because it will show me
how much you like me. Please! I'll show you how much
I like you! (*She crosses in front of him, throws herself in
his lap and buries her head on his left shoulder.* CLARENCE
stiffens.)

CLARENCE (*hoarsely—not looking at* MARY): Get up! Get up!
(SHE *pulls back her head and looks at him, then springs
from his lap with a loud cry and runs to right, covering
her face and sobbing loudly.* CLARENCE *gets up and goes
to her.*) Don't do *that*, Mary! Please don't do that!

MARY (*crying*): Now you'll think I'm just a bold and forward girl.

CLARENCE: Oh, no!

MARY: Yes, you will!—you'll think I'm bold!

CLARENCE: Oh, no—it's not that.

MARY (*half turning to him*): Was it because it's Sunday?

CLARENCE: No, it would be the same any day— (*He is about to explain, but* MARY *flares.*)

MARY (*faces him*): Oh, it's just because you didn't want me sitting on your lap?

CLARENCE: It was nice of you to do it—

MARY: It was nice of me! So you told me to get up! You just couldn't bear to have me sit there. Well, you needn't write me first. You needn't write me any letters at all because I'll tear them up without opening them! (*She turns her back on him, still crying.* FATHER *enters arch from left, a sheaf of bills in his account book under his arm; also a pencil.*) I guess I know now you don't like me. (*She breaks and starts to run toward stairs, around table.*) I never want to see you again. I—I—

(*At sight of* FATHER *she stops, only to let out a louder cry, then continues on upstairs, unable to control her sobs.* CLARENCE, *who has been standing in unhappy indecision, turns to follow her around table, but stops short, at corner of table, at sight of* FATHER, *who is standing in arch, looking at him with some amazement.* FATHER *looks toward the vanished* MARY, *and then back to* CLARENCE.)

FATHER: Clarence, that young girl is crying—she's in tears. What's the meaning of this?

CLARENCE: I'm sorry, Father, it's all my fault.

FATHER: Nonsense! What's that girl trying to do to you?

CLARENCE: What? No, she wasn't—it was—I—how long have you been here?

FATHER (*crossing to back of table—dismissing it*): Well, whatever the quarrel was about, Clarence, I'm glad you held your own. Where's your mother?

CLARENCE (*desperately*): I have to have a new suit of clothes —you've got to give me the money for it. (FATHER's *account book reaches the table with a sharp bang as he stares at* CLARENCE *in astonishment.*)

FATHER: Young man, do you realize you're addressing your father? (CLARENCE *wilts miserably.*)

CLARENCE: I'm sorry, Father—I apologize—(*he crosses right and sinks on stool just left of* FATHER's *armchair*)—but you don't know how important this is to me.

FATHER: A suit of clothes is so—? Now why should a—? (*Something dawns on* FATHER, *he looks up in direction in which* MARY *has disappeared, then looks back at* CLARENCE. *Crosses to right.*) Clarence, has your need for a suit of clothes anything to do with that young lady?

CLARENCE: Yes, Father.

FATHER: Why, Clarence! (FATHER *suddenly realizes that women have come into* CLARENCE's *emotional life, and there comes a yearning to protect this inexperienced and defenseless member of his own sex.*) This comes as quite a shock to me.

CLARENCE: What does, Father?

FATHER: You're being so grown-up. Still, I might have known that if you're going to college this fall—yes, you're at an age when you'll be meeting girls—Clarence, there are things about women that I think you ought to know. (*He goes up and closes doors, then comes down.*) Yes—it's better for you to hear this from me than to have to learn it for yourself. (*Sits on bench.*) Clarence, women aren't the angels that you think they are. Well, now—first, let me explain this to you. You see, Clarence, we men have to run this world and it's not an easy job. It takes work, and it takes thinking. A man has to be sure of his facts and figures. He has to reason things out. Now you take a woman—a woman thinks—no, I'm wrong right there— she doesn't think at all. She just gets stirred up. And she gets stirred up about the damnedest things. (*Remembering his own troubles.*) Now, I love my wife just as much as any man, but that doesn't mean I should stand for a lot of folderol. (*Looks toward arch, exploding.*) My God, I won't stand for it.

CLARENCE: Stand for what, Father?

164

FATHER (*to himself*): That is one thing I shall not submit myself to. (*Turns to* CLARENCE.) Clarence, if a man thinks a certain thing is the wrong thing to do he shouldn't do it. If he thinks it's right, he should do it. But that has nothing to do with whether he loves his wife or not.

CLARENCE: Who says it has, Father?

FATHER: They do.

CLARENCE: Who, sir?

FATHER: Women. They get stirred up—and they try to get you stirred up, too—but don't you let them, Clarence. As long as you can keep reason and logic in the argument, no matter what it's about, a man can hold his own, of course. But if they can switch you—pretty soon the argument's about whether you love them or not. I swear I don't know how they do it. Don't you let 'em, Clarence, don't you let 'em.

CLARENCE: I see what you mean so far, Father. If you don't watch yourself, love can make you do a lot of things you don't want to do.

FATHER: Exactly.

CLARENCE (*with new knowledge*): But if you do watch out and know just how to handle women—

FATHER: Then you'll be all right. All a man has to do is be firm. You know how at times I have to be firm with your mother. (*Looks again toward arch.*) Just now about this month's household accounts—

CLARENCE: But, Father, what can you do when they cry?

FATHER (*thinks for a second*): Well, that's quite a question. —You just have to make them understand that what you're doing is for their good. (*Turns back to* CLARENCE.)

CLARENCE: I see.

FATHER (*rising and putting hand on son's shoulder*): Now, Clarence—you know *all* about women. (FATHER *goes to left of table and sits down in front of his account book. He puts on his glasses, opens book and begins to sort bills.* CLARENCE *rises and looks at him.*)

CLARENCE (*rather diffidently*): But, Father—

FATHER: Yes, Clarence.

CLARENCE (*to right of table*): I thought you were going to tell me about—?

FATHER: About what?

CLARENCE: About—women.

FATHER (*after a pause—he suddenly understands to what CLARENCE is referring*): Clarence, there are some things gentlemen don't discuss! I've told you all you need to know. The thing for you to remember is—be firm! (*There is a knock at door.*) Yes, come in. (MARY *opens the door and enters.*)

MARY: Excuse me! (*She comes down, looks right, then left, sees her handkerchief, goes to couch, picks it up and continues around side of couch. CLARENCE crosses back of table to meet her, acting firm and dominating. MARY passes below him without a glance. CLARENCE wilts, then again assuming firmness, turns up in arch in an attempt to quail MARY with a look. MARY marches upstairs, ignoring him. CLARENCE turns back into room, defeated. He looks down at his clothes unhappily, then decides to be firm with his father. He straightens up and steps toward him. At this moment FATHER, staring at a bill, emits his cry of rage.*)

FATHER: Oh, God! (*CLARENCE retreats above table, then goes slowly to window. We hear door slam upstairs and sound of VINNIE's feet as she comes rushing downstairs.*)

VINNIE: What's the matter, Clare? What's wrong?

FATHER (*rises, picking up bill*): I will not send this person a check. (*VINNIE takes bill. FATHER sits again.*)

VINNIE (*looking at bill*): Why, Clare, that's the only hat I've bought since March, and it was reduced from forty dollars.

FATHER: I don't question your buying the hat or what you paid for it, but the person from whom you bought it—(*he rises and takes bill from VINNIE*)—this Mlle. Mimi—isn't fit to be in the hat business, or any other.

VINNIE: I never went there before, but it's a very nice place and I don't see why you object to it.

FATHER: I object to it because this confounded person

doesn't put her name on her bills! Mimi what? Mimi O'Brien? Mimi Jones? Mimi Weinstein?

VINNIE: How do I know? It's just Mimi.

FATHER: It can't be just Mimi. She must have some other name, confound it! I wouldn't make out a check payable to Charley or Jimmy, and I will not make out a check payable to *Mimi*. Find out what her last name is, and I'll pay her the money. (*Sits down again.*)

VINNIE: All right, Clare. All right. (*She starts out—slowly at first—then tries to hurry. She gets up about two steps.*)

FATHER: Just a minute, Vinnie, that isn't all.

VINNIE: But, Clare dear, Cora will be leaving any minute.

FATHER: Never mind Cora.

VINNIE: And it isn't polite for me—

FATHER: Never mind Cora. Sit down, Vinnie. (*He points to chair right of table.*) Sit down. (*VINNIE crosses back of table slowly—taking a peep at account book as she passes. She then sits at right. CLARENCE goes slowly into hall, looks upstairs.*) Vinnie, you know I like to live well, and I want my family to live well. But this house must be run on a sound business basis. (*VINNIE has heard this before.*) I must know how much money I am spending and what for. (*Something out the window attracts her attention.*) Now for instance, if you recall a week ago I gave you six dollars to buy a new coffeepot.

VINNIE (*quickly turning to him*): Yes, because you broke the old one. You threw it right on the floor.

FATHER: I am not talking about that. I'm merely endeavoring—

VINNIE: And it was so silly to break that nice coffeepot, Clare; there was nothing the matter with the coffee that morning. It was made just the same as always.

FATHER: It was not! It was made in a damned barbaric manner! (*CLARENCE disappears off left.*)

VINNIE: And besides, I couldn't get another imported one. That little shop has stopped selling them. They said the

167

tariff wouldn't let them. And that's your fault, Clare, because you're always voting to raise the tariff.

FATHER: The tariff protects America against cheap foreign labor. Now I find among my bills—

VINNIE: The tariff does nothing but raise the prices and that's hard on everybody, especially the farmer. (*She sounds as though she is quoting.*)

FATHER (*annoyed*): I wish to God you wouldn't talk about things you don't know a damn thing about!

VINNIE: I do too know about them. Miss Gulick says every intelligent woman should have some opinion—

FATHER: Who, may I ask, is Miss Gulick?

VINNIE: Why, Clare, you know, she's that current events woman I told you about, and the tickets are a dollar every Tuesday.

FATHER: Do you mean to tell me that a pack of idle-minded females pay a dollar apiece to listen to another female? Listen to me if you want to know anything about the events of the day.

VINNIE: But you get so excited, Clare, and besides, Miss Gulick says that our President, whom you're always belittling, prays to God for guidance and—

FATHER (*having had enough of Miss Gulick*): Vinnie, what happened to that six dollars?

VINNIE: What six dollars?

FATHER: I gave you six dollars to buy a new coffeepot and now I find that you apparently got one at Lewis and Conger's and charged it. Here's their bill. "One coffeepot—five dollars."

VINNIE (*quickly*): So you owe me a dollar and you can hand it right over. (*Holds out her hand for it.*)

FATHER: I'll do nothing of the kind. What did you do with that six dollars?

VINNIE: Why, Clare, I can't tell you now, dear. Why didn't you ask me at the time?

FATHER: Oh, my God!

VINNIE: Wait a moment! I spent four dollars and a half for

that new umbrella I told you I wanted and you said I
didn't need it but I did, very much.

FATHER: Now we are getting somewhere. (*He takes his
pencil and writes in the account book.*) One umbrella—
four dollars and fifty cents.

VINNIE: And that must have been the time I paid Mrs.
Tobin for two extra days' washing.

FATHER (*writing*): Mrs. Tobin.

VINNIE: That's two dollars more.

FATHER (*still writing*): Two dollars.

VINNIE: That makes—six dollars—and fifty cents. That's another fifty cents you owe me.

FATHER: I don't owe you anything. What you owe me is an
explanation of where my money's gone to! Now, we're
going over this account book—item by item.

VINNIE: I do the best I can to keep down expenses. And you
know yourself that Cousin Phoebe spends twice as much as
we do.

(CLARENCE *enters from left—looks upstairs, then sits on third
step. He is very despondent.*)

FATHER: Damn Cousin Phoebe—I don't wish to be told how
she throws her money around!

VINNIE: Oh, Clare, how can you? And I thought you were so
fond of Cousin Phoebe.

FATHER: I *am* fond of Cousin Phoebe, but I can do without
hearing so much about her.

VINNIE: You talk about your own relatives enough.

FATHER (*hurt*): That's not fair, Vinnie. When I talk about
my relatives I criticize them.

VINNIE: Of course, if I can't even speak of Cousin Phoebe—

FATHER (*loudly*): You can speak of her all you want to—but
I won't have Cousin Phoebe or anyone else dictating to me
how to run my house. Now this month's total—

VINNIE (*righteously*): I didn't say a word about her dictating—

FATHER (*sputters*): You said—you—

VINNIE: Why, Clare—she isn't that kind.

FATHER (*dazed*): I swear, I don't know what you said now. (*Firmly.*) You never stick to the point. I endeavor to show you how to run this house on a business basis, and you always wind up by gibbering and jabbering about everything else under the sun. Now there is a little item here of thirty-two dollars—

VINNIE (*distressed*): I don't know what you expect of me. I tire myself out chasing up and down those stairs all day long—trying to look after your comfort—to bring up our children—I do the mending and the marketing—as if that isn't enough, you expect me to be an expert bookkeeper, too. (*She begins to cry.*)

FATHER (*distressed*): Vinnie, I have no wish to be unreasonable—but don't you understand I'm doing this for your good? (VINNIE *gives him a look, then with a wail—rises and crosses to window.* FATHER *drops bills—then pencil on table—snaps off his glasses and swings chair so he faces front. Helplessly.*) I suppose I'll have to go ahead just paying the bills and hoping I've got money enough in the bank to meet them. (VINNIE *crosses to back of table.*) But it's all very discouraging.

VINNIE (*repentantly*): I'll try to do better, Clare.

FATHER (*holds his hand out to her—affectionately*): That's all I'm asking. (VINNIE *goes to just right of back of his chair. She puts her arm around his neck.*) I'll go down and make out the checks and sign them. (VINNIE *doesn't seem entirely consoled, so he attempts a lighter note to cheer her up.*) Oh, Vinnie, maybe I haven't any right to sign those checks? (*She looks at him.*) Since in the sight of the Lord I haven't any name at all. (*He laughs loudly at his own joke.* VINNIE, *taking it seriously, moves to left of his chair.*) Do you suppose the banks would feel that way about it, too—or do you think they'll take a chance?

VINNIE: That's right, Clare, to make those checks good, you'll have to be baptized.

FATHER: The bank doesn't care whether I've been baptized or not. (*He starts to pick up bills.*)

VINNIE: Well, I care. No matter what Dr. Lloyd says, I'm not sure we're really married—

FATHER (*sorry he started it*): Damn it, Vinnie, we have four children! If we're not married now, we never will be.

VINNIE: Oh, Clare, don't you see how serious this is? You've got to do something about it!

FATHER (*rises, with bills in his hand*): Well, right now I've got to do something about these damn bills you've run up. (*Sternly.*) I'm going downstairs. (*Turns to pick up book, putting bills and pencil in it.*)

VINNIE: Not before you give me that dollar and a half.

FATHER (*turning to her, astonished*): What dollar and a half?

VINNIE: The dollar and a half you owe me.

FATHER: I don't owe you any dollar and a half. I gave you some money to buy a coffeepot for *me* and somehow it turned into an umbrella for *you*.

VINNIE: Clarence Day, what kind of a man are you? Quibbling about a dollar and a half when your immortal soul is in danger! (*Religion again—so* FATHER *turns away.*) And what's more—

FATHER (*quickly*): All right. All right. All right. (*He takes three fifty-cent pieces from his change purse and gives them to her, one at a time, then puts purse back in his pocket.*)

VINNIE: Thank you, Clare. There! Now the accounts are all straight again.

(VINNIE *flounces out and upstairs.* CLARENCE *rises to let her pass.* FATHER *watches her go in astonishment, then gathers up his papers and book and starts out center toward left.*)

CLARENCE: Father—you never did tell me—may I have a new suit of clothes?

FATHER: No, Clarence! (*Starts to go, then turns back.*) I'm sorry, Clarence, but I have to be firm with you, too!

(*He stalks off.* JOHN *comes quickly downstairs, carrying a bag, which he takes out toward front door.* CLARENCE *moves to center.* JOHN *returns empty-handed and starts upstairs again.*)

CLARENCE (*getting an idea—turns up and takes* JOHN's *arm.*) John, come here a minute.

JOHN: What do you want?

CLARENCE (*pulling him farther into room*): John, have you got any money you could lend me?

JOHN: With this week's allowance I'll have about—three dollars.

CLARENCE: That's no good. I've got to have enough to buy a new suit of clothes.

JOHN: Why don't you earn some money? That's what I'm going to do. I'm going to buy a bicycle—one of those new low kinds, with both wheels the same size—you know, a safety.

CLARENCE: How are you going to earn that much?

JOHN: I've got a job—practically. Look, I found this ad in the paper. (*Takes clipping from his pocket.*) "Wanted, an energetic young man to handle household necessity that sells on sight. Liberal commissions—apply—"

CLARENCE: Liberal commissions? (*Takes clipping from* JOHN *and reads hurriedly.*) "Apply 312 West 14th Street, Tuesday, from eight to twelve." Listen John, let me have that job.

JOHN (*takes clipping*): Why should I give you my job? (*Crosses to right.*) They're hard to get.

CLARENCE (*following him*): But I've got to have a new suit of clothes.

JOHN: Maybe I could get a job for both of us? (*Doorbell rings vigorously.*) I'll tell you what I'll do. I'll ask the man.

FATHER (*enters—calls upstairs*): Cora! Vinnie, that cab's here. Hurry up! (FATHER *goes toward front door.*)

CLARENCE: John, we've both got to get down there early Tuesday—the first thing.

Life with Father

JOHN: Oh, no, you don't—I'm going alone.

CLARENCE: But, John—

JOHN: But I'll put in a good word with the boss about you.

FATHER (*off right*): They'll be right out. (CLARENCE *crosses quickly to left. We hear* FATHER *close front door.*) Cora! Vinnie! (*He comes back to foot of stairs and calls up.*) Are you coming? The cab's waiting.

VINNIE (*from upstairs*): We heard you, Clare. We'll be down in a minute. (FATHER *comes into room.*)

FATHER: John, go upstairs and hurry them down. (JOHN *goes upstairs.* FATHER *crosses back of table to window and looks out, consulting his watch.*) What's the matter with those women? Don't they know cabs cost money? Clarence, go see what's causing this infernal delay. (CLARENCE *hurries up hall.* MARY *comes sedately downstairs.*)

CLARENCE: Here they come, Father. (FATHER *crosses quickly to back of table.* CORA *and* VINNIE *follow* MARY *downstairs.* MARY *passes* CLARENCE *without a glance and goes to* FATHER. CLARENCE *goes to front of sofa.*)

MARY (*extending her arm above table*): Good-by, Mr. Day. I can't tell you how much I appreciate your hospitality.

FATHER (*shaking her hand and trying to hurry her*): Not at all! Not at all! (VINNIE *and* CORA *come into room.* JOHN *comes downstairs with another bag and exits.*)

CORA: Good-by, Clarence. (*Starts toward left—putting on gloves.*)

FATHER (*crosses to center quickly*): Cora, we can say good-by to you on the sidewalk. (MARY *moves to upper corner of table.*)

VINNIE: There's no hurry—their train doesn't go until one-thirty. (*She crosses back of table to* MARY.)

FATHER: Cabs cost money. If they have any waiting to do they should do it at Grand Central Depot. They've got a waiting-room there, it's just *for* that.

VINNIE (*to* MARY): If there's one thing Mr. Day can't stand it's to keep a cab waiting.

CORA: It's been so nice seeing you again, Clarence. (*She kisses him.*)—I hope—(*No one is in a hurry except* FATHER, *and it annoys him.* MARGARET *enters with a box of lunch.*)

MARGARET (*starting down to* CORA): Here's the lunch.

FATHER: All right. All right. Give it to me. . . . Let's get started. (*He takes it from* MARGARET—*and starts out.* MARGARET *follows* FATHER—*then exits.*)

CORA (*starting up*): Where's John? (VINNIE *goes to* CORA.)

FATHER (*as he is leaving room*): He's outside. Come on.

(CORA *and* VINNIE *follow, ad libbing good-bys, etc.* MARY *starts, crosses below table as* CORA *and* VINNIE *exit.*)

CLARENCE: Mary—aren't you going to—shake hands with me?

MARY: I don't think I'd better. You may remember that when I get too close to you, you feel contaminated. (*She starts out.*)

CLARENCE (*follows her*): Mary, you're going to write to me, aren't you?

MARY: Are you going to write first?

CLARENCE (*facing front, very much his* FATHER): No, Mary— there are times when a man must be firm. (JOHN *enters hurriedly.*)

JOHN: Mary, Mother says you'd better hurry out before Father starts yelling. It's Sunday. (MARY *crosses back of* JOHN— *then turns back to him—offering her hand—which he takes.*)

MARY: Good-by, John. I'm very happy to have made *your* acquaintance.

(*She walks out.* CLARENCE *is crushed.* JOHN *gives* CLARENCE *a questioning look—grins—and follows her.* CLARENCE *dashes into arch; just then we hear door slam. For a moment* CLARENCE'S *world has fallen about him—but he decides quickly and rushes to side table, takes a pad of writing paper and a pencil from drawer—rushes to table, sits and starts to write—in desperation.*)

CLARENCE: "Dear Mary"—

Life with Father

SCENE: *The same. Two days later. The breakfast table. The bowl of fruit is on side table. Dishes and silverware have been removed from* JOHN's *place. The fruit is ready at* FATHER's *and* CLARENCE's *places. There are two cups of coffee and the sugar-bowl on side table.* HARLAN *and* WHITNEY *are at table, ready to start breakfast. Their glasses of milk are in front of them.* CLARENCE *is near window, reading newspaper.*

NORA, *a new maid—heavily built and along toward middle age—is just entering, carrying two plates and bowls of cereal. She serves* HARLAN, *then* WHITNEY. *As she puts cereal in front of* WHITNEY *the postman's whistle blows twice and doorbell rings.* NORA *starts toward center.* CLARENCE *glances out window.*

CLARENCE: Never mind, Nora. It's the postman—I'll go. (*He runs out through arch and exits toward outside door, putting paper at* FATHER's *place as he goes.* NORA *crosses right of table.*)

WHITNEY (*to* NORA): You forgot the sugar. It goes here between me and Father.

NORA: Oh, yes.

(NORA *gets sugar bowl from side table, puts it near* FATHER's *place, then waits. We hear front door slam.* CLARENCE *comes back with three or four letters, which he looks through quickly, and then his face falls in utter dejection —moves to back of table.* FATHER *comes downstairs.*)

FATHER: Good morning, boys! (CLARENCE *crosses to his chair at table.* BOYS *rise.* ALL *say "Good morning, sir."* FATHER *comes into room.*) John not down yet? (*He shouts upstairs.*) John! Hurry down to your breakfast.

CLARENCE: John had his breakfast early, Father, and went out to see about something.

FATHER: See about what?

CLARENCE: John and I thought we'd work this summer and earn some money.

FATHER (*crosses to his place at table*): Good! Sit down, boys.

(*The two young* BOYS *sit. They use cream and sugar on cereal and put them near* FATHER'S *place again.*)

CLARENCE: We saw an ad in the paper and John went down to see about it.

FATHER: Why didn't you go, too? (NORA *crosses to center —awaits orders.*)

CLARENCE: I was expecting an answer to a letter I wrote, but it didn't come. (FATHER *sits.*) Here's the mail. (*Puts mail left of* FATHER. *He seems depressed, but sits and starts to eat.*)

FATHER (*takes his napkin and spreads it on his lap*): What kind of work is this you're planning to do?

CLARENCE: Sort of salesman, the ad said.

FATHER (*eating his fruit*): Un-hum. Work never hurt anybody. It's good for them. But if you're going to work—work hard. King Solomon had the right idea about work. (BOYS *stop eating and look at* FATHER.) "Whatever thy hand findeth to do," Solomon said, "do thy damnedest." Where's your mother? (*The* BOYS *start eating again.*)

NORA: If you please, sir, Mrs. Day doesn't want any breakfast. She isn't feeling well so she went back upstairs to lie down again.

FATHER: Now why does your mother do that to me? She knows when she doesn't come down to breakfast she just upsets my whole day. . . . Clarence, go tell your mother I'll be up to see her before I start for the office.

CLARENCE (*rises*): Yes, sir. (*He goes upstairs.*)

HARLAN: What's the matter with Mother?

FATHER: There's nothing the matter with your mother. Perfectly healthy woman. Whenever she gets an ache or a twinge, instead of being firm about it, she just gives in to it. (*Doorbell rings, then postman's whistle blows once.* NORA *answers it.*) Boys, after breakfast, you find out what your mother wants you to do today. Whitney, you take care of Harlan. (NORA *comes back with special-delivery letter on salver. Letter and envelope are on pink paper.*)

WHITNEY: Yes, Father.

NORA (*impressed*): It's a special delivery, sir.

FATHER (*taking letter*): Thank you. (*He takes letter out and puts envelope to his left, then gets out his glasses and starts to read letter.* NORA *takes salver off, then crosses to arch and exits. Then* CLARENCE *comes rushing downstairs.*)

CLARENCE: Was that the postman again?

WHITNEY: It was a special delivery.

CLARENCE (*to back of table*): Yes? Where is it?

WHITNEY: It was for Father.

CLARENCE (*again disappointed*): Oh— (*He sits at table.* FATHER *is having trouble with letter. He turns it over and looks at signature, then looks back to first page, then gives a shrug and settles down to read it. Before he has finished half the first page he says—*)

FATHER: I don't understand this at all. Here's a letter from some woman I never heard of. (*He goes on reading.* CLARENCE *sees envelope, picks it up, looks at postmark, realizes that it's from* MARY. *He is worried.*)

CLARENCE (*rises*): Father—

FATHER (*exploding*): Oh, God!

CLARENCE: What is it, Father?

FATHER: This woman claims that she sat on my lap. (CLARENCE *begins to feel uncomfortable.* FATHER *goes on reading a little further, then holds letter over in front of* CLARENCE.) What's that word? (CLARENCE *begins feverishly to read as much as possible, but* FATHER *cuts in after a moment.*) No, that word down here. (*He points.*)

CLARENCE: It looks like—"curiosity." (FATHER *withdraws letter.* CLARENCE's *eyes follow it hungrily.*)

FATHER (*reading*): "I opened your letter only as a matter of curiosity." (*He turns page.*)

CLARENCE (*in agony, after a painful moment of hoping FATHER will continue to read out loud*): Yes? Go on.

FATHER: This gets worse and worse! Just turns into a lot of sentimental lovey-dovey mush. (*He rises and crushes letter, then crosses to left. VINNIE hurries downstairs. She is dressed in a negligee. Her hair is in braids.*) Is this someone's idea of a practical joke?

VINNIE (*as she comes downstairs*): What's the matter, Clare!

FATHER: I don't know why I should always be the butt— (*Throws letter in fireplace.*)

VINNIE (*entering room*): What's wrong! (*The CHILDREN rise as MOTHER enters.*)

FATHER (*crosses up behind sofa to her—he puts his glasses away*): Nothing wrong—just a damn fool letter. How are you, Vinnie?

VINNIE: I don't feel well, Clare. I thought you needed me, but if you don't, I'll go back to bed.

FATHER (*drawing her down and putting her in her chair*): Well, now that you're here, sit down and have some breakfast with us. Sit down, Vinnie. Sit down. (*VINNIE sits, very reluctantly and protesting. CHILDREN sit. NORA enters with a tray of bacon and eggs, goes to side of table.*) Get some food in your stomach. Do you good.

VINNIE: I don't feel like eating anything, Clare.

FATHER (*heartily*): That's all the more reason why you should eat. Build up your strength. (*NORA is at side table, her back turned toward FATHER. He addresses her.*) Here-re-re—(*To CLARENCE.*) What's this one's name?

CLARENCE (*sits*): Nora.

FATHER: Nora! Some bacon and eggs to Mrs. Day. (*He crosses back of table to his chair and sits.*)

VINNIE: No, Clare! (*NORA however has gone to Vinnie's side with platter.*) No, take it away, Nora. I don't even want to smell it. (*During following, NORA puts platter of bacon and eggs on side table, then removes fruit from FATHER and*

178

CLARENCE. *She picks up bacon and eggs and serves* FATHER, *replaces bacon and eggs; picks up two cups of coffee—serves* FATHER, *then* CLARENCE, *then gets bacon and eggs and serves* CLARENCE. *Then puts platter on tray on side table. After that she takes remains of fruit from side table—puts them on tray, then takes tray and exits.*)

FATHER: Vinnie, it's just weak to give in to an ailment. Any disease can be cured by firmness. What you need is strength of character.

VINNIE (*with sick protest*): I don't know why you object to my complaining a little. I notice when you have a headache you yell and groan and swear enough.

FATHER: Of course I yell. (*Picks up serving spoon and fork.*) That's to prove to the headache that I'm stronger than it is— (*Helping himself to bacon and eggs.*) I can generally swear one right out of my system.

VINNIE: This isn't a headache. I think I've caught some kind of a germ. There's a lot of sickness around. Several of my friends have had to send for the doctor. I may have the same thing. (WHITNEY *finishes breakfast—puts napkin in ring.*)

FATHER (*uses cream and sugar—passes them to* CLARENCE): Vinnie, I'll bet this is all your imagination. You hear of a lot of other people having some disease and you get scared and think you have it yourself. So you take to your bed and send for the doctor. The doctor—all poppycock!

VINNIE: I didn't say a word about my sending for the doctor.

FATHER: I should hope not. Doctors think they know a damn lot but they don't. (HARLAN *finishes—puts napkin in ring.*)

VINNIE: But, Clare, dear, when people are seriously ill you have to do something.

FATHER: Certainly you have to do something! Cheer 'em up— that's the way to cure 'em!

VINNIE (*with slight irony*): How would you go about cheering them up?

FATHER: I? I'd tell 'em—bah! (VINNIE, *out of exasperation and*

weakness, begins to cry. FATHER *looks at her amazed.*)
What have I done?

VINNIE (*rises and moves to center*): Oh, Clare—hush up!
(HARLAN *slides out of his chair, runs over to her and puts
his arms around her.*) Harlan, dear, keep away from
Mother. You might catch what she's got. Whitney— (*She
goes to sofa and sits.*)

WHITNEY (*rises, crosses to above* HARLAN): Yes, Mother.

VINNIE: If you have finished your breakfast—I promised Mrs.
Whitehead to send over Margaret's recipe for Floating
Island Pudding. Margaret has it all written out. And take
Harlan with you.

WHITNEY (*sympathetically*): All right, Mother. I hope you
feel better.

(WHITNEY *takes* HARLAN'S *hand and leads him out.* HARLAN
keeps his eyes on Mother as long as he can. FATHER *goes
over and sits beside* VINNIE *on sofa, speaking as he goes.*
CLARENCE *also has finished and puts napkin in ring and
sits very quietly.*)

FATHER: Vinnie. (*Contritely.*) I didn't mean to upset you. I
was just trying to help! (*Pats her hand.*) When you take
to your bed I have a damned lonely time around here. So
when I see you getting it into your head that you're sick,
I want to do something about it. (*Continues to pat her
hand. He gets very hale and hearty. His hand-pats become
vigorous.*) Now, Vinnie, just because some of your friends
have given in to this is no reason why you should imagine
you're sick—

VINNIE (*snatches her hand away*): Oh! Stop, Clare! —Get out
of this house and go to your office!

(FATHER *is a little bewildered and somewhat indignant at
this rebuff to his feelings of tenderness. He gets up and
goes out into hall. A moment later, with his hat and stick,*

he marches across arch and out of house, slamming door.
VINNIE *gets up after door slams and starts toward arch.*)

CLARENCE (*rises and goes to her*): I'm sorry you're not feeling well, Mother.

VINNIE: I'll be all right, Clarence. Remember I had a touch of this last fall and I was all right the next morning.

CLARENCE: Are you sure you don't want the doctor?

VINNIE: Oh, no. I really don't need him—and besides, doctors worry your father. I don't want him to be upset. (*She starts up again.*)

CLARENCE (*following her*): Is there anything I can do for you?

VINNIE (*stops*): Ask Margaret to send me a cup of tea. I'll try to drink it. I'm going back to bed. (*She starts upstairs.*)

CLARENCE (*at foot of stairs*): Do you mind if John and I go out today, or will you need us?

VINNIE: You run along. I just want to be left alone. (*She exits top of stairs.* CLARENCE *starts for the fireplace eager to retrieve* MARY's *letter.* NORA *enters with a tray to clear table.* HE *stops.*)

CLARENCE (*back of sofa*): Oh!—Nora—will you take a cup of tea up to Mrs. Day in her room?

NORA: Yes, sir.

(NORA *exits. Then* CLARENCE *hurries to fireplace, gets crumpled letter and starts to read it feverishly. He reads quickly then draws a deep, happy breath. Door slams. He puts letter in his pocket. We see* JOHN's *hat fly by arch, and hear the whistling sound.* JOHN *enters, carrying two heavy packages which he puts on breakfast table.*)

CLARENCE (*crosses below sofa*): Did you get the job?

JOHN: Yes, for both of us. Look, I got it with me.

CLARENCE: What is it?

JOHN (*unwrapping top of one package*): Medicine.

CLARENCE (*dismayed*): Medicine! You took a job for us to go out and sell medicine!

JOHN: But it's *wonderful* medicine. (JOHN *gets a bottle out of package. He reads from bottle.*) "Bartlett's Beneficent Balm—a Boon to Mankind." Look what it cures! (*He hands bottle to* CLARENCE, *who reads from label.*)

CLARENCE: "A sovereign cure for colds, coughs, catarrh, asthma, quinsy and sore throat; (*Moves to below sofa—* JOHN *follows him.*) poor digestion, summer complaint, colic, dyspepsia, heartburn, and shortness of breath; lumbago, rheumatism, heart disease, giddiness, and women's complaints; nervous prostration, St. Vitus' Dance, jaundice and la grippe; proud flesh, pink eye, seasickness, and pimples."

(*As* CLARENCE *reads off list he has become more and more impressed, with occasional looks, toward* JOHN, *of growing confidence.*)

JOHN: See?

CLARENCE: That sounds all right!

JOHN: It's made "from a secret formula known only to Dr. Bartlett."

CLARENCE: He must be quite a doctor.

JOHN (*enthusiastically*): It sells for a dollar a bottle! And we get twenty-five cents' commission on every bottle.

CLARENCE: Where does he want us to sell it?

JOHN: He's given us the territory of all Manhattan Island.

CLARENCE: That's bully. Anybody that's sick at all ought to need a bottle of this. (*Hands bottle to* JOHN *and goes toward package.*) Let's start by calling on friends of Father and Mother.

JOHN: That's a good idea. But wait a minute. Suppose they ask us if we used it at our house.

CLARENCE: Oh, yes, it would be better if we could say we did. (NORA *enters with tray on which is a cup of tea and a napkin. She goes to table, puts tray on it—crosses to table to get sugar bowl and cream pitcher, which she puts on tray.*)

JOHN: But we can't because we haven't had it here long enough.

CLARENCE: Is that the tea for Mrs. Day?

NORA: Yes.

CLARENCE: I'll take it up to her. You needn't bother.

NORA: Thank you. Take it up right away while it's good and hot. (*She exits.*)

CLARENCE (*forgetting about medicine and concerned about* MOTHER): Mother wasn't feeling well this morning.

JOHN (*sympathetically*): What was the matter with her?

CLARENCE: I don't know—she was just complaining.

JOHN (*getting an idea—consulting bottle, quickly—crosses to* CLARENCE): Well, it says here it's good for *women's complaints.* (*They look at each other a second;* CLARENCE *takes bottle—pulls out cork and smells it.* JOHN *pulls* CLARENCE's *hand toward him so that he also can smell it. They look at each other—*JOHN *nods.* CLARENCE *crosses to table, picks up spoon and pours medicine into it. He hands bottle back to* JOHN, *puts medicine in tea and starts to stir tea.* JOHN *holds bottle a second—looks at it—then suddenly pours some more of medicine into tea. Quick curtain.*)

(*The* CURTAIN *is lowered for a few seconds to denote a lapse of three hours.*

(*When* CURTAIN *rises again, breakfast things have been cleared and the room is in order. The bowl of fruit is again on table.* VINNIE's *prayer book is on mantel.* HARLAN *is kneeling on* FATHER's *armchair, looking out window as if watching for somebody.* MARGARET *enters hurriedly down the stairs.*)

MARGARET: Has your father come yet?

HARLAN: Not yet.

MARGARET: Glory be—(NORA *enters from downstairs with a steaming teakettle and a towel and* MARGARET *meets her*

at arch.) Hurry that upstairs. The doctor's waiting for it.
(NORA *starts upstairs.* MARGARET *goes to foot of stairs.*)
And, Nora, see if there is anything else you can do! I've got
to go out.

NORA (*on third step*): Where are you going?

MARGARET: I have to go and get the minister. (NORA *goes
upstairs and exits.* MARGARET *starts taking off her apron.*)

HARLAN: There's a cab coming up the street.

MARGARET: Well, I hope it's him, poor man—but a cab
doesn't sound like your father. (*She exits.* HARLAN *watches,
then runs to downstairs staircase, and kneels as he yells
downstairs.*)

HARLAN: Yes, it's Father. Whitney got him all right. (HARLAN
*runs back toward chair—but stops in front of table, when
front door slams.* FATHER *crosses arch, and runs upstairs.*
WHITNEY *comes into arch. He is very pleased with himself.*) What took you so long?

WHITNEY: Long? I wasn't long. I went right down on the
elevated, and got Father right away and we came all the
way back in a cab.

HARLAN: I thought you were never coming.

WHITNEY: Well, the horse didn't go very fast at first. The
cabby whipped him and swore at him and still he wouldn't
gallop. Then Father spoke to the horse. (*Very pleased
with himself, he rocks on his feet and swings his hat for
a few seconds.*) How is Mother?

HARLAN: I don't know. The doctor's up there now.

WHITNEY: Well, she'd better be good and sick or Father
may be mad at me for getting him up here—(*stops and
turns quickly*)—especially in a *cab!*

FATHER (*from upstairs*): Damn! Damnation! (*We hear a door
slam and* FATHER's *angry footsteps as he comes downstairs and into the room.*)

FATHER (*pacing back and forth, indignantly*): Well, huh!
It seems to me I ought to be shown a little consideration.
I guess I've got some feelings, too!

WHITNEY: Father, Mother's awfully sick, isn't she?

FATHER (*crossing back of table toward arch*): How do I know? I wasn't allowed to stay in the same room with her!

WHITNEY: Father—who put you out, the doctor?

FATHER (*in arch, loudly*): No, it was your mother, damn it! (*He goes out and hangs up his hat and stick.* WHITNEY *crosses to sofa and puts his hat on side table, then goes to back of sofa.* HARLAN *moves to table.* FATHER *returns. He may be annoyed, but he is also worried.*) You boys keep quiet around here today. (*He paces again.*)

WHITNEY (*back of sofa, hopefully*): Father, Mother must be pretty sick.

FATHER: She must be, Whitney. I don't know—I can only guess. (DR. HUMPHREYS *comes downstairs, with his satchel. Stops on last step.*) Nobody ever tells me anything in this house.

DR. HUMPHREYS: Mrs. Day is quieter now. (*Starts to exit.*)

FATHER: Well, Doctor? How is Mrs. Day? What's the matter with her?

DR. HUMPHREYS (*crossing to* FATHER): She's a pretty sick woman, Mr. Day. I had given her a sedative—just before you arrived—after you left the room I had to give her another. Have you a telephone?

FATHER: A telephone! No—I don't believe in them. Why?

DR. HUMPHREYS: It would just have saved me a few steps. I'll be back in about ten minutes. (*He turns to go.*)

FATHER: Just a minute—I think I'm entitled to know what's the matter with my wife? (DR. HUMPHREYS *turns back.*)

DR. HUMPHREYS: What did Mrs. Day have for breakfast this morning?

FATHER: She didn't eat anything—not a thing.

DR. HUMPHREYS: Are you sure?

FATHER: I tried to get her to eat something, but she wouldn't.

DR. HUMPHREYS (*almost to himself*): I can't understand it.

FATHER: Understand what?

DR. HUMPHREYS: These violent attacks of nausea. It's almost as though she were poisoned.

FATHER: What?

DR. HUMPHREYS (*starts out*): I'll try not to be gone more than ten or fifteen minutes. (DR. HUMPHREYS *exits.*)

FATHER: But, see here—if you really— (*We hear street door close. Angrily, trying to reassure himself.*) Damn doctors! They never know what's the matter with anybody. (*Indignantly he crosses to window.*) He'd better get your mother well and damn soon or he'll hear from me!

WHITNEY (*really worried about Mother now*): Father, Mother is going to get well, isn't she?

FATHER (*the thought worries him for a moment*): Of course she's going to get well.

HARLAN (*running to* FATHER—*puts his arms around him*): I hope Mother gets well soon. When Mother stays in bed it's lonesome.

FATHER: Yes, it is, Harlan. It's lonesome. (*With his arm around* HARLAN'S *shoulder, they move to center. When they stop,* HARLAN *is downstage of* FATHER.) What were you boys supposed to do today?

WHITNEY: I was to learn the rest of my catechism.

FATHER (*smoothing* HARLAN'S *tie and collar*): Well, if that's what your mother wanted you to do, you'd better do it.

WHITNEY (*positively*): I know it. (*Then dubiously.*) I think.

FATHER: You'd better be sure.

WHITNEY: I can't be sure unless somebody hears me—will you hear me?

FATHER: Yes, Whitney—yes, I'll hear you. (WHITNEY *goes to mantel and gets prayer book.* FATHER *crosses to sofa and sits. Puts on his glasses.*)

HARLAN (*follows him and sits beside* FATHER): If Mother is still sick will you read to me tonight?

FATHER: Of course I'll read to you. (*He pats* HARLAN'S *knee and they laugh. He is going to enjoy these moments with his sons.* WHITNEY *opens prayer book and hands it to* FATHER.)

WHITNEY: Here it is, Father. Just the end of it. Mother knows I know the rest. Look, start here. (*Points to question, then steps back.*)

FATHER (*so that his youngest son may also enjoy these moments with him,* FATHER *holds book so that* HARLAN *can
look at it, and as* WHITNEY *finishes each answer* HARLAN
quickly looks up to FATHER *as if to say "Pretty good, Eh!"*
—*reading*): "How many parts are there in a Sacrament?"

WHITNEY (*reciting*): "Two: the outward visible sign, and the
inward spiritual grace." (FATHER *nods in approval and
smiles at* HARLAN.)

FATHER: "What is the outward visible sign or form in Baptism?"

WHITNEY: "Water; wherein the person is baptized, in the
Name of the Father and of the Son and of the Holy Ghost."
—You haven't been baptized, Father, have you?

FATHER (*ignoring it*): "What is the inward and spiritual
grace?"

WHITNEY: If you don't have to be baptized, why do I have
to be confirmed?

FATHER (*rather sharply*): "What is the inward and spiritual
grace?"

WHITNEY: "A death unto sin, and a new birth unto righteous-
ness; for being by nature born in sin, and the children of
wrath, we are hereby made the children of grace." Is that
why you get mad so much, Father—because you're a child
of wrath?

FATHER: Whitney, mind your manners! You're not supposed
to ask questions of your elders! (FATHER *isn't enjoying
himself now.*) "What is required of persons to be baptized?"

WHITNEY (*a little frightened*): "Repentance, whereby"—
whereby—

FATHER: You don't know it well enough, Whitney. (*He shuts
book and hands it to him, sharply. Snaps off his glasses and
crosses to right.*) You'd better study it some more.

WHITNEY: Now?

FATHER: No—no, you don't have to do it now. (WHITNEY
puts book on mantel.) Let's see, now, what can we do?

WHITNEY (*edging up towards arch*): I was working with my

tool chest out in the back yard. (HARLAN *rises as* WHITNEY *passes him.*)

FATHER: Better not do any hammering with your mother sick upstairs. You'd better stay here.

WHITNEY: I wasn't hammering—I was doing wood carving.

FATHER: Well, Harlan—how about you—shall we play a game of tiddlywinks?

HARLAN (*moving up beside* WHITNEY): I was helping Whitney.

FATHER: Oh—all right. (*The* BOYS *start out slowly—but as soon as* FATHER *looks away, they run and exit.* FATHER *goes to arch—calls down stairway softly.*) Boys—boys, don't do any shouting out there. We all have to be very quiet around here today. (*We hear* BOYS *say "Yes, Father."* FATHER *stands in hall surveying room; looking and feeling very lonesome, then he looks up toward* VINNIE, *worried. Then he starts upstairs but changes his mind. Returns and goes to rail of basement stairs, and calls quietly.*) Margaret! (*There is no answer and he raises his voice a little.*) Margaret! (*There is no answer and he raises his voice a little.*) Margaret! (*Still no answer and he lets loose.*) Margaret! Why don't you answer when you hear me calling? (*At this moment* MARGARET, *wearing hat and shawl, appears in arch, having come through front door.*) Mar—

MARGARET: Sh-sh—(FATHER *turns quickly and sees* MARGARET.)

FATHER: Oh, there you are!

MARGARET (*reprovingly, but deferentially*): We must all be quiet, Mr. Day—Mrs. Day is very sick.

FATHER (*testily*): I know she's sick. That's what I wanted you for. You go up and wait outside her door in case she needs anything. (MARGARET *starts to go up.* FATHER *swings to* MARGARET's *right at foot of stairs.*) And what were you doing out of the house, anyway?

MARGARET (*on stairs*): I was sent for the minister.

FATHER (*startled*): The minister?

MARGARET: Yes, sir. He's outside now, paying off the cab.

(FATHER *moves to side of arch. Door off stage closes.*
MARGARET *bows as if to the minister and exits upstairs.*
DR. LLOYD *appears in arch and goes to* FATHER, *offering
his hand, which* FATHER *takes.*)

DR. LLOYD: I was deeply shocked to hear of Mrs. Day's
illness. I hope I can be of some service. Will you take me
up to her?

FATHER: Mrs. Day is resting now and she can't be disturbed.

DR. LLOYD: But I've been summoned.

FATHER (*after a moment's thought*): The doctor will be
back in a few minutes and we'll see what he has to say
about it. (*Another short pause.* FATHER *doesn't relish a
visit with the minister but, of course, he is polite.*) You'd
better come in and wait.

DR. LLOYD: Thank you. (DR. LLOYD *comes into room and
sits on bench, putting his hat on table.*) Mrs. Day has
been a tower of strength in the parish. Everyone liked her
so much. Yes, she was a fine woman.

FATHER (*at table*): I wish to God you wouldn't talk about
Mrs. Day as if she were dead. (*He moves toward back
of sofa.* NORA *comes downstairs hurriedly.*)

NORA: Mr. Day—is the doctor back yet?

FATHER (*crossing to arch*): No. Does she need him?

NORA: She's kind of restless, sir. She's talking in her sleep
and twisting and turning. (*She exits.*)

FATHER (*looks upstairs—then crosses back of table to window*): That doctor said he'd be right back.

MARGARET (*coming downstairs*): The doctor's coming. I
was watching for him out the window. (*She goes to front
door.* FATHER *crosses front of table. A moment later we
hear* DR. HUMPHREYS *say, "Thank you Margaret."* DR.
HUMPHREYS *enters, starts toward stairs.* DR. LLOYD *rises.*)

FATHER: Well, Doctor, seems to me that was a pretty long
ten minutes. (DR. HUMPHREYS *enters room but stops
short at* FATHER's *remark and tone.*)

DR. HUMPHREYS (*testily*): See here, Mr. Day, if I'm to be

responsible for Mrs. Day's health, I must be allowed to handle this case in my own way.

FATHER: Well, you can't handle it while you're out of the house. (MARGARET *shows in* DR. SOMERS, *who stops.* MARGARET *exits upstairs.*)

DR. HUMPHREYS (*flaring*): I left this house because—(*seeing* DR. SOMERS)—Mr. Day, this is Dr. Somers.

DR. SOMERS (*crossing to* FATHER—*offering his hand, which* FATHER *takes*): How do you do.

DR. HUMPHREYS: I felt that Mrs. Day's condition warranted getting Dr. Somers here as quickly as possible—for a consultation. I hope that meets with your approval?

FATHER (*a little awed*): Why, yes, of course. Anything that can be done.

DR. HUMPHREYS: Upstairs, Doctor! (*The two* DOCTORS *go upstairs.* FATHER *crosses arch, a little shaken.*)

DR. LLOYD: Mrs. Day is in good hands now. There's nothing you and I can do at the moment to help.

FATHER: Dr. Lloyd—(*Indicates to* DR. LLOYD *to sit.* DR. LLOYD *sits on bench.*) There's something that's troubling Mrs. Day's mind. (*Sits on bench.*) I think you know what I refer to. (FATHER *looks toward upstairs.*)

DR. LLOYD: Yes—you mean the fact that you've never been baptized?

FATHER (*stormily turning on him*): I gathered you knew about it—from your sermon last Sunday. (FATHER *looks at him a second with indignant memory, then cools down.*) But let's not get angry. I think something should be done about it.

DR. LLOYD: Yes, Mr. Day.

FATHER: When those doctors get through up there I want you to talk to Mrs. Day. I want you to tell her something.

DR. LLOYD: Yes, I'll be glad to.

FATHER: You're just the man to do it. She shouldn't be upset about this—and I want you to tell her that my being baptized would just be a lot of damned nonsense.

DR. LLOYD: But, Mr. Day!

FATHER: No, she'd take your word on a thing like that—and we've got to do everything we can to help her now.

DR. LLOYD (*rises*): Mr. Day, baptism is one of the sacraments of the church—

FATHER (*rises*): You're her minister and you're supposed to bring her comfort and peace of mind.

DR. LLOYD: The solution is so simple. It would take only your consent to be baptized.

FATHER: That's out of the question—and I'm surprised that a grown man like you should suggest such a thing. (FATHER *crosses left. The* DOCTORS *start downstairs.*)

DR. LLOYD (*following him*): If you're really concerned about Mrs. Day's peace of mind, don't you think—?

FATHER: Now see here—if— (*He turns so he sees the* DOCTORS *entering.* FATHER *crosses to meet* DR. HUMPHREYS.) Well, Doctor, how is Mrs. Day? What have you decided?

DR. HUMPHREYS: Is there a room we could use for our consultation? (DR. SOMERS *has gone to back of table.*)

FATHER (*a little uneasy*): Of course. (MARGARET *comes downstairs.* DR. HUMPHREYS *moves to* DR. SOMERS. FATHER *moves up to arch, the storm breaking on* MARGARET.) Margaret!—you go back upstairs! I don't want Mrs. Day left alone.

MARGARET (*still on stairs*): There is something I have to do for the doctor. I'll go back up as soon as I get it started.

FATHER: Well, hurry. (MARGARET *comes down left, but stops as* FATHER *speaks.*) And, Margaret—show these—gentlemen—downstairs to the billiard room.

MARGARET: Yes, sir. This way, Doctors—please—downstairs. (MARGARET *exits, followed by* DR. SOMERS.)

FATHER (*as* DR. HUMPHREYS *starts to follow*): Dr. Humphreys, you know now, don't you—this isn't serious—is it?

DR. HUMPHREYS: After we've had our consultation, we'll talk to you, Mr. Day.

FATHER (*annoyed at being put off*): But surely you must—?

DR. HUMPHREYS: Rest assured Dr. Somers will do everything that is humanly possible. (*Crosses behind* FATHER, *exits.*)

191

FATHER (*swinging around—now he is really very worried*):
Why,—you don't mean—

DR. HUMPHREYS (*off stage*): We'll try not to be long.

(FATHER *looks upstairs—then down lower stair well—where
doctors have gone—as he looks up again he catches* DR.
LLOYD'*s eye.* FATHER *is obviously frightened—but he tries
not to show it*).

FATHER (*quietly*): This Dr. Somers—I've heard his name
often—he's very well thought of, isn't he?

DR. LLOYD: Oh, yes, indeed.

FATHER: If Vinnie's seriously—if anyone could help her, he
could—don't you think?

DR. LLOYD: A very fine physician. (FATHER, *very worried,
looks away.*) But there's a greater help, ever present in
the hour of need. Let us turn to Him in prayer. Let us
kneel and pray. (FATHER *looks at him, straightens up,
walks to side of room—then turns toward* DR. LLOYD.) Let
us kneel and pray. (*After a moment* FATHER *finally bows
his head.* DR. LLOYD *looks at him, astonished, and not
kneeling himself, speaks simply in prayer.*) Oh, Lord,
look down from Heaven—behold, visit, and relieve this
thy servant who is grieved with sickness, and extend
unto her thy accustomed goodness. We know she has
sinned against thee in thought, word, and deed. Have
mercy on her, Oh, Lord, have mercy on this miserable
sinner. (FATHER *is annoyed.*) Forgive her, Oh, Lord—!

FATHER (*losing control*): She's not a miserable sinner and
you know it! (FATHER *now shouts directly to the Deity.
It's not a prayer—it's man to man.*) Oh, God! You know
Vinnie's not a miserable sinner! She's a damn fine woman.
She shouldn't be made to suffer.

(VINNIE *appears on stairway in her nightgown. She is very
weak.*)

VINNIE: What's the matter, Clare, what's wrong?

FATHER (*not hearing her*): It's got to stop, I tell you, it's got to stop! Have mercy, I say!

VINNIE (*at foot of stairs*): What's the matter, Clare?

FATHER: Have mercy, damn it!

VINNIE (*coming into room*): What's wrong? (FATHER *turns and sees* VINNIE *and rushes to her. They meet dead center.*)

FATHER: Vinnie—Vinnie, what are you doing down here? You shouldn't be out of bed—you get right back upstairs.

VINNIE (*her arm around his neck*): Oh, Clare. I heard you call. Do you need me?

FATHER (*quietly*): Vinnie—I know now how much I need you. Get well, Vinnie. I'll be baptized. I promise. I'll be baptized.

VINNIE (*puts other arm around his neck*): You will?

FATHER: I'll do anything.

VINNIE: Oh, Clare—

FATHER: We'll go to Europe together, just we two. You won't have to worry about the children or the household accounts. (VINNIE *starts to faint.*) Vinnie! (*He picks her up in his arms.*)

DR. LLOYD: Don't worry, Mr. Day—she'll be all right now. Bless you for what you have done.

FATHER: What did I do?

DR. LLOYD: You promised to be baptized.

FATHER (*his concern over* VINNIE's *fainting has made him forget, and he is genuinely surprised at* DR. LLOYD's *statement*): I did? (*Suddenly he remembers and stamps his foot.*) Oh, God! (*With* VINNIE *in his arms, he turns and stomps toward stairs.*)

Act III

Scene 1

Scene: *The same. A month later. Midafternoon. The clock says four-fifteen. Bowl of fruit is not on table.* Vinnie *is on sofa, working on her petit-point.*

Margaret *enters, as usual uncomfortable at being upstairs. She is trying to brush her apron, fix her hair and sleeves, all at once.*

Margaret: You wanted to speak to me, ma'am?

Vinnie: Yes, Margaret, about tomorrow morning's breakfast— we must plan it very carefully.

Margaret (*puzzled*): Mr. Day hasn't complained to me about his breakfasts lately. As a matter of fact, I've been blessing my luck!

Vinnie: Oh, no, it's not that. But tomorrow morning I'd like something for his breakfast that would surprise him.

Margaret (*doubtfully*): Surprising Mr. Day is always a bit of a risk, ma'am. My motto with him has always been let well enough alone.

Vinnie: But if we think of something he especially likes, Margaret; what would you say to kippers?

Margaret: Well, I've served him kippers, but I don't recall his ever saying he liked them.

Vinnie: He's never said he didn't like them, has he?

Margaret: They've never got a stamp on the floor out of him one way or the other.

Vinnie: If Mr. Day doesn't say he doesn't like a thing you can assume that he does. Let's take a chance on kippers, Margaret.

MARGARET: Very well, ma'am. (MARGARET *starts out.*)

VINNIE (*innocently*): And, Margaret—you'd better have enough breakfast for two extra places.

MARGARET (*knowingly, comes back again*): Oh—so that's it! We're going to have company again?

VINNIE: Yes, my cousin Miss Cartwright and her friend are coming back from Springfield. I'm afraid they'll get here just about breakfast time.

MARGARET: Well, in that case I'd better make some of my Sunday morning hot biscuits, too.

VINNIE: Yes. We know Mr. Day likes those.

MARGARET: I've been getting him to church with them for the last fifteen years. (MARGARET *starts out. Door slams. She looks toward it.*) Oh, it's Mr. Clarence, ma'am. (MARGARET *goes out.* CLARENCE *enters with a large box, wrapped.*

CLARENCE (*to back of table*): Here it is, Mother. (*After he puts box on table, he puts his hat on side table.*)

VINNIE (*rises, crosses to back of table—puts her petit-point on side table*): Oh, it was still in the store! They hadn't sold it! I'm so relieved. Didn't you admire it, Clarence?

CLARENCE (*hedging*): Well, it is unusual.

VINNIE (*unwrapping package*): You know I saw this down there the day before I got sick. I was walking through the bric-a-brac section and it caught my eye. I was so tempted to buy it. And all the time I lay ill I just couldn't get it out of my head. I can't understand how it could stay in the store all this time without somebody snatching it up. (*She takes it out of package. It is a large china pug dog.* CLARENCE *moves empty box to table. He has taken lid of box as* VINNIE *takes it off and puts it on table.*) There! Isn't that the darlingest thing you ever saw! It does need a ribbon, though. I've got the very thing somewhere. Oh, yes, I know. (*She leaves dog on table and goes to side table, gets ribbon out of drawer, singing "Sweet Marie" softly as she goes.*)

CLARENCE: Isn't John home yet?

VINNIE: I haven't seen him—why?

CLARENCE: Well, you know we've been working, and John went down to collect our money.

VINNIE (*crossing to back of table again, ties ribbon on dog*): That's fine. Oh, Clarence, I have a secret for just the two of us! Who do you think is coming to visit us tomorrow?— Cousin Cora and Mary!

CLARENCE: Yes, I know.

VINNIE: How did you know?

CLARENCE: I happened to get a letter. (*Front door slams. Enter* JOHN *carrying two packages of medicine.*)

VINNIE (*holding up dog*): John, did you ever see anything so sweet?

JOHN: What *is* it?

VINNIE: It's a pug dog. Your father would never let me have a real one, but he can't object to one made of china. This ribbon needs pressing. I'll take it down and have Margaret do it right away. (VINNIE *exits, taking dog with her*)

CLARENCE: What did you bring home more medicine for? (*Then, with sudden fright, he moves toward* JOHN.) Dr. Bartlett paid us off, didn't he?

JOHN: Yes.

CLARENCE: You had me worried for a minute. (*Heaving a great sigh of relief—then happily moves down center.*) When I went down to McCreery's to get the pug dog for Mother, I ordered the daisiest suit you ever saw. Dr. Bartlett owed us sixteen dollars apiece, and the suit was only fifteen. Isn't that lucky? Come on, give me my money. (*Crosses back to* JOHN.)

JOHN (*has moved center when* CLARENCE *mentioned suit— very diffidently*): Clarence, Dr. Bartlett paid us off in medicine.

CLARENCE (*aghast*): You let him pay us off with that old Beneficent Balm?

JOHN (*proudly*): Well, he thanked us, too—"for our services to mankind."

CLARENCE (*in agony*): What about me? I belong to mankind. What about my suit?

JOHN (*sympathetically—crosses, puts packages on bench*): You'll just have to wait for your suit.

CLARENCE: I can't wait! I've got to have it tomorrow—and besides, they're making the alterations. I've got to pay for it this afternoon. Fifteen dollars!

JOHN (*helpfully*): Offer them fifteen bottles of medicine. (CLARENCE *gives it a little desperate thought.*)

CLARENCE: They wouldn't take it. McCreery's don't sell medicine. (*He moves towards mantel, then paces up and down.*)

JOHN: That's too bad. (JOHN *crosses to window and looks out.*) Here comes Father.

CLARENCE: I'll have to brace Father for that fifteen dollars. I hate to do it, but I've got to—that's all—I've got to! (*Crosses as if to window, but stops when door slams.*)

JOHN (*picking up packages*): I'm not going to be here when you do. (*Door slams.*) I'd better hide this somewhere, anyway.

(*He starts up arch.* FATHER *enters and looks into room, before* JOHN *can get out, so he hides packages behind him.* FATHER *has his newspaper with him.*)

CLARENCE (*at right of table*): Good afternoon, sir.

FATHER: How's your mother, Clarence? Where is she?

CLARENCE: She's all right. She's downstairs with Margaret. Oh, Father . . .

(FATHER *exits, and we hear him calling downstairs.* JOHN *rushes upstairs—hiding packages as best he can.*)

FATHER (*off stage*): Vinnie! I'm home. (FATHER *reappears in arch, minus hat and stick, carrying newspaper.*)

CLARENCE: Father, Mother will be well enough to go to church with us next Sunday.

FATHER: That's fine, Clarence. That's fine. (*He starts toward his chair.*)

CLARENCE (*stepping in front of* FATHER): Father, have you noticed that I haven't been kneeling down in church lately?

FATHER (*good-naturedly*): Don't let your Mother catch you at it.

CLARENCE (*very abruptly*): Then I've got to have a new suit of clothes.

FATHER (*after a puzzled look*): Clarence, you're not even making sense!

CLARENCE: But a fellow doesn't feel right in cut-down clothes—especially your clothes. That's why I can't kneel down in church—I can't do anything in them you wouldn't do.

FATHER: Well, that's a damn good thing. If my old clothes make you behave yourself I don't think you should ever wear anything else.

CLARENCE (*desperately*): Oh, no! You're you—and I'm me! I want to be myself! Besides, you're older and there are things I've got to do that I wouldn't do at your age.

FATHER: Clarence, you should never do anything I wouldn't do.

CLARENCE: Oh—yes, look, for instance. Suppose I should want to kneel down in front of a girl?

FATHER: Why in heaven's name should you want to do a thing like that?

CLARENCE: Well, I've got to get married some time. I've got to propose to a girl *sometime*.

FATHER (*exasperated*): Before you're married, I hope, you'll be earning your own clothes. Don't get the idea into your head I'm going to support you and a wife, too. Besides, at your age, Clarence—

CLARENCE (*hastily—desperately*): Oh, I'm not going to be married right away, but for fifteen dollars I can get a good suit of clothes. (VINNIE *enters.*)

FATHER (*bewildered and irritated, loudly*): Clarence! You're beginning to talk as crazy as your mother. (VINNIE *comes right down to* FATHER's *side, putting her hand on his shoulder—paying no attention to his last remark—kindly.*) Oh, hello, Vinnie. (*He kisses her.*) How're you feeling?

VINNIE: I'm fine. Clare! You don't have to hurry home from the office every day like this. (CLARENCE *throws himself in chair by window, sick with disappointment. He pays no attention to following scene.*)

FATHER (*crossing to sofa*): Business the way it is, no use going to the office at all.

VINNIE: But you haven't been to your club for weeks.

FATHER (*sits and takes out his glasses*): Can't stand the damn place. You do look better, Vinnie. What did you do today?

VINNIE (*moves to back of sofa*): I took a long walk and dropped in to call on Mrs. Whitehead.

FATHER (*opens paper and starts to read*): Well, that's fine.

VINNIE (*suddenly excited*): It was the most fortunate thing that ever happened. I've got wonderful news for you! Who do you think was there? Mr. Morley!

FATHER (*not placing him*): Morley?

VINNIE: You remember—that nice young minister who substituted for Dr. Lloyd one Sunday?

FATHER (*looking up from paper*): Oh, yes—bright young fellow, preached a good sensible sermon.

VINNIE: It was the only time I ever saw you put five dollars in the plate!

FATHER: Ought to be more ministers like him. I could get along with that young man without any trouble at all. (*He goes back to his paper.*)

VINNIE: Well, Clare, his parish is in Audubon—you know, way up above Harlem.

FATHER (*reading paper*): Is that so?

VINNIE: Isn't that wonderful? Nobody knows you up there. You'll be perfectly safe!

FATHER (*repeats without thinking*): Safe? (*Suddenly getting the thought.*) Vinnie, what the devil are you talking about?

VINNIE: I've been all over everything with Mr. Morley and he's agreed to baptize you.

FATHER (*good-naturedly*): Oh, he has—the young whipper-snapper! Damn nice of him! (*Goes back to his paper.*)

VINNIE (*moving a little left*): We can go up there any morning, Clare—we don't even have to make an appointment.

FATHER (*his attention still on paper*): Vinnie, you're making a lot of plans for nothing. Who said I was going to be baptized at all?

VINNIE (*aghast*): Why, Clare! You did!

FATHER (*looking up*): Now, Vinnie!—

VINNIE: You gave me your promise—your Sacred Promise. (*Crossing to point out spot and then down to sofa.*) You stood right on that spot and said "I'll be baptized. I promise—I'll be baptized!"

FATHER: What if I did?

VINNIE (*amazed*): Aren't you a man of your word?

FATHER (*rises, with righteous indignation*): Vinnie, that was under entirely different circumstances. We all thought you were dying, so naturally I said that to cheer you up. As a matter of fact, the doctor told me that's what cured you. So it seems to me pretty ungrateful of you to press this matter any further.

VINNIE: You gave me your Sacred Promise!

FATHER (*getting annoyed*): Vinnie, you were sick when I said that. Now you're well again. (*MARGARET enters with pug dog, which now has the freshly pressed ribbon tied around its neck. She puts it on table. FATHER doesn't notice her.*)

MARGARET: Is that all right, Mrs. Day?

VINNIE (*dismissingly, keeping her attention on FATHER*): That's fine, Margaret, thank you. (*MARGARET exits. VINNIE goes right on talking as though there had been no interruption.*) My being well has nothing to do with it! You gave me your word! You gave the Lord your word. (*FATHER throws paper on sofa, then puts glasses away.*) If you had seen how eager Mr. Morley was to bring you into the fold. (FATHER *swings around end of sofa toward arch. She follows him.*) And you're going to march yourself up to his church some morning before you go to the office and be christened. (FATHER *sees pug dog, and stops.*) If you think for one minute that I'm going to . . .

FATHER (*now staring at it intently*): What in the name of heaven is that?

VINNIE (*on his left*): If you think I'm going to let you add the sin of breaking your Solemn and Sacred Promise—

FATHER: I demand to know what that repulsive object is!

VINNIE: It's perfectly plain what it is—it's a pug dog!

FATHER: What's it doing in this house?

VINNIE (*trying unsuccessfully to be defiant*): I wanted it and I bought it.

FATHER: You paid good money for that?

VINNIE: Clare, we're not talking about that! We're talking about you! Don't try to change the subject!

FATHER: How much did you pay for that atrocity?

VINNIE: I don't know. I sent Clarence down for it. Listen to me, Clare—

FATHER: Clarence, what did you pay for that?

CLARENCE (*rises*): I didn't pay anything. I charged it.

FATHER (*looking at* VINNIE): Charged it! I might have known. (*To* CLARENCE.) How much was it?

CLARENCE: Fifteen dollars.

FATHER: Fifteen dollars for that eyesore?

VINNIE (*crossing to back of table taking dog in her arms*): Don't you call that lovely work of art an eyesore! That will look beautiful sitting on a red cushion by the fireplace in the parlor. (*She puts dog down on table.*)

FATHER: If that sits in the parlor, I won't! Furthermore, I don't even want it in the same house with me. Get it out of here! (*He starts for arch.*)

VINNIE (*crossing up and stopping him*): You're just using that for an excuse. You're not going to get out of this room until you set a date for your baptism.

FATHER (*starts to stairs—speaking as he is going up*): Well, I'll tell you one thing: I'll never be baptized as long as that hideous monstrosity is in this house. (*He stomps upstairs and off.*)

VINNIE (*calling after him*): All right! (*She goes to pug dog back of table. She makes up her mind.*) All right! It goes back this afternoon and he's christened first thing in the morning. (*Puts dog in box.*)

CLARENCE: But, Mother—

VINNIE: Clarence, you heard your father say that he'd be baptized as soon as I got this pug dog out of the house. (*Takes ribbon from dog.*) You hurry right back to McCreery's with it—and be sure they credit us with fifteen dollars. (*The "fifteen dollars" rings a bell in* CLARENCE's *mind.*)

CLARENCE (*at table*): Oh, Mother, while I was at McCreery's I happened to see a suit I liked very much and the suit was only fifteen dollars.

VINNIE (*regretfully*): Well, Clarence, I'm afraid your suit will have to wait until after I get your father christened.

CLARENCE (*hopefully*): No. I meant that since the suit cost just the same as the pug dog, if I exchanged the pug dog for the suit—

VINNIE: Why, yes, then your suit wouldn't cost Father anything! . . . That's very bright of you, Clarence, to think of that!

CLARENCE (*crossing to back of table*): I'd better start right away before McCreery's closes. (*He picks up box cover.*)

VINNIE: Yes. Let's see. If we're going to take your Father all the way up to Audubon—Clarence, you stop at Ryerson and Brown's on your way back and tell them to have a cab here at eight o'clock tomorrow morning.

CLARENCE: Mother, a cab! Do you think you ought to?

VINNIE: Well, we can't walk to Audubon.

CLARENCE (*warningly*): But you know what a cab does to Father.

VINNIE: This is an important occasion.

CLARENCE (*with a shrug*): All right. A brougham or a victoria?

VINNIE: Get one of their best cabs—the kind they use at funerals.

CLARENCE: Mother! Those cost two dollars an hour! And if Father gets mad—

VINNIE: If your father starts to argue in the morning, you remember—

CLARENCE: Oh, he agreed to it! We both heard him!

VINNIE (*regretfully*): I did have my heart set on this. (*An idea comes to her.*) Still—if they didn't sell him in all that time— (*She gives dog a reassuring pat. Then rolls string and ribbon around her finger. She begins to sing "Sweet Marie" happily. FATHER comes down the stairs. CLARENCE puts lid on box, then takes his hat and box and goes happily and quickly out. FATHER is startled at CLARENCE rushing by him. We hear door slam.*) I hope you notice that Clarence is returning the pug dog?

FATHER: That's a sign you're getting your faculties back. (*FATHER starts toward sofa, but stops. VINNIE is still singing quietly to herself in a satisfied way. She puts ribbon and string on side table.*) Good to hear you singing again, Vinnie. (*Suddenly remembering.*) Oh!—on my way uptown I stopped in at Tiffany's and bought you a little something. Thought you might like it. (*He takes out of his pocket a small ring box and holds it out to her. She runs to take it as soon as he says Tiffany's. FATHER goes to sofa—takes up paper and sits.*)

VINNIE (*opens it eagerly*): Oh, Clare. What a lovely ring! (*She takes ring out and examines it. Then puts it on her finger and admires it.*)

FATHER: I'm glad if it pleases you, Lavinia.

VINNIE: Oh, Clare. (*Crosses back of sofa, putting ring box on table as she passes. Kisses him.*) I don't know how to thank you.

FATHER: It's thanks enough for me to have you up and around again. (*VINNIE moves to center, admiring ring.*)

When you take to your bed this house is like a tomb. There's no excitement! (*He snaps open his paper.*)

VINNIE: Clare, this is the loveliest ring you ever bought me. (*Crosses and sits beside him.*) Now that I have this, you needn't buy me any more rings.

FATHER (*rather pleased. He starts to straighten ribbon of his glasses*): Well, if you don't want any more.

VINNIE (*still looking at ring*): What I'd really like now is a nice diamond necklace.

FATHER (*aghast*): Vinnie, do you know how much a diamond necklace costs?

VINNIE: I know, Clare, but don't you see—your getting me this ring shows that I mean a little something to you. Now a diamond necklace—

FATHER: Good God—if you don't know how I feel about you by this time— (*He looks away.*) We've been married for twenty years and I've loved you every minute of it.

VINNIE (*hardly believing her ears*): What did you say, Clare?

FATHER (*turning to her sharply*): I said we've been married twenty years and I've loved you every minute. (*He looks away. VINNIE's eyes fill with tears, at FATHER's definite statement of his love.*) But if I have to buy out jewelry stores to prove it—if I haven't shown it in my words and actions I might as well— (*He turns back and sees VINNIE crying—speaks with resigned helplessness.*) What have I done now?

VINNIE: It's all right, Clare—I'm just so happy.

FATHER: Happy?

VINNIE: You said you loved me—and this beautiful ring—that's something else I never expected. (*She puts her arm through his and cuddles her head on his shoulder. FATHER is pleased.*) Oh, Clare, I love surprises.

FATHER (*seriously*): That's another thing I have never understood about you, Vinnie. Now I like to know what to expect. Then I'm prepared to meet it.

VINNIE (*her head on his shoulder*): Yes, I know. But, Clare, life would be pretty dull if we always knew what was coming.

FATHER: Well, it's certainly not dull around here—in this house you never know what's going to hit you tomorrow. (*He laughs heartily at his own joke.*)

VINNIE: (*to herself*): Tomorrow! (*She starts to sing, "Sweet Marie," softly,* FATHER *listening to her happily.*) "Every daisy in the dell, Knows my *secret*, knows it well, And yet I dare not *tell* (*she turns her eyes up towards him*) Sweet Marie!"

SCENE 2

SCENE: *The same. The next morning. Breakfast. The clock says eight-thirty. The bowl which had fruit in it now has flowers in it.*

VINNIE'S *prayer book is now on side table. The fruit is at* VINNIE'S *place.* FATHER *and the two elder* BOYS *are eating kippers. The young* BOYS *have their porridge as usual. The* WHOLE FAMILY *except* JOHN *and* VINNIE *is at table eating quietly but in good spirits. The* BOYS *are dressed in their Sunday clothes.* CLARENCE *is still in black suit.* MAGGIE, *the new maid, is at side table, back to audience, with a plate of hot biscuits on a tray. There are two letters at right of* FATHER'S *place.*

JOHN (*entering from upstairs*): Mother says she'll be right down. (*He sits at table.* MAGGIE *comes down to serve* FATHER, *leaving tray on side table. As* FATHER *takes a biscuit, he glances up at her and shows some little surprise.*)

FATHER: Who are you? What's your name?

MAGGIE: Margaret, sir.

FATHER: Can't be Margaret. We've got one Margaret in the house.

MAGGIE: At home they call me Maggie, sir.

FATHER: All right, Maggie. (MAGGIE *continues serving biscuits to* CLARENCE *and* JOHN, *then leaves them on table to left of* JOHN—*then crosses to center and waits.*) Boys, if her name's Margaret, that's a good sign. Maybe she'll stay awhile. You know, your mother used to be just the same about cooks as she is about maids. Never could keep them, for some reason. Well, one day about fifteen years ago—yes, it was right after you were born, John—my, you were a homely baby. (THEY *all laugh, at* JOHN's *expense.*) I came home that night all tired out and what did I find?—no dinner because the cook had left. Well, I decided I'd had just about enough of that, so I marched over to the employment agency myself, and said to the woman in charge, "Where do you keep the cooks?" She tried to hold me up with a lot of red tape folderol but I just walked into the room where the girls were waiting, looked 'em over, saw Margaret, pointed at her and said "I'll take that one." I walked her home with me, she cooked dinner that night and she's been cooking for us ever since. (*He takes a bite of fish.*) Damn good cook, too. (*He stamps on floor three times.*)

VINNIE (*enters—dressed in a very handsome white dress*): Good morning, Clare— (*She crosses to chair and puts her bonnet on it. Then crosses and sits at table. She is a little self-conscious of her dress because of the occasion.*) Good morning, boys. (*All* BOYS *rise—and say "Good morning."* FATHER *rises—crosses above table to* VINNIE's *chair, drawing it out for her. He notices that she is very dressed up.*)

FATHER: Good morning, Vinnie. (*After she sits, he starts above table to his chair, noticing boys' clothes as he passes.*) Sit down, boys. (*He stands by his chair for just a moment, speaking happily.*) Everybody's all dressed up. —What's on the program? (*He sits.*)

VINNIE (*dodging the real issue*): This afternoon May Lewis's mother is giving a party for all the children in May's dancing class. Harlan's going to that.

HARLAN: I don't want to go, Mother.

VINNIE: Why, Harlan, don't you want to go to a party and get ice cream and cake?

HARLAN: May Lewis always tries to kiss me. (*This is greeted with family laughter.*)

FATHER (*genially*): When you're a little older, Harlan, you won't object to girls wanting to kiss you. (*He laughs—then suddenly.*) Will he, Clarence? (*They all laugh at* CLARENCE *who blushes.* MARGARET *comes in hurrying. She is a little anxious.*)

MARGARET: What's wanting? (*She goes between* JOHN *and* VINNIE.)

FATHER: Margaret, these kippers are *good*. (MARGARET *makes her usual deprecatory gesture.*) Haven't had kippers for a long time. I'm glad you remembered I like them.

MARGARET: Yes, sir. (MARGARET *and* VINNIE *exchange knowing looks.* MARGARET *goes out happy.*)

FATHER: What got into Margaret this morning? Hot biscuits, too!

VINNIE: She knows how fond you are of them. (*There is a second's pause, then doorbell rings.* MAGGIE *goes to answer it. Nervously.*) Well, who can that be? It can't be the postman, because he's been here.

FATHER (*with sly humor*): Clarence has been getting a good many special deliveries lately. Is that business deal going through, Clarence? (FAMILY *has a laugh at* CLARENCE *again.* MAGGIE *comes back into room with a suit box.*)

MAGGIE: This is for you, Mr. Day. Where shall I put it?

CLARENCE (*hastily*): Oh, that's for me, I think. Take it upstairs, please, Maggie. (*She starts to do so.*)

FATHER (*getting out his glasses*): Wait a minute, Maggie, bring it here. Let's see it. (MAGGIE *brings it to table, toward* FATHER. CLARENCE *rises as she gets near him, and takes box from her.* MAGGIE *exits.*)

CLARENCE: (*just showing it, but trying to get it away*): See, it's for me, Father—Clarence Day, Jr. (*He hurries up to arch, but stops short as Father speaks.*)

FATHER: Let me look! (CLARENCE *does so, slowly. He fears*

an explosion.) It's from McCreery's and it's marked charge.
What is it? (CLARENCE *looks to Mother.*)

VINNIE: It's all right, Clare. It's nothing for you to worry
about.

FATHER: Well, at least I think I should know what's being
charged to me. What is it?

VINNIE: Now, Clare, stop your fussing. It's a new suit of
clothes for Clarence. It isn't costing you a penny.

FATHER: It's marked "Charge $15." It's costing me fifteen
dollars. And I told Clarence . . .

VINNIE: Clare, can't you take my word? It isn't costing you
a penny.

FATHER (*taking off glasses*): I'd like to have you explain
why it isn't?

VINNIE (*triumphantly*): Because Clarence took the pug dog
back and got the suit instead.

FATHER: Yes, and they'll charge me fifteen dollars for the
suit.

VINNIE: Nonsense, Clare, we gave them the pug dog for
the suit. Don't you see?

FATHER: Then they'll charge me fifteen dollars for the pug
dog.

VINNIE: But, Clare, they can't. We haven't got the pug dog.

FATHER (*she has him winging for a second*): Just a minute,
Vinnie, there's something wrong with your reasoning.
(*He slaps his napkin on table, swings his chair so he faces
front, while he tries to figure it out.*)

VINNIE (*laughs lightly*): I'm surprised at you, Clare, and
you're supposed to be so good at figures. (FATHER *looks
at* VINNIE *resentfully.*) Why, it's perfectly clear to me.

FATHER (*emphatically*): My dear Vinnie, they'll charge me
for one thing or the other.

VINNIE (*firmly*): Don't you let them!

FATHER (*gets up and crosses to left staring at* VINNIE—*then
he walks over to window, in his irritation saying*): Well,
McCreery's aren't giving away suits and they aren't giving

away pug dogs. Can't you get it through your—? (*Looking out window.*) Oh! Oh! Oh, God!

VINNIE: What is it, Clare? What's wrong?

FATHER (*backs away to near his chair at table*): Don't anyone answer the door.

VINNIE: Who is it? Who's coming?

FATHER: Those damn women are back!

JOHN: What women?

FATHER: Cora and that little idiot. (CLARENCE *dashes madly upstairs, clutching box with his new suit.* VINNIE *rises— moves up towards arch*): They're moving in on us again, bag and baggage. (*Doorbell rings.*) Don't let them in! (JOHN *puts napkin in ring.*)

VINNIE (*comes down to back of her chair*): Clarence Day, as if we could turn our own relatives away! (*She goes up to arch.*)

FATHER: Tell them to get back in that cab and drive right on to Ohio. If they're extravagant enough to take cabs when horse cars go right by our door— (MAGGIE *crosses hall to answer bell.*)

VINNIE (*coming down to her chair again*): Now, Clare—you be quiet and behave yourself. They're here and there's nothing you can do about it. (*She starts toward hall—at side of arch.*)

FATHER (*shouting*): Why do they always pounce on us without warning—the damn gypsies!

VINNIE (*from arch, loudly to* CLARE): Shh! Shh!— (*Immediately following this, in her best welcoming tone and with arms extended.*) Cora! (JOHN, HARLAN *and* WHITNEY *rise.*)

CORA (*entering—kisses* VINNIE): How are you, Vinnie. (*As she moves right.*) We've been so worried about you. (CORA *greets* HARLAN *and* WHITNEY *as she passes below table. They answer her.* MARY *enters, kisses* VINNIE. *They come into room.* MARY *looks around room for* CLARENCE.) Harlan—and Whitney! (MAGGIE *follows in and stands at arch and waits for orders.*) And Cousin Clare. (CORA *kisses* FATHER *on cheek.*) Here we are again! (FATHER *gives her a quick frosty smile.* WHITNEY *and* HARLAN *sit—and put napkins in rings.* CORA *crosses to upper corner of table.*) And John!

JOHN: Hello, Cousin Cora.

CORA: Where is Clarence?

MARY: Yes, where is Clarence?

VINNIE: John, go tell Clarence that Cousin Cora and *Mary* are here.

JOHN (*exits upstairs*): Yes, Mother.

VINNIE: You got here just in time to have breakfast with us.

CORA: We had breakfast at the depot.

VINNIE: Well, as a matter of fact, we'd just finished.

FATHER (*with cold dignity*): I haven't finished my breakfast!

VINNIE: Well, then sit down, Clare. (FATHER *returns to his chair slowly, in stony silence. To* CORA *and* MARY.) Margaret gave us kippers this morning and Clare's so fond of kippers . . . Why don't we all sit down? (VINNIE *indicates empty places and* GIRLS *sit.* CORA *in* JOHN's *chair.* MARY *in* CLARENCE's.) Maggie, clear those things away. (*She indicates dishes in front of girls.* MAGGIE *does so, puts dishes on tray then exits with them.* FATHER *puts on glasses, opens letter and starts to read it.*) Clare, don't let your kippers get cold. (VINNIE *sits at table, moving her chair up so it is almost on level with* CORA's. *There is a second's uncomfortable pause.*) Now—tell us all about Springfield.

(JOHN *comes downstairs and exits.*)

CORA: We had a wonderful month—but tell us about you, Cousin Vinnie. You must have had a terrible time.

VINNIE: Yes, I was pretty sick, but I'm all right again now.

CORA: What was it?

VINNIE: Well, the doctors don't know exactly, but they did say this, whatever it was they've never seen anything like it before.

CORA: You certainly look well enough now. Doesn't she, Cousin Clare?

FATHER (*angered by letter*): Oh, God! (JOHN *starts upstairs with bags.*)

VINNIE: What's the matter, Clare? What's wrong?

FATHER (*seeing* JOHN *on stairs*): John! John! (JOHN *is half-way up stairs with bags. He comes running down, leaves bags in hall and goes to* FATHER.)

JOHN: Yes, Father?

FATHER (*quietly, looking at letter*): Have you been going around this town selling medicine?

JOHN (*a little frightened*): Yes, Father.

FATHER: Dog medicine?

JOHN: No, Father, not dog medicine.

FATHER (*looking at* JOHN): It must have been dog medicine.

JOHN: It wasn't dog medicine, Father—

FATHER (*indicating letter he has been reading*): Mrs. Sprague writes me that you sold her a bottle of this medicine and her little boy gave some of it to their dog and it killed him! Now she wants ten dollars for a new dog.

JOHN: He shouldn't have given it to a dog. It's for humans— (FATHER *looks at* JOHN.) Why, it was Bartlett's Beneficent Balm—made from a secret formula.

FATHER: Have you been going around to our friends and neighbors selling them some damned Dr. Munyon patent nostrum?

JOHN: It's good medicine, Father. I can prove it by Mother.

FATHER (*quietly*): Vinnie, what do you know about this?

VINNIE: Nothing, Clare; but I'm sure that John . . .

JOHN: No. I mean that day Mother—

FATHER (*firmly*): That's enough. You're going to every house where you sold a bottle of that concoction and buy it all back.

JOHN (*dismayed*): But it's a dollar a bottle.

FATHER (*putting letter in envelope*): I don't care how much it costs. I'll give you the money. How many bottles did you sell?

JOHN (*almost afraid to tell*): A hundred and twenty-eight.

FATHER (*roaring*): A hundred and twenty-eight!

VINNIE: Clare, I always told you John would make a good businessman.

FATHER (*looks at* VINNIE *for a second—calmly*): Well, John, I'll give you the money to buy it all back. A hundred and twenty-eight dollars. And ten more for Mrs. Sprague. (*Throws letter on table.*) That's a hundred and thirty-eight dollars. (*Getting louder.*) But it's coming out of your allowance. That means you'll not get another penny until that hundred and thirty-eight dollars is all paid up.

(FATHER *picks up newspapers angrily and sits quietly—nothing must be done to take audience's attention from* JOHN. JOHN *starts toward hall, counting on his fingers; when he is in back of table, he turns and addresses his* FATHER *in dismay.* JOHN'S *allowance is about $25 a year.*)

JOHN: I'll be twenty-one years old. (FATHER *ignores him, so* JOHN *turns and goes on upstairs with bags.*)

VINNIE (*quietly*): Clare, you know you've always encouraged the boys to earn their own money.

FATHER: I'll handle this, Vinnie. (*He buries himself in his newspaper, so that his face is not seen by audience. There is a pause.*)

CORA (*breaking through the constraint*): Of course, Aunt Judith sent her love to all of you—

VINNIE: I haven't seen Judith for years. You'd think living so close to Springfield—maybe I could run up there before the summer's over?

CORA: She'll be leaving for Pleasantville any day now. Grandpa Ebbetts has been failing very fast and that's why I have to hurry back.

VINNIE: Hurry back? Well, you and Mary can stay with us a few days, at least?

CORA: No, Cousin Vinnie, I hate to break the news to you,

but we can't even stay overnight. We're leaving on the five o'clock train this afternoon.

VINNIE (*disappointedly*): Oh! What a pity! (FATHER *lowers paper and takes off glasses.*)

FATHER (*heartily*): Cora, it certainly is good to see you again. (*To* MARY.) Young lady, I think you've been enjoying yourself—you look prettier than ever. (MARY *laughs and blushes.*)

WHITNEY: I'll bet Clarence will think so. (FATHER *laughs and starts eating again. Doorbell rings.*)

FATHER: That can't be another special delivery for Clarence! (MAGGIE *crosses hall.* FATHER *to* MARY.) Seems to me, while you were in Springfield our postman's been kept pretty busy. Sure you girls won't have any breakfast?

MARY (*rises—goes to arch, looking upstairs for* CLARENCE): No, thank you.

CORA: Oh, no, thank you, Clare, we had our breakfast.

FATHER: At least you ought to have a cup of coffee with us. Vinnie, why didn't you think to order some coffee for the girls. (MAGGIE *appears again and goes to* VINNIE.)

CORA: No no! Thank you, Cousin Clare. (VINNIE *is very self-conscious, knowing that the moment has arrived.*)

MAGGIE: It's the cab, ma'am. (MAGGIE *exits.*)

FATHER (*still eating*): The cab? What cab?

VINNIE: The cab that's to take us to Audubon.

FATHER: Who's going to Audubon? (*Picks up his coffee cup and takes a sip.*)

VINNIE: We all are. Cora, the most wonderful thing has happened.

CORA: What, Cousin Vinnie?

VINNIE (*happily*): Clare's going to be baptized this morning.

FATHER (*just about to take another drink of coffee—not believing his ears*): Vinnie—what—what are you saying?

VINNIE (*with gentle determination*): I'm saying you're going to be baptized this morning!

FATHER (*putting down cup*): I am not going to be baptized this morning, or any other morning!

VINNIE (*getting a little excited*): You promised yesterday
that as soon as I sent that pug dog back you'd be baptized.

FATHER (*also getting excited*): I promised no such thing!

VINNIE: You certainly did!

FATHER: I never said anything remotely like that!

VINNIE: Clarence was right here and heard it! You ask him!

FATHER: Clarence be damned! I know what I said! I don't
remember exactly, but it wasn't that!

VINNIE: Well, I remember! That's why I ordered the cab!

FATHER: The cab? (*Suddenly remembering.*) Oh, my God,
that cab! (*Rises—looks out window, then moves to table.*)
Vinnie, you send that right back.

VINNIE (*rises*): I'll do no such thing. I'm going to see that
you go to heaven!

FATHER: I can't go to heaven in a cab!

VINNIE: Well, you can start in a cab. I'm not sure whether
they'll ever let you in heaven, but I know they won't
unless you're baptized.

FATHER (*with dignity*): They can't keep me out of heaven
on a technicality.

VINNIE: Clare, stop quibbling! You might just as well face
it—you've got to make your peace with God.

FATHER (*excitedly*): Until you stirred Him up, I had no
trouble with God. (*He crosses right—then down center
again. CORA has been following argument with lively interest. MARY has been paying no attention—now she moves
towards foot of stairs—then starts towards VINNIE.*)

MARY: Mrs. Day? (*VINNIE answers her quickly, as if expecting MARY to supply her with an added argument.
FATHER also is interested in what she may say.*)

VINNIE: Yes, Mary?

MARY: Where do you suppose *Clarence* is?

FATHER (*crossing to her*): You keep out of this, young lady!
If it hadn't been for you, no one would have known
whether I was baptized or not. (*MARY breaks into a loud
burst of tears—runs to arch.*) Damn! Damnation!

VINNIE (*crossing to them, quickly*): Harlan, Whitney, get

your Sunday hats. (*Calls upstairs.*) John! Clarence! (*She runs back of sofa to chair for her bonnet.* HARLAN *and* WHITNEY *rise and push their chairs under table, then start out. They stop as* FATHER *speaks.* WHITNEY *at corner of table,* HARLAN *almost in front of* FATHER.)

FATHER (*with hurt dignity*): Vinnie, are you mad? Was it your plan that my own children should witness this indignity?

VINNIE (*picking up her bonnet*): Why, Clare, they'll be proud of you!

FATHER (*pointing at* HARLAN, *exploding*): I suppose Harlan is to be my godfather! (*With determination, he crosses to* VINNIE.) Vinnie, it's no use. (WHITNEY *and* HARLAN *move slowly up to arch.* JOHN *starts downstairs, slowly.*) I can't go through with this thing, and I won't. That's final.

VINNIE: All right, Clare dear, if you feel that way about it—

FATHER (*turning away*): I do!

VINNIE: We won't take the children with us. (FATHER *turns back to* VINNIE. JOHN *enters room.* WHITNEY *moves up to arch after* JOHN *enters.* HARLAN *to back of sofa.*)

JOHN (*coming down*): Yes, Mother?

FATHER (*dodging an argument*): Oh, John! Vinnie, I haven't time for anything like that this morning. I've got to take John down to the office and give him the money to buy back that medicine. (*To* JOHN.) When I think of you going around this town selling dog medicine— (WHITNEY *goes to table near sofa.*)

JOHN (*insistently*): It wasn't dog medicine, Father.

FATHER: That's enough. We're starting downtown this minute!

VINNIE: You're doing no such thing! (FATHER *turns to* VINNIE.) You gave me your Sacred Promise that day I almost died . . .

JOHN (*proudly—a chance to justify himself*): Yes, and she would have died if we hadn't given her some of that medicine. That proves it's good medicine. (MARY *has stopped crying and becomes interested.*)

FATHER (*turning slowly to* JOHN—*aghast*): You gave your mother some of that dog medicine!

VINNIE: Oh, no, John, you didn't!

JOHN (*sees something is wrong*): Yes, we did, Mother. We put some in your tea that morning. (VINNIE *sits, a little stunned.* CORA *rises.*)

FATHER: You did what? Without her knowing it? (JOHN *nods.*) Do you realize you might have killed your mother? You *did* kill Mrs. Sprague's dog. (*After a solemn pause.*) John, you've done a very serious thing. I'll have to give considerable thought as to how I'm going to punish you for this.

VINNIE: But Clare, dear!

FATHER: No, Vinnie. When I think of that day—with this house full of doctors— Why, Cora, we even sent for the minister. (*Really moved.*) Vinnie, we might have lost you! (*He dismisses the thought.*) It's all right now, thank God, you're well again. (*Pats her shoulder and moves toward* JOHN.) But what *I* went through that afternoon . . . the way I felt—I'll never forget it.

VINNIE: Don't talk that way, Clare. You've forgotten it already.

FATHER (*turning to her*): What do you mean?

VINNIE: That was the day you gave me your Sacred Promise.

FATHER: I wouldn't have promised if I hadn't thought you were dying—and you wouldn't have almost have died if John hadn't given you that dog medicine. Don't you see, the whole thing's illegal. (JOHN *goes slowly up to arch.*)

VINNIE: Suppose I had died! (HARLAN *goes behind her chair, frowning at* FATHER *and putting arm around her.*) It wouldn't make any difference to you. You don't care whether we meet in heaven or not—(WHITNEY *goes down to her, also frowning at* FATHER)—you don't care whether you ever see me and the children again. (*She almost succeeds in crying.*)

FATHER (*distressed*): Now, Vinnie, you're not being fair to me.

VINNIE (*nobly resigned*): It's all right, Clare. If you don't love us enough, there's nothing we can do about it.

FATHER (*exasperated*): That has nothing to do with it!—I love my family as much as any man. (*Walking away in distress.*) There's nothing within reason I wouldn't do for you and you know it! The years I've struggled and worked just to prove— (*He has reached window and sees cab. A slight pause. He turns back, and speaks in a very sympathetic tone.*) Vinnie, you're not well enough to go all the way up to Audubon.

VINNIE (*perkily*): I'm well enough to go if we ride.

FATHER: That trip would take all morning. And those cabs cost a dollar an hour.

VINNIE: That's one of their best cabs. That costs two dollars an hour. (FATHER *stares at her a second, horrified, half turns to window—then explodes.*)

FATHER: Then why aren't you ready? Get your hat on! (*He crosses center.*) Damn! Damnation! (FATHER *exits for his hat and stick. Doorbell rings loudly.* VINNIE *dashes for prayer book which is on side table—putting on her bonnet as she runs.*)

WHITNEY (*takes* HARLAN's *hand*): Let's watch them start! (*Running up to sofa—with* HARLAN.) Come on, Cousin Cora, let's watch them start. (*They exit.*)

CORA (*following them off*): I wouldn't miss it. (VINNIE *starts out.* MARY *runs to window.*)

JOHN (*contrite*): Mother—I didn't mean to almost kill you.

VINNIE (*going to* JOHN): Now, don't you worry about what your father said. (*Tenderly.*) It's all right, dear. (*She kisses him and starts to exit, then stops.*) It turned out fine! (*She exits. We hear sound of hurrying feet upstairs.* JOHN *looks upstairs, then at* MARY.)

JOHN: Mary! Here comes Clarence!

(JOHN *exits.* MARY *hurriedly sits in* FATHER's *chair.* CLARENCE *comes rushing down steps in his new cream-colored suit. He goes into room and quickly adjusts his new clothes.*)

Then rushes right to MARY. *Without saying a word he kneels in front of her. They both are starry-eyed.* FATHER, *with hat and stick, comes into arch and sees* CLARENCE *and* MARY.)

FATHER: Oh, God! (CLARENCE *springs up in embarrassment.* VINNIE *re-enters hurriedly.*)

VINNIE: What's the matter? What's wrong? (FATHER *steps down and points his cane at* CLARENCE.)

CLARENCE (*quickly*): Nothing's wrong, Mother—nothing's wrong. (*Hurriedly for want of something to say.*) Going to the office, Father?

FATHER: No, I'm going to be baptized, damn it! (*He slams his hat on angrily and stalks out, crossing in front of* VINNIE. VINNIE *gives a triumphant nod and follows him. Curtain starts down and as it falls,* CLARENCE *again kneels at* MARY'S *feet.*)

YOU CAN'T TAKE IT WITH YOU

INTRODUCTION

The day after *You Can't Take It with You* opened in New York, John Mason Brown, distinguished dramatic critic and author, wrote:

> In a world in which the sanity usually associated with sunshine is sadly overvalued, *You Can't Take It with You* is something to be prized. It is moonstruck, almost from beginning to end. It is blessed with all the happiest lunacies Moss Hart and George S. Kaufman have been able to contribute to it. The Sycamore family is the most gloriously mad group of contented eccentrics the modern theatre has yet had the good fortune to shadow.[1]

It had a run of 837 performances and won the Pulitzer Prize for the 1936–1937 season. It has been widely played since that time. England saw a production in Manchester on December 13, 1937, and London on December 22, 1937. It has been anthologized frequently.

As we read it now after a quarter century has elapsed, we can understand why thousands of theatregoers flocked to it all through 1937 and later, and why it has retained its interest for us, long after hundreds of other plays that have appeared on Broadway have been forgotten. Edmond M. Gagey expressed it well:

> Whatever its failings, it [i.e., Broadway comedy] kept its humor and its sanity at a time when civilization

---

[1] *Two on the Aisle*, p. 177.

seemed to be going to smash under the impacts of depression and war. Its impudent escapism is admirably expressed in the Pulitzer Prize-winner *You Can't Take It with You* (1936).[2]

In 1936 America was still in the Depression and the world was only three years away from World War II. The story of a family living near Columbia University who managed not only to survive in those terrible days but to enjoy life hugely appealed to thousands of playgoers both here and abroad. Its very absurdities and improbabilities endeared the play even more. Eager to forget the bad news at home and the ever-increasing threats from abroad, playgoers found this a kind of poor man's Shangri-La on Morningside Heights.

Coupled with the pleasure derived from observing the antics of a harebrained but happy family living on practically nothing a week was the delight in viewing another cleverly wrought product of one of the most expert writing teams in American dramatic history.

THE PLAYWRIGHTS

George S. Kaufman was born in Pittsburgh, Pennsylvania, on November 16, 1889. After an early career as a reporter and drama critic, he turned to writing plays rather than reviewing them.

By 1936 he had written one play, *The Butter and Egg Man* (1925), by himself, and twenty-four in collaboration with such authors as Irving Pichel, Larry Evans, Marc Connelly, Edna Ferber, Katherine Dayton, Alexander Woollcott, Ring Lardner and Morris Ryskind. His name has been on Broadway marquees since 1921, when his first collaboration, *Dulcy*, written with Marc Connelly, appeared. It was a rare year during the next three decades that did not have a Kaufman play on Broadway.

His talents lay in many directions. *Beggar on Horseback*

[2] *Revolution in American Drama*, p. 229.

(1924), again with Marc Connelly, was acclaimed for its expressionism, a form of interpretative drama that developed in Germany after World War I.[3] With *The Bandwagon* (1931), written in collaboration with Howard Dietz, he set a new standard of excellence in the field of the topical revue. His musical *Of Thee I Sing* (1931) was the first of its kind to win a Pulitzer Prize. After the première of *Of Thee I Sing*, Gilbert Gabriel, critic of the New York *American*, exclaimed:

> We first-nighters . . . were in at the liberation of musical comedy from twaddle and treacle and garden-party truck. We were laughing gratefully along at a new date in stage history.[4]

Moss Hart was born in New York City on October 24, 1904, and seems to have selected writing as a goal in his high-school days. After trying various occupations, he wrote *Once in a Lifetime* in 1930. With Kaufman's work on the script and successful staging of the play it became a hit of the 1930–1931 season. Other collaborations with Kaufman were *Merrily We Roll Along* (1934) and *I'd Rather Be Right* (1937). His recent autobiography, *Act One* (1959), became a best seller.

Both authors know their stage business well and have an ear for dialogue that is realistic and laugh-provoking. Some critics have found the theme of *You Can't Take It with You* rather threadbare, but Kaufman and Hart have never professed to be philosophers.[5]

This play is an example of clever theatrical craftsmanship, of strikingly funny situations, of dialogue that is humorous and stageworthy and of a view of life that may have been in the hearts of many in the unhappy days that had not yet seen the last of the Depression and were shortly to witness the beginning of World War II.

---

[3] Barnard Hewitt, *Theatre U.S.A.*, p. 355.
[4] *Ibid.*, p. 387.
[5] Frank Hurburt O'Hara, *Today in American Drama*, p. 225. See also Joseph Wood Krutch, *The American Drama Since 1918*, pp. 136–152.

ADDITIONAL READING

Brown, John Mason. *Two on the Aisle,* New York: Norton, 1938. Pages 177–180 contain a review of the play.

Flexner, Eleanor. *American Playwrights, 1918–1938.* New York: Simon and Schuster, 1938. Pages 225–227 contain a discussion of the play. Pages 198–233 contain a study of Kaufman's work up to 1938.

Gagey, Edmond M. *Revolution in American Drama,* pp. 229–231. New York: Columbia, 1947.

Hewitt, Barnard. *Theatre U.S.A.: 1668 to 1957,* pp. 336–337. New York: McGraw-Hill, 1959.

Krutch, Joseph Wood. *The American Drama Since 1918.* New York: Random House, 1939. Pages 136–152 contain an analysis of Kaufman's technique.

Kunitz, Stanley J., and Haycraft, Howard. *Twentieth Century Authors,* pp. 623–624, 748–749. New York: Wilson, 1942.

Kunitz, Stanley J. *Twentieth Century Authors.* First Supplement, pp. 512–513. New York: Wilson, 1955.

Mantle, Burns. *Contemporary American Playwrights,* pp. 8–20. New York: Dodd, Mead, 1938.

Mantle, Burns, ed. *The Best Plays of 1936–37.* New York: Dodd, Mead, 1937. Contains an outline of the play and introductory comments.

Morehouse, Ward. *Matinee Tomorrow,* pp. 262, 269, 301. New York: McGraw-Hill, 1949.

O'Hara, Frank Hurburt. *Today in American Drama,* pp. 224–378. Chicago: University of Chicago, 1938.

Shipley, Joseph T. *Guide to Great Plays,* pp. 377–378. Washington, D.C.: Public Affairs, 1956.

YOU CAN'T TAKE IT WITH YOU

BY MOSS HART AND GEORGE S. KAUFMAN

ACT I

SCENE 1

The home of MARTIN VANDERHOF—*just around the corner from Columbia University, but don't go looking for it. The room we see is what is customarily described as a living room, but in this house the term is something of an understatement. The every-man-for-himself room would be more like it. For here meals are eaten, plays are written, snakes collected, ballet steps practiced, xylophones played, printing presses operated—if there were room enough there would probably be ice skating. In short, the brood presided over by* MARTIN VANDERHOF *goes on about the business of living in the fullest sense of the word. From* GRANDPA VANDERHOF *down, they are individualists. This is a house where you do as you like, and no questions asked.*

At the moment, GRANDPA VANDERHOF'S *daughter,* MRS. PE-NELOPE SYCAMORE, *is doing what she likes more than any-*

thing else in the world. She is writing a play—her eleventh. Comfortably ensconced in what is affectionately known as Mother's Corner, she is pounding away on a typewriter perched precariously on a rickety card table. Also on the table is one of those plaster of Paris skulls ordinarily used as an ash tray, but which serves PENELOPE *as a candy jar. And, because* PENNY *likes companionship, there are two kittens on the table, busily lapping at a saucer of milk.*

PENELOPE VANDERHOF SYCAMORE *is a round little woman in her early fifties, comfortable looking, gentle, homey. One would not suspect that under that placid exterior there surges the Divine Urge—but it does, it does.*

After a moment her fingers lag on the keys; a thoughtful expression comes over her face. Abstractedly she takes a piece of candy out of the skull, pops it into her mouth. As always, it furnishes the needed inspiration—with a furious burst of speed she finishes a page and whips it out of the machine. Quite mechanically, she picks up one of the kittens, adds the sheet of paper to the pile underneath, replaces the kitten.

As she goes back to work, ESSIE CARMICHAEL, MRS. SYCA-MORE'S *eldest daughter, comes in from the kitchen. She is a girl of about twenty-nine, very slight, a curious air of the pixie about her. She is wearing ballet slippers—in fact, she wears them throughout the play.*

ESSIE (*enters as* PENNY *crosses back with skull, and fanning herself, takes paper out of typewriter*): My, that kitchen's hot.

PENNY (*finishing a bit of typing*): What, Essie? (*Rises and crosses to right.*)

ESSIE (*crossing to right table*): I say the kitchen's awful hot. That new candy I'm making—it just won't ever get cool.

PENNY: Do you have to make candy today, Essie? It's such a hot day.

ESSIE: Well, I got all those new orders. Ed went out and got a bunch of new orders. (*Leg-limbering exercise on chair.*)

PENNY: My, if it keeps on I suppose you'll be opening up a store.

ESSIE: That's what Ed was saying last night (*she leans body forward*), but I said no, I want to be a dancer.

PENNY (*returning to her desk*): The only trouble with dancing is, it takes so long. You've been studying such a long time.

ESSIE (*slowly drawing a leg up behind her as she talks*): Only—eight—years. After all, Mother, you've been writing plays for eight years. We started about the same time, didn't we?

PENNY (*at her desk*): Yes, but you shouldn't count my first two years, because I was learning to type.

(*From the kitchen comes a colored maid named RHEBA—a very black girl somewhere in her thirties. She carries eight napkins.*)

RHEBA (*as she enters*): I think the candy's *hardening up* now, Miss Essie. (*Puts napkins on chair.*)

ESSIE: Oh, thanks, Rheba. I'll bring some in, Mother—I want you to try it. (*Goes into kitchen.*)

(PENNY *returns to her work, sits—puts fresh paper in and types—as* RHEBA *removes table centerpiece and goes to buffet.*)

RHEBA (*taking a tablecloth from buffet drawer*): Finish the second act, Mrs. Sycamore?

PENNY: Uh? What?

RHEBA (*returning to table, she throws tablecloth over back of a chair and removes table cover*): I said, did you finish the second act?

PENNY (*moves with script, papers, and pencil*): Oh, no, Rheba. I've just got Cynthia entering the monastery.

RHEBA: She was at the Kit Kat, wasn't she?

PENNY (*crosses to table*): Well, she gets tired of the Kit Kat Club, and there's this monastery, so she goes there.

RHEBA: Do they let her in?

PENNY: Yes, I made it Visitors' Day, so of course anybody can come.

RHEBA (*as she spreads tablecloth*): Oh.

PENNY: So she arrives on Visitors' Day, and—just stays.

RHEBA: You mean she stays all night?

PENNY: Oh, yes. She stays six years. (*Crosses to her desk and sits.*)

RHEBA: Six years? (*Starting for kitchen.*) My, I bet she busts that monastery wide open. (*She is gone.*)

PENNY (*half to herself, as she types*): "Six Years Later . . ."

(PAUL SYCAMORE *comes up from the cellar. He is in his mid-fifties, but with a kind of youthful air. His quiet charm and mild manner are distinctly engaging. He is carrying a frying pan containing several small firecrackers. He is smoking a cigarette.*)

PAUL (*turning back as he comes through door*): Mr. De Pinna! (*A voice from below: "Yah?"*) Mr. De Pinna, will you bring up one of those new skyrockets, please? I want to show them to Mrs. Sycamore. (*An answering "Sure!" from cellar as he crosses toward* PENNY, *who rises.*) Look, Penny—what do you think of these little firecrackers we just made? We can sell them ten strings for a cent. Listen. (*He puts one down in the pan on table and lights it. It goes off with a good bang.*) Nice, huh?

PENNY: Yes. Paul, dear, were you ever in a monastery?

PAUL (*puts half of firecrackers in pan, quite calmly as he crosses to her*): No, I wasn't. . . . Wait till you see the new rockets. Gold stars, then blue stars, and then bombs, and then a balloon. Mr. De Pinna thought of the balloon.

(DE PINNA *enters.*)

PENNY: Sounds lovely. Did you do all that today?

PAUL: Sure. We made up— Oh, here we are. (DE PINNA *comes up from cellar. He is a bald-headed little man with a serious manner, carrying two good-sized skyrockets.* PAUL *takes one to show* PENNY.) Look, Penny. Costs us eighteen cents to make and we sell 'em for fifty. How many do you figure we can make before the Fourth of July, Mr. De Pinna?

DE PINNA: Well, we've got two weeks yet—what day you going to take the stuff up to Mount Vernon?

PAUL (*picking up his pan and firecrackers*): About a week. You know, we're going to need a larger booth this year— got a lot of stuff made up. (PAUL *starts out.*) Come on, we're not through yet. (DE PINNA *follows.*)

DE PINNA: Look, Mr. Sycamore (*examining rocket in his hand*), I'm afraid the powder chamber is just a little bit close to the balloon.

PAUL: Well, we got the stars and the bombs in between.

DE PINNA: But that don't give the balloon time enough. A balloon needs plenty of time.

PAUL: Come on—come on. Let's go down in the cellar and try it. (*He exits.*)

DE PINNA (*starting off*): All right.

PENNY (*rising and crossing two steps*): Mr. De Pinna, if a girl you loved entered a monastery, what would you do?

DE PINNA: Oh I don't know, Mrs. Sycamore . . . it's been so long.

(PENNY *sits at her desk, as* DE PINNA *exits. She starts to type again as* RHEBA *enters from kitchen bringing a pile of plates and salt and pepper shakers.*)

RHEBA (*crossing down to table*): Miss Alice going to be home to dinner tonight, Mrs. Sycamore? (*She puts pile of plates on table.*)

PENNY (*deep in her thinking*): What? I don't know, Rheba. Maybe.

RHEBA: Well, I'll set a place for her, but she's only been home one night this week.

PENNY: Yes, I know.

RHEBA (*puts down a plate or two*): Miss Essie's making some mighty good candy today. She's doing something new with coconuts.

PENNY: Uh-huh. That's nice.

RHEBA: Let's see . . . six and Mr. De Pinna, and if Mr. Kolenkhov comes that makes eight, don't it? (PENNY *types. A whistling sound of a rocket followed by a series of explosions comes up from cellar.* PENNY *and* RHEBA, *however, don't even notice it.* RHEBA *goes right on.*) Yes, I'd better set for eight. (*Puts napkins from chair to table. Puts down one more plate, looks over her setting of the table, and starts off.*)

PENNY (*rising*): Rheba, I think I'll put this play away for a while and go back to the war play.

(ESSIE *returns from kitchen carrying a plate of freshly made candy.*)

RHEBA: Oh, I always liked that one—the war play. Boom, boom! (*She exits.*)

ESSIE (*crossing over to* PENNY): They'll be better when they're harder, Mother, but try one—I want to know what you think.

PENNY: Oh, they look lovely. (*She takes one.*) What do you call them?

ESSIE: I think I'll call 'em Love Dreams. (*She places them on table.*)

PENNY: Yes, that's nice. . . . (*Nibbling on one of the candies.*) I'm going back to my war play, Essie. What do you think?

ESSIE (*dances back to buffet*): Oh, are you, Mother?

PENNY (*puts script down*): Yes, I sort of got myself into a monastery and I can't get out.

ESSIE (*pointing her toe*): Oh, well, it'll come to you, Mother. Remember how you got out of that brothel. . . . (*She looks at snake solarium, a glass structure looking something like a goldfish aquarium, but containing, believe it or not, snakes.*) The snakes look hungry. Did Rheba feed them?

(RHEBA *enters carrying silverware.*)

PENNY (*as* RHEBA *re-enters, puts silverware down on table and sets two places*): I don't know. Rheba, did you feed the snakes yet?

RHEBA: No, Donald's coming and he always brings flies with him. (ESSIE *dances to buffet.*)

PENNY: Well, try to feed them before Grandpa gets home. You know how fussy he is about them. (*Crossing to desk, she picks up file box with kittens in it.*)

RHEBA (*starts to go*): Yes'm.

PENNY (*handing* RHEBA *the kittens*): And here, take Groucho and Harpo into the kitchen with you. (RHEBA *exits.*) Believe I'll have another Love Dream. (*Sits at her desk.*)

(PAUL *emerges from cellar again.*)

PAUL (*enters and crosses to* ESSIE): Mr. De Pinna was right about the balloon. It was too close to the powder.

ESSIE: Want a Love Dream, Father? They're on the table.

PAUL (*starts for stairs*): No, thanks. I gotta wash.

PENNY: I'm going back to the war play, Paul.

PAUL: Oh, that's nice. We're putting some red stars after the bombs and *then* the balloon. That ought to do it. (*He goes upstairs.*)

ESSIE: You know, Mr. Kolenkhov says I'm his most promising pupil.

PENNY: You'd think with forty monks and one girl that *some*-thing would happen.

(ED CARMICHAEL *comes downstairs. He is a nondescript young man in his mid-thirties. He removes his coat as he crosses to xylophone.*)

ED: Essie! Heh! Essie! (PENNY *sits as music starts. He hums a snatch of melody as he heads for the far corner of the room —the xylophone corner. Arriving there, he picks up the sticks and continues the melody on the xylophone. Immediately* ESSIE *is up on her toes, performing intricate ballet steps to* ED's *accompaniment.*)

ESSIE (*rising on toes—dancing*): I like that, Ed. Did you write it? (PENNY *types.*)

ED (*pauses in his playing and shakes his head*): No, Beethoven. (*Music continues.*)

ESSIE (*never coming down off her toes*): Lovely. Got a lot of *you* in it. . . . I made those new candies this afternoon, Ed.

ED (*playing away*): Yah?

ESSIE (*a series of leaping steps*): You can take 'em around tonight.

ED: All right. . . Now, here's the finish. This is me. (*He works up to an elaborate crescendo, but* ESSIE *keeps pace with him, right to the finish, pirouetting to the last note.*) How's that?

ESSIE: That's fine. Remember it when Kolenkhov comes, will you?

PENNY (*who has been busy with her scripts*): Ed, dear. Why don't you and Essie have a baby? I was thinking about it just the other day.

(ED *puts xylophone hammers down—comes down from alcove.*)

ED (*as* ESSIE *busies herself with her slippers*): I don't know— we could have one if you wanted us to. What about it, Essie? Do you want to have a baby?

ESSIE: Oh, I don't care. I'm willing if Grandpa is. (*She goes off into kitchen.*)

ED (*calling after her*): Let's ask him.

PENNY (*running through a pile of scripts*): Labor play (ED *works printing press with a bang*), religious play (*another bang.* RHEBA *enters with silverware. Puts table cover on buffet arm*) sex play—(*still another bang*)—I know it's here some place.

DE PINNA (*coming out of cellar, bound for kitchen to wash up*): I was right about the balloon. It was too close to the powder.

ED (*who has crossed to his press*): Anything you want printed, Mr. De Pinna? How about some more calling cards?

DE PINNA: No, thanks. I've still got the *first* thousand.

ED: Well, call on somebody, will you?

DE PINNA: All right! (*Exits*)

ED (*coming downstage—type stick in hand*): What have we got for dinner, Rheba? I'm ready to print the menu.

RHEBA: Let's see. Corn flakes, watermelon, some of these candies Miss Essie made, and some kind of meat—I forget. (*Sets silverware.*)

ED: I think I'll set it up in boldface Cheltenham tonight. (*Going to printing press.*) You know, if I'm going to take those new candies around I'd better print up some descriptive matter after dinner.

PENNY: Do you think anybody reads those things, Ed, that you put in the candy boxes? . . . Oh, here's the war play. (*She pulls a script out of pile.*) "Poison Gas." (*The doorbell rings.*) I guess that's Donald. (RHEBA *smiles and starts for hall door.*) Look at Rheba smile.

ED: The boy friend, eh, Rheba?

(RHEBA *is out of sight.*)

PENNY: They're awfully cute, Donald and Rheba. Sort of like Porgy and Bess.

DONALD (*off stage*): Hello, Rheba.

RHEBA: Donald! (RHEBA *has opened door and* DONALD *now looms up in arch, straw hat in hand.*)

DONALD: Evening, everybody!

ED: Hi, Donald! How've you been?

DONALD (*coming into room*): I'm pretty good, Mr. Ed. How you been, Mrs. Sycamore?

PENNY: Very well, thank you. (*Rises.*) Donald?

DONALD: Yes, ma'am?

PENNY: Were you ever in a monastery?

DONALD: No-o. I don't go no place much. I'm on relief.

PENNY: Ah, yes, of course. (*Sits.*)

DONALD (*crossing to* RHEBA—*pulling a bottle out of side pocket*): Here's the flies, Rheba. Caught a big mess of them today.

RHEBA (*taking the jar*): You sure did. (RHEBA *goes into the kitchen.* DONALD *moves toward* PENNY.)

DONALD: I see you've been working, Mrs. Sycamore.

PENNY: Yes, indeed, Donald.

DONALD: How's Grandpa?

PENNY: Just fine. He's over at Columbia this afternoon. The commencement exercises.

DONALD (*crossing to table*): My . . . my. The years certainly do roll 'round. M-m-m. (*Takes a candy.*)

ED (*with his typesetting*): M–E–A–T. . . . What's he go there for all the time, Penny?

PENNY: I don't know, it's so handy—just around the corner.

(PAUL *comes downstairs, an impressive-looking tome under his arm.*)

PAUL: Oh, Donald! Mr. De Pinna and I are going to take the fireworks up to Mount Vernon next week. Do you think you could give us a hand?

DONALD: Yes, sir, only I can't take no money for it this year, because if the Government finds out I'm working they'll get sore.

PAUL: Oh! (DONALD *drifts up to buffet and feeds bits of candy to the snakes*). Ed, I got a wonderful idea in the bathroom just now. I was reading Trotsky. It's yours, isn't it?

ED: Yah, I left it there.

PENNY: *Who* is it?

PAUL (*moving toward* PENNY): You know, Trotsky. The
Russian Revolution. (*Shows her book.*)

PENNY: Oh.

PAUL: Anyhow, it struck me it was a great fireworks idea.
Remember "The Last Days of Pompeii"?

PENNY: Oh, yes. Palisades Park. (*With a gesture of her arms
she loosely describes a couple of arcs, indicative of the
eruption of Mt. Vesuvius.*) That's where we met.

PAUL: Well, I'm going to do the Revolution! A full-hour
display.

DONALD: Say!

PENNY: Paul, that's wonderful!

ED: The red fire is the flag, huh?

PAUL: Sure! And the Czar, and the Cossacks!

DONALD: And the freeing of the slaves?

PAUL: No, no, Donald—the Russian Revolution. (*The sound
of the front door slamming. A second's pause, then* GRANDPA
enters living room. GRANDPA *is about seventy-five, a wiry
little man whom the years have treated kindly. His face is
youthful, despite the lines that sear it; his eyes are very
much alive. He is a man who made his peace with the
world long, long ago, and his whole attitude and manner
are quietly persuasive of this.*) Hello, Grandpa. (*DONALD
crosses to door.* ED *moves near xylophone.* PAUL *sits above
table.*)

GRANDPA (*putting his hat on newel post and surveying the
group*): Well, sir, you should have been there. That's all I
can say—you should have been there.

PENNY: Was it a nice commencement, Grandpa?

GRANDPA: Wonderful. They get better every year. (*He peers
into snake solarium.*) You don't know how lucky you are
you're snakes. (*Crosses to alcove for his house coat.*)

ED: Big class this year, Grandpa? How many were there?

GRANDPA: Oh, must have been two acres. *Everybody* graduated. (*Removes street coat.*) Yes, sir. And much funnier
speeches than they had last year. (*Moves to his chair,
putting on house coat.*)

DONALD: You want to listen to a good speech you go up and hear Father Divine.

GRANDPA: I'll wait—they'll have him at Columbia. (*Sits.*)

PENNY: Donald, will you tell Rheba Grandpa's home now and we won't wait for Miss Alice.

(DE PINNA *enters from kitchen, rolling down his sleeves.*)

DONALD: Yes'm . . . (*As he exits through kitchen door.*) Rheba, Grandpa's home . . . we can have dinner.

PAUL: We made a new skyrocket today, Grandpa. Wait till you see it.

DE PINNA: Evening, Grandpa.

GRANDPA (*starting to remove his shoes*): Evening, Mr. De Pinna.

PAUL: Didn't we make a fine rocket today, Mr. De Pinna?

DE PINNA (*as he exits through cellar door*): We certainly did.

PAUL: Wonder why they don't have fireworks at commencements?

GRANDPA: Don't make enough noise. You take a good commencement orator and he'll drown out a whole carload of fireworks. (ED *gets a new pair of hammers.*) And say just as much, too.

PENNY: Don't the graduates ever say anything?

GRANDPA: No, they just sit there in cap and nightgown, get their diplomas, and then along about forty years from now they suddenly say, "Where am I?"

ESSIE (*entering from kitchen, carrying a plate of tomatoes for the evening meal*): Hello, Grandpa. Have a nice day?

GRANDPA: Hello-have-a-nice-day. Don't I even get kissed?

ESSIE (*kissing him*): Excuse me, Grandpa.

GRANDPA: I'll take a tomato, too. (ED *strikes three tentative notes on xylophone.* GRANDPA *takes a tomato and sits with it in his hand, weighing it.*) You know I could have used a couple of these this afternoon. . . .

ESSIE (*offering plate to* PAUL): Father?

(*Again* ED *strikes the keys of his xylophone.*)

PAUL: No, thanks.

(ESSIE *crosses to* PENNY.)

ESSIE: Mother?

PENNY: No, thanks, dear.

GRANDPA: Play something, Ed.

ED: All right. (ED *at once obliges on the xylophone. Immediately* ESSIE *is up on her toes, drifting through the mazes of a toe dance, placing plate of tomatoes on the table as she dances.*)

ESSIE (*after a moment of dancing "The Dying Swan"*): There was a letter came for you, Grandpa. Did you get it?

GRANDPA (*cutting a tomato*): Letter for me? I don't know anybody.

ESSIE: It was for you, though. Had your name on it.

GRANDPA: That's funny. Where is it?

ESSIE: I don't know. Where's Grandpa's letter, Mother?

PENNY (*who has been deep in her work*): What, dear?

ESSIE (*dancing dreamily away*): Where's that letter that came for Grandpa last week?

PENNY: I don't know. (*Then brightly.*) I remember seeing the kittens on it. (ESSIE *starts to floor.*)

GRANDPA: Who was it from? Did you notice?

ESSIE: Yes, it was on the outside.

GRANDPA: Well, who was it?

ESSIE (*first finishing the graceful flutterings of "The Dying Swan"*): United States Government. (*The music ends.*)

GRANDPA: Really? Wonder what *they* wanted.

ESSIE (*rising*): There was one before that, too, from the same people. There was a couple of them.

GRANDPA: Well, if any more come I wish you'd give them to me.

ESSIE (*exits through kitchen door on her toes*): Yes, Grandpa.

GRANDPA (*rises—shoes in hand*): I think I'll go out to Westchester tomorrow and do a little snake-hunting. (*Starts up to alcove for slippers.* ED *looks over xylophone, figuring out tune.*)

PAUL (*who has settled down with his book some time before this*): "God is the State; the State is God."

GRANDPA (*coming down—slippers in one hand, album in the other*): What's that?

PAUL: "God is the State; the State is God."

GRANDPA: Who says that?

PAUL: Trotsky.

GRANDPA: Well, that's all right—I thought *you* said it. (*Sits.*)

ED: It's nice for printing, you know. Good and short. (*He reaches into type case.*) G-O-D—space—I-S—space—T-H-E—space—

(*The sound of the outer door closing, and* ALICE SYCAMORE *enters the room. She is a lovely, fresh young girl of about twenty-two. She is plainly* GRANDPA's *granddaughter, but there is something that sets her apart from the rest of the family. For one thing, she is in daily contact with the world; in addition, she seems to have escaped the tinge of mild insanity that pervades the rest of them. But she is a Sycamore for all that, and her devotion and love for them are plainly apparent. At the moment she is in a small, nervous flutter, but she is doing her best to conceal it.*)

ALICE (*as she makes the rounds, kissing her mother, her father, her grandfather*): And so the beautiful princess came into the palace, and kissed her mother, and her father and her grandfather—

GRANDPA: Hello, darling!

ALICE: Hi, Grandpa—and what do you think? They turned into the Sycamore family. Surprised? (*Removes her hat.* ED *gets another set of hammers.*)

ESSIE (*enters, examining* ALICE's *dress*): Oh, Alice, I like it.

ALICE: Do you?

ESSIE: It's new, isn't it?

PENNY: Looks nice and summery.

ESSIE: Where'd you get it?

ALICE: Oh, I took a walk during lunch hour.

GRANDPA: You've been taking a lot of walks lately. That's the second new dress this week.

ALICE (*takes off gloves*): I just like to brighten up the office once in a while. I'm known as the Kay Francis of Kirby & Co. . . . Well, what's new around here? In the way of plays, snakes, ballet dancing or fireworks. Dad, I'll bet you've been down in that cellar all day. (ED *sees if hammers are straight.*)

PAUL: Huh?

PENNY: I'm going back to the war play, Alice. (ESSIE *does dance step exercise.*)

ALICE: Really, Mother? (*She takes her hat to the hatrack. ED strikes a note on xylophone.*)

ESSIE: Ed, play Alice that Beethoven thing you wrote.

(ED *at xylophone. He plays.* ESSIE *is up on her toes.*)

GRANDPA: You know, you can mail a letter all the way from Nicaragua now for two pesetas.

PAUL: Really?

PENNY (*reading from her script*): "Kenneth! My virginity is a priceless thing to me."

ALICE: Listen, people. . . . Listen. (*The music dies out. She gets a scattered sort of attention.*) I'm not home to dinner. A young gentleman is calling for me. (ED *fixes a xylophone hammer.*)

ESSIE: Really, who is it?

PENNY: Well, isn't that nice?

ALICE: I did everything possible to keep him from coming here but he's calling for me.

PENNY: Why don't you both stay for dinner?

ALICE: No, I want him to take you in easy doses. I've tried to prepare him a little, but don't make it any worse than you can help. Don't read him any plays, Mother, and don't let a snake bite him, Grandpa, because I like him. And I wouldn't dance for him, Essie, because we're going to the Monte Carlo Ballet tonight.

GRANDPA: Can't do *anything*. Who *is* he—President of the United States?

ALICE: No, he's vice-president of Kirby & Co. Mr. Anthony Kirby, Jr.

ESSIE: The boss's son?

PENNY: Well!

ALICE: The boss's son. Just like the movies.

ESSIE: That explains the new dresses.

ED: And not being home for dinner for three weeks.

ALICE: Why, Sherlock Holmes!

PENNY (*rises, all aglow—script in hand*): Are you going to marry him?

ALICE: Oh, of course. Tonight! Meanwhile I have to go up and put on my wedding dress. (PENNY *laughs, crosses to desk.*)

ESSIE: Is he good looking?

ALICE (*vainly consulting her watch*): Yes, in a word . . . Oh, dear! What time is it?

PENNY (*preoccupied with scripts*): I don't know. Anybody know what time it is?

PAUL: Mr. De Pinna might know.

ED: It was about five o'clock a couple of hours ago.

ALICE: Oh, I ought to know better than to ask you people. . . . Will you let me know the minute he comes, please?

PENNY: Of course, Alice.

ALICE: Yes, I know, but I mean the *minute* he comes.

PENNY: Why, of course.

ALICE: Well, be sure.

(ALICE *looks apprehensively from one to the other; then disappears up the stairs.*)

PENNY: Well, what do you think of that?

GRANDPA: She seems to like him, if you ask me.

ESSIE: I should say so. She's got it bad.

(ED *crosses into the room.*)

PENNY: Wouldn't it be wonderful if she married him? We could have the wedding right in this room.

PAUL: Now, wait a minute, Penny. This is the first time he's ever called for the girl.

(ESSIE *does stretching exercise.*)

PENNY: You only called for me once.

PAUL: Young people are different nowadays.

ESSIE: Oh, I don't know. Look at Ed and me. He came to dinner *once* and just stayed. (*Points toe.*)

PENNY: Anyhow, I think it's wonderful. Don't you, Grandpa?

GRANDPA: She certainly seems happy about it.

PENNY: He must be crazy about her. Maybe he's the one who is taking her out every night. (*Doorbell.*) There he is! Never mind, Rheba, I'll answer it. (*She is fluttering to the door.*) Now remember what Alice said, and be *very* nice to him.

GRANDPA (*rising*): All right—let's take a look at him.

(PAUL *rises.* ED *puts on his coat and comes into room. They all stand awaiting the stranger's appearance.*)

PENNY (*at the front door, milk and honey in her voice*): Well! Welcome to our little home!

HENDERSON: How do you do?

PENNY: I'm Alice's mother. Do come right in! Here we are! (*She reappears in archway, piloting the stranger, holding his hand.*) This is Grandpa, and that's Alice's father, and Alice's sister and her husband, Ed Carmichael. (*The family all give courteous little nods and smiles as they are introduced.*) Well! Now give me your hat and make yourself right at home. (PENNY *takes his hat.*)

THE MAN (*reaching for his card*): I'm afraid you must be making a mistake.

241

PENNY: How's that?

THE MAN: My card.

PENNY (*reading*): "Wilbur C. Henderson. Internal Revenue Department."

(PAUL *and* GRANDPA *exchange looks.*)

HENDERSON: That's right.

GRANDPA: What can we do for you?

HENDERSON: Does a Mr. Martin Vanderhof live here?

GRANDPA: Yes, sir. That's me.

HENDERSON (*moving toward table*): Well, Mr. Vanderhof, the Government wants to talk to you about a little matter of income tax.

PENNY: Income tax?

HENDERSON: You mind if I sit down?

GRANDPA: No, no. Just go right ahead.

HENDERSON (*settling himself in a chair at the table*): Thank you. (GRANDPA *sits. From above stairs the voice of* ALICE *floats down.*)

ALICE: Mother! Is that Mr. Kirby?

PENNY (*going to stairs*): No. No, it isn't, darling. It's—an internal something or other. (*To* HENDERSON.) Pardon me.

DE PINNA (*entering, carrying a firecracker*): Mr. Sycamore . . . oh, excuse me.

PAUL: What is it?

DE PINNA (*crossing to* PAUL): These things are not going off. Look. (*He strikes a match.*)

PAUL: Not here, Mr. De Pinna. Grandpa's busy.

DE PINNA: Oh!

(*They start for hall.*)

PAUL: Pardon me.

(*They start again for hall,* DE PINNA *looking at* HENDERSON *until* PAUL *and* DE PINNA *exit.*)

HENDERSON (*pulling a sheaf of papers from his pocket*): Now, Mr. Vanderhof (*a quick look toward hall*), we've written you several letters about this, but have not had any reply.

GRANDPA: Oh, that's what those letters were.

ESSIE (*sitting on couch*): I told you they were from the Government.

HENDERSON: According to our records, Mr. Vanderhof, you have never paid an income tax.

GRANDPA: That's right.

HENDERSON: Why not?

GRANDPA: I don't believe in it.

HENDERSON: Well—you own property, don't you?

GRANDPA: Yes, sir.

HENDERSON: And you receive a yearly income from it?

GRANDPA: I do.

HENDERSON: Of—(*he consults his records*)—between three and four thousand dollars.

GRANDPA: About that.

HENDERSON: You've been receiving it for years.

GRANDPA: I have. 1901, if you want the exact date.

HENDERSON: Well, the Government is only concerned from 1914 on. That's when the income tax started. (*Pause.*)

GRANDPA: Well?

HENDERSON: Well—it seems, Mr. Vanderhof, that you owe the Government twenty-four years' back income tax.

ED (*coming down as* ESSIE *joins him*): Wait a minute! You can't go back that far—that's outlawed.

HENDERSON (*calmly regarding him*): M-m-m! What's *your* name?

ED: What difference does that make?

HENDERSON: Ever file an income tax return?

ED: No, sir.

HENDERSON: Ah! What was your income last year?

ED: Ah—twenty-eight dollars and fifty cents, wasn't it, Essie?

ESSIE: Yes, sir.

HENDERSON: If you please! (*Dismissing* ED *and* ESSIE. *They drift to the rear.*) Now, Mr. Vanderhof, you know there's quite a penalty for not filing an income tax return.

PENNY: Penalty?

GRANDPA: Look, Mr. Henderson, let me ask you something.

HENDERSON: Well?

GRANDPA: Suppose I pay you this money—mind you, I don't say I'm going to pay it—but just for the sake of argument —what's the Government going to do with it?

HENDERSON: How do you mean?

GRANDPA: Well, what do I get for my money? If I go into Macy's and buy something, there it *is*—I see it. What's the Government give me?

HENDERSON: Why, the Government gives you everything. It protects you.

GRANDPA: What from?

HENDERSON: Well—invasion. Foreigners that might come over here and take everything you've got.

GRANDPA: Oh, I don't think they're going to do that.

HENDERSON: If you didn't pay an income tax, they would. How do you think the Government keeps up the Army and Navy? All those battleships . . .

GRANDPA: Last time we used battleships was in the Spanish-American War, and what did we get out of it? Cuba—and we gave that back. I wouldn't mind paying if it were something sensible.

HENDERSON: Sensible? Well, what about Congress, and the Supreme Court, and the President? We've got to pay *them*, don't we?

GRANDPA: Not with my money—no, sir.

HENDERSON (*furious; rises, picks up papers*): Now wait a minute! I'm not here to argue with you. All I know is that you haven't paid an income tax and you've got to pay it!

GRANDPA: They've got to show me.

HENDERSON (*yelling*): We don't have to show you! I just told you! All those buildings down in Washington (*to* PENNY— *she nods*), and interstate commerce, and the Constitution!

GRANDPA: The Constitution was paid for long ago. And interstate commerce—what *is* interstate commerce, anyhow?

HENDERSON (*looks at* PENNY—*at* ED—*at* GRANDPA; *with murderous calm, crosses and places his hands on table*): There are forty-eight states—see? And if there weren't interstate commerce, nothing could go from one state to another. See?

GRANDPA: Why not? They got fences?

HENDERSON (*to* GRANDPA): No, they haven't got fences. They've got *laws!* (*Crossing to arch.*) My God, I never came across anything like *this* before!

GRANDPA: Well, I might pay about seventy-five dollars, but that's all it's worth.

HENDERSON: You'll pay every cent of it, like everybody else!

ED (*who has lost interest*): Listen, Essie—listen to this a minute.

(*The xylophone again;* ESSIE *goes into her dance.*)

HENDERSON: (*going right ahead, battling against the music*): And let me tell you something else! You'll go to jail (PENNY *rises*) if you don't pay, do you hear that? That's the law, and if you think you're bigger than the law, you've got another think coming. You're no better than anybody else, and the sooner you get that through your head, the better . . . you'll hear from the United States Government, that's all I can say. . . . (*The music has stopped. He is backing out of the room.*)

GRANDPA (*quietly*): Look out for those snakes.

HENDERSON (*jumping; exits*): Jesus! (*An explosion from the hall. He exits through hall door.*)

ED: How was that, Essie?

ESSIE: Fine, Ed.

PAUL (*entering from hall with* DE PINNA): How did that sound to you folks? (ESSIE *sits on couch.*)

GRANDPA: I liked it.

PENNY: My goodness, he was mad, wasn't he?

GRANDPA: It's not his fault. It's just that the whole thing is so silly.

245

PENNY: He forgot his hat.

GRANDPA: Say, what size is that hat?

PENNY: Seven and an eighth.

GRANDPA: Just right for me.

DE PINNA: Who was that fellow, anyway? (*Doorbell. As bell rings* DE PINNA *makes for cellar door to get his coat.*)

PENNY: That *must* be Mr. Kirby.

PAUL: Better make sure this time.

PENNY: Yes, I will. (*She disappears.*)

ESSIE (*rises*): I hope he's good looking.

(*The family is again standing awaiting the newcomer.*)

PENNY (*heard at the door*): How do you do?

MAN'S VOICE: Good evening.

PENNY (*taking no chances*): Is this Mr. Anthony Kirby, Jr.?

TONY: Yes.

(GRANDPA *rises.*)

PENNY (*giving her all*): Well, Mr. Kirby, come right in! We've been expecting you. Come right in! (*They come into sight;* PENNY *expansively addresses the family.*) This is *really* Mr. Kirby! Now, I'm Alice's mother, and that's *Mr.* Sycamore, and Alice's grandfather, and her sister Essie, and Essie's husband. (DE PINNA *waves for recognition. There are a few mumbled greetings.*) There! Now you know *all* of us, Mr. Kirby. Give me your hat and make yourself right at home.

(TONY KIRBY *comes a few steps into the room. He is a personable young man, not long out of Yale, and, as we will presently learn, even more recently out of Cambridge. Although he fits all the physical requirements of a boss's son, his face has something of the idealist in it. All in all, a very nice young man.*)

TONY: Thank you.

(*Again the voice of the vigilant* ALICE *floats down from upstairs.* "Is that Mr. Kirby, Mother?")

PENNY (*shouting upstairs*): Yes, Alice. It is. He's *lovely!*

ALICE (*aware of storm signals*): I'll be right down.

PENNY (*puts* TONY's *hat on desk*): Do sit down, Mr. Kirby.

TONY (*as* PAUL *places chair for him*): Thank you. (*A glance at dinner table.*) I hope I'm not keeping you from dinner?

GRANDPA: No, no. Have a tomato? (*He and* PAUL *sit.*)

TONY: No, thank you.

PENNY (*producing candy-filled skull, crosses to* TONY): How about a piece of candy?

TONY (*eying the container*): Ah—no, thanks. (DE PINNA *again steps forward.*)

PENNY: Oh, I forgot to introduce Mr. De Pinna. This is Mr. De Pinna, Mr. Kirby. (*An exchange of "How do you do's?"*)

DE PINNA: Wasn't I reading about your father in the newspaper the other day? Didn't he get indicted or something?

TONY (*smiling*): Hardly that. He just testified before the Securities Commission.

DE PINNA: Oh.

PENNY (*sharply*): Yes, of course. I'm sure there was nothing crooked about it, Mr. De Pinna. As a matter of fact—(*she is now addressing* TONY; *drawing forward her desk chair, she sits*)—Alice has often told us what a lovely man your father is.

TONY (*sitting*): Well, I know Father couldn't get along without Alice. She knows more about the business than any of us.

ESSIE: You're awful young, Mr. Kirby, aren't you, to be vice-president of a big place like that?

TONY: Well, you know what that means, vice-president. All I have is a desk with my name on it.

PENNY: Is that all? Don't you get any salary?

TONY: Well, a little. More than I'm worth, I'm afraid.

PENNY: Now you're just being modest.

GRANDPA: Sounds kind of dull to me—Wall Street. Do you like it?

TONY: Well, the hours are short. And I haven't been there very long.

GRANDPA: Just out of college, huh?

TONY: Well, I knocked around for a while first. Just sort of had fun.

GRANDPA: What did you do? Travel?

TONY: For a while. Then I went to Cambridge for a year.

GRANDPA (*nodding*): England.

TONY: That's right.

GRANDPA: Say, what's an English commencement like? Did you see any?

TONY: Oh, very impressive.

GRANDPA: They are, huh?

TONY: Anyhow, now the fun's over, and—I'm facing the the world.

PENNY: Well, you've certainly got a good start, Mr. Kirby. Vice-president, and a rich father.

TONY: Well, that's hardly my fault.

PENNY (*brightly*): So now I suppose you're all ready to settle down and—get married.

PAUL: Come now, Penny, I'm sure Mr. Kirby knows his own mind.

PENNY: I wasn't making up his mind for him—was I, Mr. Kirby?

TONY: That's quite all right, Mrs. Sycamore.

PENNY (*to the others*): You see?

ESSIE: You mustn't rush him, Mother.

PENNY: Well, all I meant was he's bound to get married (ALICE *starts downstairs*), and suppose the wrong girl gets him?

(*The descending* ALICE *mercifully comes to* TONY's *rescue at this moment. Her voice is heard from stairs.* TONY *rises.*)

ALICE: Well, here I am, a vision in blue. (*She comes into the room—and very lovely indeed.*) Apparently you've had time to get acquainted. (ESSIE *takes a step to the rear,* TONY *and* PAUL *rise.*)

PENNY (*rises and pushes chair back*): Oh, yes, indeed. We were just having a delightful talk about love and marriage.

ALICE: Oh, dear. (*She turns to* TONY.) I'm sorry. I came down as fast as I could.

TONY: I didn't mind in the least.

RHEBA (*enters, bringing a platter of sliced watermelon*): Damn those flies in the kitchen. (ALICE *looks at* PENNY *and back to* TONY.) Oh, Miss Alice, you look beautiful. Where you going?

ALICE (*making the best of it*): I'm going out, Rheba.

RHEBA (*noticing* TONY—*looks at him*): Stepping, huh?

(*The doorbell sounds.* RHEBA *puts platter on table and crosses to hall door.*)

ESSIE: That must be Kolenkhov.

ALICE (*uneasily; she crosses to left*): I think we'd better go, Tony.

TONY (*crossing to desk*): All right.

(*Before they can escape, however,* DONALD *emerges from kitchen bearing a tray.*)

DONALD: Grandpa, you take cream on your corn flakes? I forget.

GRANDPA: Half and half, Donald.

(DONALD *exits. The voice of* BORIS KOLENKHOV *booms from outer door.*)

KOLENKHOV: Ah, my little Rhebishka!

GRANDPA: Yes, that's Kolenkhov, all right.

RHEBA (*with a scream of laughter*): Yessuh, Mr. Kolenkhov!

KOLENKHOV: Good evening, everybody!
ALL: Good evening.

(He appears in archway, his great arm completely encircling the delighted RHEBA. MR. KOLENKHOV is one of RHEBA's pets, and if you like Russians he might be one of yours. He is enormous, hairy, loud, and very, very Russian. His appearance in the archway still further traps ALICE and TONY. RHEBA exits.)

KOLENKHOV *(as he comes forward)*: Grandpa, what do you think? I have had a letter from Russia! The Second Five-Year Plan is a failure! *(Throws hat on buffet. Lets out a laugh that shakes the rafters.)*
ESSIE: I practiced today, Mr. Kolenkhov!
KOLENKHOV *(with a deep Russian bow and a click of heels)*: My Pavlowa!
ALICE *(crossing down)*: Well, if you'll excuse us, Mr. Kolenhov. *(PENNY hands TONY his hat.)*
KOLENKHOV: My little Alice! *(He kisses her hand.)* Never have I seen you look so magnificent.
ALICE: Thank you, Mr. Kolenkhov. *(KOLENKHOV steps back.)* Tony, this is Mr. Kolenkhov, Essie's dancing teacher. Mr. Kirby.
TONY: How do you do?
KOLENKHOV: How do you do? *(A click of the heels and a bow from KOLENKHOV.)*
ALICE *(determined, this time)*: Will you pardon us, Mr. Kolenkhov—we're going to the Monte Carlo Ballet.
KOLENKHOV *(at the top of his tremendous voice)*: The Monte Carlo Ballet! It *stinks*.
ALICE *(panicky now)*: Yes. . . . Well—good-by, everybody. Good-by.
TONY: Good-by. I'm so glad to have met you all.

(A chorus of answering "Good-bys" from the family. The young people are gone. The sound of hall door closing.)

You Can't Take It with You

DE PINNA: Good-by.

KOLENKHOV (*still furious*): Monte Carlo Ballet!

PENNY: Isn't Mr. Kirby lovely? . . . Come on, everybody! Dinner's ready! (PAUL *indicates chair.*)

ED (*pulling up chair from alcove*): I thought he was a nice fellow, didn't you? (*Gets another chair from hall.*)

ESSIE (*doing her toe steps*): Mm. (*Bending.*) And so good looking.

PENNY: And he had such nice manners. Did you notice, Paul? Did you notice his manners?

PAUL: I certainly did. You were getting pretty personal with him.

PENNY: Oh, now, Paul. . . . Anyhow, he's a very nice young man. (DE PINNA *brings chair from alcove.*)

DE PINNA (*as he seats himself*): He looks like a cousin of mine. (ESSIE *bends.*)

KOLENKHOV: Bakst! Diaghileff! *Then* you had the *ballet!*

PENNY: I think if they get married here I'll put the altar where the snakes are. You wouldn't mind, Grandpa, would you?

GRANDPA: Not if the snakes don't.

ESSIE (*crossing to chair back of table and sitting*): Oh, no, they'll want to get married in a church. His family and everything.

DE PINNA: I like a church wedding.

ED: Yes, of course they would. } (*Together.*)

KOLENKHOV: Of course.

GRANDPA (*tapping on a plate for silence*): Quiet, everybody! Quiet! (*They are immediately silent. . . . Grace is about to be pronounced.* GRANDPA *pauses a moment for heads to bow then raises his eyes heavenward. He clears his throat and proceeds to say Grace.*) Well, Sir, we've been getting along pretty good for quite a while now, and we're certainly much obliged. Remember, all we ask is to just go along and be happy in our own sort of way. Of course we want to keep our health but as far as anything else is concerned, we'll leave it to You. Thank You. (*The heads come up as*

251

RHEBA *and* DONALD *enter through kitchen door with steaming platters.*) So the Second Five-Year Plan is a failure, eh, Kolenkhov?

KOLENKHOV: Catastrophic! And wait until they try the Third Five-Year Plan!

PENNY (*On the cue "Thank You."*): Of course his family is going to want to come. Imagine. Alice marrying a Kirby!

ESSIE: Think of that. Isn't it exciting?

ED: I'll play the wedding march on the xylophone.

PAUL: What have we got for dinner? I'm hungry.

SCENE 2

Late the same night. The house is in darkness save for a light in the hall. An accordion is heard off stage, then suddenly a good loud BANG! from the cellar. Somewhere in the nether regions, one of the Sycamores is still at work.

As the accordion player finishes the song the sound of a key in the outer door. The voices of ALICE and TONY drift through.

ALICE (*off stage*): I could see them dance every night of the week. I think they're marvelous.

TONY: They are, aren't they? But of course just walking inside any theater gives *me* a thrill.

ALICE (*as they come into sight in hallway*): Well, it's been *so* lovely, Tony, I hate to have it over.

TONY: Oh, is it over? Do I have to go right away?

ALICE: Not if you don't want to.

TONY: I don't.

ALICE: Would you like a cold drink?

TONY: Wonderful. (ALICE *pauses to switch on lights.*)

ALICE: I'll see what's in the icebox. Want to come along?

TONY: I'd follow you to the ends of the earth.

ALICE (*at door*): Oh just the kitchen is enough.

(They exit through kitchen door. A pause, and the lights go on.)

TONY: Why, I like it. You've done it very simply, haven't you?

ALICE: Yes, we didn't know whether to do it Empire or Neo-Grecian.

TONY: So you settled for Frigidaire.

ALICE: Yes, it's so easy to live with. *(They return. ALICE crosses to table. She is carrying two glasses. TONY, a bottle of ginger ale and a bottle opener.)* Lucky you're not hungry, Mr. K. An icebox full of corn flakes. That gives you a rough idea of the Sycamores. *(TONY follows her to table.)*

TONY *(working away with the opener)*: Of course, why they make these bottle openers for Singer midgets I never did . . . *(As bottle opens.)* All over my coat.

ALICE *(as she hands him a glass)*: I'll take mine in a glass, if you don't mind.

TONY *(pouring)*: There you are. A foaming beaker. *(Pours his own.)*

ALICE: Anyhow, it's cold.

TONY *(as ALICE sits at table)*: Now if you'll please be seated, I'd like to offer a toast.

ALICE: We are seated.

TONY: Miss Sycamore *(he raises his glass on high)* . . . to you.

ALICE: Thank you, Mr. Kirby. *(Lifting her own glass.)* To you. *(She drinks and puts glass down.)*

TONY: You know something?

ALICE: What?

TONY *(puts his glass down and sighs happily)*: I wouldn't trade one minute of this evening for . . . all the rice in China.

ALICE: Really?

TONY: Cross my heart.

ALICE *(a little sigh of contentment, then shyly)*: Is there much rice in China?

TONY: Terrific. Didn't you read *The Good Earth*? (*She laughs. They are silent for a moment. He sighs and looks at his watch.*) Well, I suppose I ought to go.

ALICE: Is it very late?

TONY (*looks at his watch*): Very. (ALICE *gives a little nod. Time doesn't matter.*) I don't want to go.

ALICE: I don't want you to.

TONY: All right, I won't. (*Sits at table—silence again.*) When do you get your vacation?

ALICE: Last two weeks in August.

TONY: I might take mine then, too.

ALICE: Really?

TONY: What are you going to do?

ALICE: I don't know. I hadn't thought much about it.

TONY: Going away, do you think?

ALICE: I might not. I like the city in the summertime.

TONY: I do too.

ALICE: But you always go up to Maine, don't you?

TONY: That's right. (*Rises.*) Oh—but I'm sure I *would* like the city in the summertime, if— Oh, you know what I mean, Alice. I'd love it if *you* were here.

ALICE: Well—it'd be nice if you were here, Tony. (*Rises and moves to right.*)

TONY: You know what you're saying, don't you?

ALICE: What?

TONY: That you'd rather spend the summer with me than anybody else.

ALICE (*with her back to* TONY): Was I?

TONY (*crossing few steps to right*): Well, if it's true about the summer, how would you feel about—the winter?

ALICE (*seeming to weigh the matter, turns to* TONY): Yes, I'd—like that too.

TONY (*tremulous*): Then there's spring and autumn. If you could—see your way clear about those, Miss Sycamore? (*Crossing to* ALICE.)

ALICE (*again a little pause*): I might.

TONY: I guess that's the whole year. We haven't forgotten anything, have we?

ALICE: No.

TONY: Well, then— (*Another pause; their eyes meet.* TONY *starts to embrace* ALICE. *And at this moment,* PENNY *is heard from stairway.* TONY *crosses to back of* GRANDPA'S *chair.*)

PENNY (*off stage*): Is that you, Alice? What time is it? (*She comes into room, wrapped in a bathrobe.*) Oh! (*In sudden embarrassment.*) Excuse me, Mr. Kirby. I had no idea— that is, I—(*she senses the situation*)—I didn't mean to interrupt anything.

TONY: Not at all, Mrs. Sycamore.

ALICE (*quietly*): No, Mother.

PENNY: I just came down for a manuscript—(*fumbling at her desk*)—then you can go right ahead. Ah, here it is. "Sex Takes a Holiday." Well—good night, Tony.

TONY: Good night, Mrs. Sycamore.

PENNY: Oh, I think you can call me Penny, don't you, Alice? At least I hope so. (*With a little laugh she vanishes upstairs.* TONY *turns back to* ALICE. *Before* PENNY'S *rippling laugh quite dies, BANG! from the cellar.* TONY *jumps.*)

TONY: What's that?

ALICE (*quietly*): It's all right, Tony. That's Father.

TONY: Oh—this time of night?

ALICE (*ominously—turns to* TONY): Any time of night. Any time of day. (*She stands silent. In the pause,* TONY *gazes at her fondly.*)

TONY (*crossing to* ALICE): You know, you're more beautiful, more lovely, more adorable than anyone else in the whole world.

ALICE (*as he starts to embrace her, she backs away*): Don't, Tony.

TONY: What? (*As* ALICE *shakes her head.*) My dear, just because your mother . . . all mothers are like that, Alice, and Penny's a darling. You see I'm even calling her Penny.

ALICE: I don't mean that. (*She faces him squarely.*) Look,

Tony, this is something I should have said a long time ago, but I didn't have the courage. (*Turns away.*) I let myself be swept away because . . . I loved you so.

TONY (*crosses to* ALICE): Darling!

ALICE: No, wait, Tony. I want to make it clear to you. Listen, you're of a different world . . . a whole different kind of people. Oh I don't mean money or socially . . . that's too silly. But your family and mine . . . it just wouldn't work, Tony. It just wouldn't work. (ALICE *moves in front of* TONY.)

(*The sound of the outer door closing.*)

ED (*heard in hallway off stage*): All right, have it your way. She can't dance. That's why they pay her all that money . . . because she can't dance.

ESSIE (*still not in sight*): Well, I don't call that dancing what she does. (*She appears in archway followed by* ED.) Oh, hello! How was the ballet? (*Throwing her hat on desk.*)

ALICE: It was fine, Essie.

TONY: Wonderful.

ED (*following* ESSIE *into room*): Hello there.

TONY: Hello.

ESSIE: Look, what do you think? Ed and I just saw Fred Astaire and Ginger Rogers. Do you think she can dance, Mr. Kirby? (*Crossing over to* TONY.)

TONY: Why, yes. I always thought so.

ESSIE: What does she *do* anyhow? (*Crossing to* TONY.) Now look, you're Fred Astaire, and I'm Ginger Rogers. (*Puts herself close to* TONY.)

ALICE: Essie, please!

ESSIE: I only want to use him for a minute. Now look, Mr. Kirby . . . (*Putting her arms around* TONY's *neck.*)

ALICE: Essie, you're just as good as Ginger Rogers. We all agree.

ESSIE: You see, Ed?

You Can't Take It with You

ED (*crossing to arch—backing up*): Yeh. . . . Come on, Essie
. . . we're butting in here.

ESSIE: Oh, they've been together all evening. . . . (*Crosses to
arch.*) Good night, Mr. Kirby. Good night, Alice.

TONY: Good night, Mrs. Carmichael.

ED: Good night. Essie, did you ask Grandpa about us having a baby? (*Crossing to stairs.*)

ESSIE: Oh, yes—he said to go right ahead.

(*They are out of sight upstairs.*)

ALICE: You see, Tony? That's what it would be like.

TONY (*crossing over to* ALICE): Oh, I didn't mind that. Anyhow, we're not going to live with your family. It's just
you and I.

ALICE: No it isn't . . . it's never quite that. I love them, Tony
. . . I love them deeply. Some people could break away,
but I couldn't. I know they do rather strange things. . . .
But they're gay and they're fun and . . . I don't know . . .
there's a kind of nobility about them.

TONY: Alice, you talk as though only you could understand
them. That's not true. Why every family has got curious
little traits. What of it? My father raises orchids at ten
thousand dollars a bulb. Is that sensible? My mother believes in spiritualism. That's just as bad as your mother
writing plays, isn't it?

ALICE: It goes deeper, Tony. Your mother believes in spiritualism because it's fashionable, and your father raises
orchids because he can afford to. My mother writes plays
because eight years ago a typewriter was delivered here
by mistake.

TONY: Darling, what *of* it?

ALICE: And—and look at Grandpa. Thirty-five years ago he
just quit business one day. He started up to his office in
the elevator and came right down again. He just stopped.
He could have been a rich man, but he said it took too
much time. So for thirty-five years, he's just collected

snakes, and gone to circuses and commencements. It never occurs to any of them . . .

(GRANDPA *comes downstairs*.)

GRANDPA (*pausing in doorway*): Hello there, children!

TONY (*turns to* GRANDPA): Good evening, Mr. Vanderhof.

ALICE: Hello, Grandpa.

GRANDPA (*coming into the room*): How's the weather? Looks like a nice summer evening.

ALICE: Yes, it's lovely, Grandpa.

GRANDPA: Well, I'm off. Good-by, Mr. Kirby. . . . I've got a date with the policeman on the corner.

TONY: Policeman?

GRANDPA: We've got a standing date—twelve-thirty every night. Known him since he was a little boy. He's really a doctor, but after he graduated, he came to me and said he didn't want to be a doctor—he had always wanted to be a policeman. So I said, "You go ahead and be a policeman, if that's what you want to be," and that's what he did. . . . How do you like my new hat?

TONY: It's very nice, Mr. Vanderhof.

GRANDPA (*regarding hat*): Yeh, I like it. The Government gave it to me. (*Exits.*)

DONALD (*entering from kitchen with an accordion slung over his shoulder*): Oh, excuse me. I didn't know you folks was in here.

ALICE (*resigned*): It's all right, Donald.

DONALD: Rheba kind of fancied some candy and I . . . Oh, there it is. (*Crossing to buffet.*) You all don't want it, do you?

ALICE: No, Donald.

DONALD (*crossing to right*): Thanks. . . . Did you have a nice evening?

ALICE: Yes, Donald.

DONALD (*edging over another step*): Nice dinner?

ALICE: Yes, Donald.

DONALD (*another step to the right*): Was the ballet nice?

ALICE: Yes, Donald.

DONALD: That's nice. (*He exits through kitchen door.*)

ALICE (*rising*): Now! Now, do you see what I mean? Could you explain Donald to your father? Could you explain Grandpa? You couldn't, Tony, you couldn't! I love you, Tony, but I love them too! And it's no use, Tony! It's no use! (*She is weeping now in spite of herself.*)

TONY (*takes her hands; quietly*): There's only one thing you've said that matters, that makes any sense at all. You love me.

ALICE: But, Tony, I know so well . . .

TONY: But, darling, don't you think other people have had the same problem? Everybody's got a family.

ALICE (*through her tears*): But not like mine.

TONY: That doesn't stop people who love each other . . . Darling! Darling, won't you trust me and go on loving me, and forget everything else?

ALICE: How can I?

TONY: Because nothing can keep us apart. You know that. You must know it. They want you to be happy, don't they? They *must*.

ALICE: Of course they do. But they can't change, Tony. I wouldn't want them to change.

TONY (*releases her hands*): They won't have to change. They're charming, lovable people, just as they are. Everything will work out . . . you're worrying about something that may never come up.

ALICE: Oh, Tony, am I?

TONY: All that matters right now is that we love each other. That's so, isn't it?

ALICE (*whispering*): Yes.

TONY: Well, then! (*They embrace, sigh and kiss.*)

ALICE (*in his arms*): Tony, Tony!

TONY (*as they break*): Now! I'd like to see a little gayety around here. Young gentleman calling, and getting engaged and everything.

ALICE (*smiling up into his face*): What do I say?

TONY: Well, first you thank the young man for getting engaged to you.

ALICE (*crossing to below table*): Thank you, Mr. Kirby, for getting engaged to me.

TONY (*following her*): And then you tell him what it was about him that first took your girlish heart.

ALICE (*leaning against table*): The back of your head.

TONY: Huh?

ALICE: Uh-huh. It wasn't your charm, and it wasn't your money . . . it was the back of your head. I just liked it.

TONY: What happened when I turned around?

ALICE: Oh, I got used to it after a while.

TONY (*tenderly*): Oh, Alice, think of it. We're pretty lucky, aren't we?

ALICE: I know that *I* am. I'm the luckiest girl in the world.

TONY: I'm not exactly unlucky myself. (*He holds her in his arms; they kiss, sigh.*) Oh, dear, I guess I ought to . . . (*Backing away, he looks at his watch.*) Good night, darling. Until tomorrow.

ALICE (*crosses to* TONY—*they kiss*): Good night.

TONY: Isn't it wonderful we work in the same office? Otherwise I'd be hanging around *here* all day.

ALICE (*starts with* TONY *for the hall*): Won't it be funny in the office tomorrow—seeing each other and just going on as though nothing had happened?

TONY: Thank God I'm vice-president. (*Turns up.*) I can dictate to you all day (*accordion*) "Dear Miss Sycamore: I love you, I love you, I love you." (*They embrace.*)

ALICE: Oh, darling! You're such a fool.

TONY (*an arm about her as he starts toward hallway*): Why don't you meet me in the drugstore in the morning—before you go up to the office? I'll have millions of things to say to you. (*Picks up his hat as they head for the door.*)

ALICE (*off stage*): All right.

TONY: And then lunch, and then dinner tomorrow night.

ALICE: Oh, Tony! What will people say?

TONY: It's got to come out sometime. In fact, if you know a good housetop, I'd like to do a little shouting. (*She laughs—a happy little ripple. They are out of sight in hall-way by this time; their voices become inaudible.*)

(PAUL, *at this point, decides to call it a day down in the cellar. He comes through door, followed by* DE PINNA. *He is carrying a small metal container, filled with powder.*)

PAUL (*crossing to table*): Yes, sir, Mr. De Pinna, we did a good night's work.

DE PINNA (*following*): That's what. Five hundred Black Panthers, three hundred Willow Trees, and eight dozen Junior Kiddie Bombers. (ALICE *comes back from hallway, still under the spell of her love.*)

PAUL: Pretty good! . . . Why, hello, Alice. You just come in?

ALICE (*softly; leans against wall*): No. No, I've been home quite a while.

PAUL: Have a nice evening?

ALICE (*almost singing it*): I had a beautiful evening, Father.

PAUL: Say, I'd like you to take a look at this new red fire. Will you turn out the lights, Mr. De Pinna? I want Alice to get the full effect. (DE PINNA *goes up to switch.*)

ALICE (*who hasn't heard a word*): What, Father?

PAUL: Take a look at this new red fire. It's beautiful. (DE PINNA *switches lights out;* PAUL *touches a match to the powder. The red fire blazes, shedding a soft glow over the room.*) There! What do you think of it? Isn't it beautiful?

ALICE (*radiant; her face aglow, her voice soft*): Yes. Oh, Father, everything's beautiful, it's the most beautiful red fire in the world! (*She rushes to him and throws her arms about him, almost unable to bear her own happiness.*)

Act II

As curtain rises, GRANDPA *is seated at right of the table,* PAUL *at back table, and a newcomer,* GAY WELLINGTON, *is seated at left of table.* PENNY *stands with one of her scripts at left of table and* ED *is standing to right of table.* DONALD *stands back of* GAY WELLINGTON *holding tray of used dinner dishes.* GAY *is drinking as curtain rises.* ED *stands at right holding type stick.*

GAY: All right, I said to him, you can take your old job. . . . (*She drinks.*)

PENNY: I'm ready to read you the new play, Miss Wellington, any time you are.

GAY (*pours*): Just a minute, dearie. Just a minute. (*Drinks again.* ED *is preoccupied with type stick.*)

PENNY: The only thing is—I hope you won't mind my mentioning this, but—you don't drink when you're acting, do you, Miss Wellington? I'm just asking, of course.

GAY (*crossing to* PENNY): I'm glad you brought it up. Once a play opens, I never touch a drop. Minute I enter a stage door, the bottle gets put away until intermission.

(RHEBA *enters and crosses to table carrying a tray.*)

GRANDPA: Have you been on the stage a long time, Miss Wellington?

GAY: All my life. I've played everything. Ever see "Peg o' My Heart"?

GRANDPA: Yes.

GAY: I saw it too. Good show. . . . My! Hot night, ain't it?

DONALD: You want me to open the window, Miss Wellington?

GAY: No, the hell with the weather. . . . Say, he's cute.

(RHEBA, *clearing table at this moment, throws* GAY *a black look, bangs a glass on her tray and exits.*)

DONALD (*starting off after* RHEBA): She's just acting, Rheba, that's all; she don't mean anything. (*Exits.*)

PENNY (*making the best of it, crossing over to her desk*): Well, any time you're ready, we'll go up to my room and start. I thought I'd read the play up in my room. (*Crosses up to stairs;* ED *drifts up to xylophone.*)

GAY (*circling—takes glass from table*): All right, dearie, I'm ready. (*Suddenly her gaze becomes transfixed. She shakes her head as though to dislodge the image, then looks again and receives verification. Puts gin bottle and glass on table.*) When I see snakes, it's time to lay down. (*She makes for couch.* ESSIE *starts downstairs.*)

PENNY (*crossing to couch*): Oh, dear! Oh, dear! Oh, but those are real, Miss Wellington! (DONALD *enters bearing a tray.* PAUL *rises.*) They're Grandpa's. Those are real! (GAY *has passed right out cold.*) Oh, dear! I hope she is not going to— Miss Wellington!

ED: She's out like a light.

PAUL: Better let her sleep it off.

DONALD: Rheba, Miss Wellington just passed out. (*Exits.*)

RHEBA (*off stage*): Good.

PENNY: Do you think she'll be all right?

GRANDPA: Yes, but I wouldn't cast her in the religious play.

PENNY: Well, I suppose I'll just have to wait.

(ED *bangs the hand press.*)

GRANDPA: Next time you meet an actress on the top of a bus, Penny, I think I'd *send* her the play instead of bringing her home to read it.

263

(*Another bang.* PENNY *covers* GAY *with couch cover.*)

ESSIE: Ed, I wish you'd stop printing and take those Love Dreams around. You've got to get back in time to play for me when Kolenkhov comes. (*A bang of the hand press again.*)

GRANDPA: Kolenkhov coming tonight? (*Goes to bookcase for stamp album and returns to table.*)

ESSIE (*executing a few toe steps*): Yes, tomorrow night's his night, but I had to change it on account of Alice.

GRANDPA: Oh! . . . Big doings around here tomorrow night, huh?

PENNY (*crossing to desk*): Isn't it exciting? You know I'm so nervous—you'd think it was me he was engaged to instead of Alice. (*Sitting in desk chair. Takes script and pencil.* GRANDPA *busies himself with album.*)

ESSIE (*doing leg exercise*): What do you think they'll *be* like—his mother and father? . . . Ed, what are you doing now?

ED: Penny, did you see the new mask I made last night? (*He reveals a new side of his character by suddenly holding a homemade mask before his face.*) Guess who it is?

PENNY: Don't tell me now, Ed. Wait a minute. . . . Helen of Troy?

ED (*disappointed*): It's Mrs. Roosevelt. (ESSIE *on toes.* ED *puts mask down and exits into kitchen.* PAUL, *meanwhile, comes from buffet with a steel-like contraption in his hand. It's a Meccano set model of the* Queen Mary. *He puts it down on floor and proceeds to sit down beside it.*)

PAUL: You know the nice thing about these Meccano sets, you can make so many different things with them. Last week it was the Empire State Building.

GRANDPA: What is it this week?

PAUL: Queen Mary.

GRANDPA: Hasn't got the right hat on.

(DE PINNA *enters from hall.* PENNY *sits.* ED *comes in from kitchen bringing a pile of candy boxes beautifully wrapped and tied together for purposes of delivery.*)

ED: Look, Mr. De Pinna—would you open the door and see if there's a man standing in front of the house?

DE PINNA: Why, what for?

ED: Well, the last two days, when I've been out delivering candy, I think a man's been following me.

ESSIE: Ed, you're crazy.

ED: No, I'm not. He follows me, and he stands and watches the house.

DE PINNA: Really? (*Striding out.*) I'll take a look and see.

GRANDPA: I don't see what anybody would follow *you* for, Ed.

PENNY: Well, there's a lot of kidnapping going on, Grandpa.

GRANDPA: Yes, but not of Ed.

ED (*as* DE PINNA *returns from hall*): Well? Did you see him?

DE PINNA: There's nobody out there at all.

ED: You're sure?

DE PINNA: Positive. I just saw him walk away.

(PAUL *puts the model back on the buffet.*)

ED: You see?

ESSIE: Oh, it might have been anybody, walking along the street. Ed, will you hurry and get back?

ED (*picking up his boxes*): Oh, all right. (*Exits.*)

DE PINNA: Want to go down now, Mr. Sycamore, and finish packing up the fireworks?

PAUL: Yeh, we've got to take the stuff up to Mt. Vernon in the morning. (PAUL *and* DE PINNA *exit.*)

(*The voice of* ALICE, *happily singing, is heard as she descends stairs.*)

ALICE (*as she comes into the room, finishing song*): Mother, may I borrow some paper? I'm making out a list for Rheba tomorrow night.

PENNY: Yes, dear. (*Drunken mutter from* GAY.) Here's some.

ALICE (*as she sights* GAY): Why, what happened to your actress friend? Is she giving a performance?

PENNY: No, she's not acting, Alice. She's really drunk. (ESSIE *dances to right of* GRANDPA's *chair.*)

ALICE: Essie, dear, you're going to give Rheba the kitchen all day tomorrow, aren't you? Because she'll need it.

ESSIE: Of course, Alice. I'm going to start some "Love Dreams" now, so I'll be 'way ahead. (*She goes into kitchen.*)

ALICE: Thanks, dear. . . . (*Crossing to* PENNY.) Look, Mother, I'm coming home at three o'clock tomorrow. Will you have everything down in the cellar by that time? The typewriter, and the snakes, and the xylophone, and the printing press . . .

GRANDPA: And Miss Wellington.

ALICE: And Miss Wellington. That'll give me time to arrange the table, and fix the flowers.

GRANDPA: The Kirbys are certainly going to get the wrong impression of this house.

ALICE: You'll do all that, won't you, Mother?

PENNY: Of course, dear. . . .

ALICE: And I think we'd better have cocktails ready by seven-fifteen, in case they happen to come a little early. . . . I wonder if I ought to let Rheba cook the dinner. What do you think, Grandpa?

GRANDPA: Now, Alice, I wouldn't worry. From what I've seen of the boy I'm sure the Kirbys are very nice people, and if everything isn't so elaborate tomorrow night, it's all right too.

ALICE: Darling, I'm not trying to impress them, or pretend we're anything that we aren't. I just want everything to— to go off well.

GRANDPA (*putting his hand over* ALICE's): No reason why it shouldn't, Alice.

PENNY: We're all going to do everything we can to make it a nice party.

ALICE: Oh, my darlings, I love you. You're the most wonderful family in the world, and I'm the happiest girl in the world. I didn't know anyone could be so happy. Why, this past week has been like—floating. He's so wonderful, Grandpa. Why, just seeing him—you don't know what it does to me.

GRANDPA: Just seeing him. Just seeing him for lunch, and dinner, and until four o'clock in the morning, and at nine o'clock *next* morning you're at the office again and there he is. Just seeing him, huh?

ALICE: I don't care! I'm in love! (*Kisses* GRANDPA *and starts out. She swings open kitchen door.*) Rheba! Rheba! (*She goes into kitchen.*)

GRANDPA: Nice, isn't it? Nice to see her so happy.

PENNY (*rises—crosses to table*): Yes, I remember when I was engaged to Paul—how happy I was. And you know, I still feel that way.

GRANDPA: I know. . . . Nice the way Ed and Essie get along too, isn't it?

PENNY: And Donald and Rheba, even though they're *not* married. . . . Do you suppose Mr. De Pinna will ever marry anyone, Grandpa?

GRANDPA (*a gesture toward couch*): Well, there's Miss Wellington.

PENNY: Oh, dear, I *wish* she'd wake up. If we're going to read the play tonight—

(DE PINNA *comes up from cellar bringing along a rather large-sized unframed painting.*)

DE PINNA: Mrs. Sycamore, look what I found! (*He turns canvas around, revealing a portrait of a somewhat lumpy and largely naked discus thrower.*) Remember? (*He props picture on chair above table.*)

PENNY (*backs away*): Why, of course. It's my painting of you as The Discus Thrower. Look, Grandpa.

GRANDPA: I remember it. Say, you've gotten a little bald, haven't you, Mr. De Pinna?

DE PINNA (*running a hand over his completely hairless head*): Is it very noticeable? Well, there's still some right here.

PENNY: Well, it was a long time ago—just before I stopped painting. Let me see—that's eight years.

DE PINNA: Too bad you never finished it, Mrs. Sycamore.

PENNY (*looking back at picture*): I always meant to finish it, Mr. De Pinna, but I just started to write a play one day and that was that. I never painted again.

GRANDPA: Just as well, too. *I* was going to have to strip next.

DE PINNA (*meditatively*): My goodness, who would have thought, that day I came to deliver the ice, that I was going to stay here for eight years?

GRANDPA: The milkman was here for five, just ahead of you.

DE PINNA: Say, why did he leave, anyhow? I forget.

GRANDPA: He didn't leave. He died.

DE PINNA: Oh, yes.

PENNY: He was such a nice man. Remember the funeral, Grandpa? We never knew his name and it was kind of hard to get a certificate.

GRANDPA: What was the name we finally made up for him?

PENNY: Martin Vanderhof. We gave him *your* name.

GRANDPA: Oh, yes, I remember. (*Rises and goes to alcove. DE PINNA lights pipe.*)

PENNY: It was a lovely thought, because otherwise he never would have got all those flowers.

GRANDPA: Certainly was. And it didn't hurt *me* any. Not bothered with mail any more, and I haven't had a telephone call from that day to this. (*He catches fly on painting and feeds it to snakes. Returns to his chair; sits, reads paper.*)

PENNY: Yes, it was really a wonderful idea.

DE PINNA (*points to picture*): I wish you'd finish that sometime, Mrs. Sycamore. I'd kind of like to have it.

PENNY: You know what, Mr. De Pinna? I think I'll do some work on it. Right tonight.

DE PINNA: Say! Will you? (*Doorbell.*)

PENNY (*peering at the prostrate* GAY): I don't think she's going to wake up anyhow. . . . Look, Mr. De Pinna! You go down in the cellar—(RHEBA *enters, crosses to hall door.*)—and put on your costume. And bring up the easel. (DE PINNA *starts off.*) Is it still down there?

DE PINNA (*excited*): I think so! (*He exits.*)

PENNY (*crossing to stairs*): Now, where did I put my palette and brushes?

(*The voice of* KOLENKHOV *is heard at door, booming as usual.*)

KOLENKHOV: Rhebishka! My little Rhebishka!

RHEBA (*delighted, as usual*): Yassuh, Mr. Kolenkhov!

PENNY (*as she goes upstairs*): Hello, Mr. Kolenkhov. Essie's in the kitchen.

KOLENKHOV: Madame Sycamore, I greet you! (*His great arm again encircling* RHEBA, *he drags her protestingly into room.*) Tell me, Grandpa—what should I do about Rhebishka! I keep telling her she would make a great toe dancer—(*breaking away, she laughs*)—but she laughs only!

RHEBA (*starts off*): No, suh! I couldn't get up on my toes, Mr. Kolenkhov! I got corns! (*She goes into kitchen.*)

KOLENKHOV (*calling after her*): Rhebishka, you could wear diamonds! (*Throws his hat on buffet.*) A great girl, Grandpa. (*Suddenly he sights portrait of* DE PINNA.) What is that?

GRANDPA: It's a picture of Mr. De Pinna. Penny painted it.

KOLENKHOV (*summing it up*): It stinks. (*Sits at table.*)

GRANDPA: I know. (*He indicates figure on couch.*) How do you like that?

KOLENKHOV (*half rising, peering over*): What is *that*?

GRANDPA: She's an actress. Friend of Penny's. (GAY *mutters.*)

KOLENKHOV: She is drunk—no?

GRANDPA: She is drunk—yes. . . . How are *you*, Kolenkhov?

KOLENKHOV: Magnificent! Life is chasing around inside of me, like a squirrel.

GRANDPA: 'Tis, huh? . . . What's new in Russia? Any more letters from your friend in Moscow?

KOLENKHOV (*nods*): I have just heard from him. I saved for you the stamp.

GRANDPA: Thanks, Kolenkhov.

KOLENKHOV: They have sent him to Siberia.

GRANDPA: They have, eh? How's he like it?

KOLENKHOV: He has escaped. He has escaped and gone back to Moscow. He will get them yet if they do not get him. The Soviet Government! I could take the whole Soviet Government and—grrah! (*He crushes Stalin and all in one great paw, just as* ESSIE *comes in from kitchen.* KOLENKHOV *rises.*)

ESSIE: I'm sorry I'm late, Mr. Kolenkhov. I'll get into my dancing clothes right away.

KOLENKHOV (*crossing to stairs*): Tonight you will really work, Pavlowa. (*As* ESSIE *goes upstairs.*) Tonight we will take something new.

GRANDPA: Essie making any progress, Kolenkhov?

KOLENKHOV (*first making elaborately sure that* ESSIE *is gone, then in a voice that would carry to Long Island*): Confidentially, she stinks! (*Lights cigarette.*)

GRANDPA: Well, as long as she's having fun . . .

(DONALD *ambles in from kitchen, chuckling, carrying tray. He crosses down to table.*)

DONALD: You sure do tickle Rheba, Mr. Kolenkhov. She's laughing her head off out there. (*Gathers up remaining cups, bottle, and glass.*)

KOLENKHOV (*sits at table*): She is a great woman. . . . Donald, what do you think of the Soviet Government?

DONALD (*puzzled*): The what, Mr. Kolenkhov?

KOLENKHOV (*gesture*): I withdraw the question. What do you think of *this* Government?

DONALD: Oh, I like it fine. I'm on relief, you know.

KOLENKHOV: Oh, yes. And you like it?

DONALD: Yassuh, it's fine. (*Starts to go off.*) Only thing is you got to go round to the place every week to get it, and sometimes you got to stand in line pretty near half an hour. Government ought to be run better than that—don't you think, Grandpa?

GRANDPA (*as he fishes envelope out of his pocket, opens letter*): Government ought to stop sending me letters. Want me to be at the United States Marshal's office Tuesday morning at ten o'clock. Look at that. (*Throws letter to* KOLENKHOV.)

KOLENKHOV (*peering at letter*): Ah! Income tax! They have got you, Grandpa.

GRANDPA (*puts letter back in pocket*): Mm. I'm supposed to give 'em a lot of money so as to keep Donald on relief.

DONALD: You don't say, Grandpa? You going to pay it from now on?

GRANDPA: That's what they want.

DONALD: You mean I can come right *here* and get it instead of standing in that line?

GRANDPA: No, Donald. I'm afraid you will have to waste a full half hour of your time every week.

DONALD: Well, I don't like it. It breaks up my week. (*Exits.*)

KOLENKHOV: He should have been in Russia when the Revolution came. Then he would have stood in line . . . a bread line. Ah, Grandpa, what they have done to Russia. Think of it! The Grand Duchess Olga Katrina, a cousin of the Czar, she is a waitress in Childs Restaurant! I ordered baked beans from her, only yesterday. It broke my heart. A crazy world, Grandpa.

GRANDPA: Oh, the world's not so crazy, Kolenkhov. It's the people *in* it. Life's pretty simple if you just relax.

KOLENKHOV (*rising*): How can you relax in times like these?

GRANDPA: Well, if they'd relax there wouldn't *be* times like these. That's just my point. Life is kind of beautiful if you let it come to you. (*Crossing to buffet for his target and darts.*) But the trouble is, people forget that. I know I did. I was right in the thick of it . . . . fighting, and scratching and clawing. Regular jungle. One day it just kind of struck me, I wasn't having any fun. (GRANDPA, *having hung his target on cellar door, returns to table.*)

KOLENKHOV: So you did what?

GRANDPA (*standing below the table*): Just relaxed. Thirty-five years ago, that was. And I've been a happy man ever since. (*Throws a dart and sits.*)

ALICE (*entering from kitchen*): Good evening, Mr. Kolenkhov.

KOLENKHOV (*crossing to* ALICE, *he bows low over her hand*): Ah, Miss Alice! I have not seen you to present my congratulations.

ALICE: Thank you.

KOLENKHOV: May you be very happy and have many children. That is my prayer for you.

ALICE: That's quite a thought. (*She exits upstairs, humming a fragment of song.*)

KOLENKHOV: Ah, love! Love is all that is left in the world, Grandpa.

GRANDPA: Yes, but there is plenty of that.

KOLENKHOV: And soon Stalin will take that away, too, I tell you, Grandpa. . . .

(PENNY *enters downstairs. She has on an artist's smock over her dress, a flowing black tie, and a large blue velvet tam-o'-shanter, worn at a rakish angle. She carries a palette and an assortment of paints and brushes.*)

PENNY: Seems so nice to get into my art things again. They still look all right, don't they, Grandpa?

GRANDPA: Yes, indeed.

KOLENKHOV: You are a breath of Paris, Madame Sycamore.

(DONALD *enters, table cover over his arm.*)

PENNY: Oh, thank you, Mr. Kolenkhov.

DONALD: I didn't know you was working for the WPA.

PENNY: Oh, no, Donald. You see, I used to paint all the time—(*The outer door slams and* ED *comes in.*)

ED (*in considerable excitement*): It happened again! There was a fellow following me every place I went!

PENNY: Nonsense, Ed. It's your imagination.

ED: No, it isn't. It happens every time I go out to deliver candy.

GRANDPA: Maybe he wants a piece of candy.

ED: It's all right for you to laugh, Grandpa, but he keeps following me.

KOLENKHOV (*somberly*): You do not know what following is. In Russia *everybody* is followed. I was followed right out of Russia.

PENNY: Of course. You see, Ed—the whole thing is just imagination.

(DE PINNA *comes up from cellar, ready for posing. He is wearing Roman toga, headband, and sandals. He is carrying* PENNY's *easel, a discus, a small platform for posing purposes, and a racing form. Takes off coat as he goes up to alcove.*)

ED: Well, maybe. (*Takes off coat.*)

(DONALD *removes napkins and tablecloth and spreads table cover. Puts cover on chair.*)

PENNY: Ah, here we are!

DE PINNA (*crosses to left, places easel*): Where do you want this? Over there?

PENNY (*putting portrait on easel*): Put it here, Mr. De Pinna. (DE PINNA *strikes a pose on model stand.*)

KOLENKHOV: Ed, for tonight's lesson we use the first movement of "Scheherazade."

ED: Okay.

PENNY (*studying* DE PINNA's *figure*): Mr. De Pinna, has something happened to your figure during these eight years?

DE PINNA (*pulling in his stomach*): No, I don't think it's any different. (*With a sudden snort,* GAY *comes to.* DE PINNA *breaks pose and looks at* GAY.)

PENNY (*crossing to below table—immediately alert*): Yes, Miss Wellington? Yes? (*For answer,* GAY *peers first at* PENNY, *then at* DE PINNA.)

GAY: Wo-o-o! (*And with that she goes right back to sleep.*)

PENNY (*exchanges look with* DE PINNA *and then returns to her painting*): Oh, dear.

(ESSIE *comes tripping downstairs—very much the ballet dancer. She is in full costume—ballet skirt, tight white satin bodice, a garland of roses in her hair.*)

ESSIE (*crosses to xylophone*): Sorry, Mr. Kolenkhov. I couldn't find my slippers.

KOLENKHOV (*having previously removed his coat, he now takes off his shirt, displaying an enormous hairy chest beneath his undershirt*): We have a hot night for it, my Pavlowa, but art is only achieved through perspiration.

PENNY: Why, that's wonderful, Mr. Kolenkhov. Did you hear that, Grandpa—art is only achieved through perspiration.

GRANDPA: Yes, but it helps if you've got a little talent with it. (*He takes up a handful of feathered darts.*) Only made two bull's-eyes last night. Got to do better than that. (*He hurls a dart at board; then his eye travels to* GAY, *whose posterior offers an even easier target. Looks to* PENNY *for approval, then returns to his game and hurls one more dart and sits. Reads his paper.* ED *strikes a few notes.*)

KOLENKHOV: You are ready? We begin! (*With a gesture he orders the music started; under* KOLENKHOV's *critical eye* ESSIE *begins the mazes of the dance. Meanwhile* DE PINNA's *free hand now holds a copy of racing form, the total effect*

being a trifle un-Grecian.) Now! Pirouette! Pirouette!
(ESSIE *hesitates.*) Come, come! You can do that! It's eight
years now! (ESSIE *pirouettes.*) At last. Entre chat! Entre
chat! (ESSIE *leaps into the air, her feet twirling.* KOLENKHOV
turns to GRANDPA.) No, Grandpa, you cannot relax with
Stalin in Russia. The Czar relaxed, and what happened to
him?

GRANDPA: He was too late!

ESSIE (*still leaping away*): Mr. Kolenkhov! Mr. Kolenkhov!

KOLENKHOV: If he had not relaxed the Grand Duchess Olga
Katrina would not be selling baked beans today.

ESSIE (*imploringly*): Mr. Kolenkhov!

KOLENKHOV: I'm sorry. We go back to the pirouette.

PENNY: Could you pull in your stomach, Mr. De Pinna?
(*Doorbell.*) That's right.

KOLENKHOV: A little freer. A little freer with the hands. The
whole body must work. Ed, help us with the music. (RHEBA
enters. Crosses to hall door.) The music must be free, too.
(*By way of guiding* ED, KOLENKHOV *hums the music at the
pace that it should go. He is even pirouetting a bit himself.
From the front door comes the murmur of voices, not quite
audible over the music. Then the stunned figure of* RHEBA
comes into archway, her eyes popping.)

RHEBA (*heavy whisper*): Mrs. Sycamore . . . Mrs. Sycamore.

PENNY: What, Rheba?

(RHEBA *edges over to right. With a gesture that has a grim
foreboding in it, motions toward the still invisible reason for
her panic. There is a second's pause, and then the reason
is revealed in all its horror. The* KIRBYS, *in full evening
dress, stand in archway—all three of them,* MR. *and* MRS.
KIRBY, *and* TONY. DE PINNA *rushes to cellar door carrying
his model stand with him.* KOLENKHOV *runs to alcove to
squirm into his shirt and coat.* ESSIE *makes for alcove, also.*
ED *pushes xylophone in place and hastily dons his coat.*
RHEBA *crosses to buffet.* DONALD *comes forward still carrying soiled dinner linen.* PENNY *utters a stifled gasp; she puts*

the painting against wall with the easel, then removes her smock and tam. GRANDPA, *alone of them all, rises to the situation. With a kind of Old World grace, he puts down his newspaper and makes the guests welcome.*)

TONY: Good evening.

GRANDPA (*rising and crossing to back of table*): How do you do?

KIRBY (*uncertainly*): How do you do?

TONY: Are we too early?

GRANDPA: No, no. Come right in. It's perfectly all right—we're glad to see you. (*His eyes still on the* KIRBYS, *he gives* DONALD *a good push toward kitchen, by way of a hint.* DONALD *goes promptly with a quick little stunned whistle that sums up his feelings.* RHEBA *looking back exits.*)

PENNY: Why—yes. Only—we thought it was to be tomorrow night.

MRS. KIRBY: Tomorrow night!

KIRBY: What!

GRANDPA: Now, it's perfectly all right. Just make yourselves at home. (*Crossing to back of table. Placing chair.*)

KIRBY: Tony, how could you possibly—

TONY: I—I don't know. I thought—

MRS. KIRBY: Really, Tony! This is most embarrassing.

GRANDPA: Not at all. Why, we weren't doing a thing.

PENNY: No, no. Just a quiet evening at home.

GRANDPA: That's all. . . . Now don't let it bother you. This is Alice's mother, Mrs. Sycamore.

PENNY: How do you do.

GRANDPA: Alice's sister, Mrs. Carmichael . . . Mr. Carmichael . . . Mr. Kolenkhov. (KOLENKHOV *comes forward, bows and discovers his shirt tail is exposed. Thrusts it into his trousers. At this point* DE PINNA *takes an anticipatory step forward, and* GRANDPA *is practically compelled to perform the introduction. Crossing to* DE PINNA.) And—Mr. De Pinna.

THE KIRBYS: How do you do?

DE PINNA: Don't mind my costume. I'll take it right off.

GRANDPA: Mr. De Pinna, would you tell Mr. Sycamore to come right up? Tell him that Mr. and Mrs. Kirby are here.

PENNY (*her voice a heavy whisper*): And be sure to put his pants on.

DE PINNA (*whispering right back*): All right. . . . Excuse me. (*He vanishes—discus, racing form, and all. At this point* PENNY *hastily throws a couch cover over* GAY. PENNY *pushes* GAY's *posterior with her knee.* GRANDPA *places chair.*)

MRS. KIRBY (*crosses to* GRANDPA's *chair*): Thank you.

PENNY (*crossing to arch*): I'll tell Alice that you're— (*She is at foot of stairs.*) Alice! Alice, dear! (*The voice of* ALICE *from above, "What is it?"*) Alice, will you come down, dear? We've got a surprise for you. (*She comes back into the room, summoning all her charm.*) Well!

GRANDPA: Mrs. Kirby, may I take your wrap? (*Removes it.*)

MRS. KIRBY: Well—thank you. If you're perfectly sure. (*She turns*) that we're not— (*Suddenly she sees snakes and lets out a scream.*)

GRANDPA: Oh, don't be alarmed, Mrs. Kirby. They're perfectly harmless.

MRS. KIRBY: Thank you. (*She sinks into a chair, weakly.*)

GRANDPA: Ed, take 'em into the kitchen.

(TONY *takes his father's hat to hall and returns to the room.* ED *at once obeys. Takes snake solarium to kitchen.*)

PENNY (*putting Japanese bowl on buffet*): Of course we're so used to them around the house—

MRS. KIRBY: I'm sorry to trouble you, but snakes happen to be—

KIRBY: I feel very uncomfortable about this. Tony, how could you have done such a thing?

TONY: I'm sorry, Dad. I thought it was tonight.

KIRBY: It was very careless of you. *Very!*

PENNY: Oh, now, anybody can get mixed up, Mr. Kirby.

277

GRANDPA: Penny, how about some dinner for these folks? They've come for dinner, you know.

MRS. KIRBY: Oh, please don't bother. (ED *enters.*) We're really not hungry at all.

PENNY (*crosses to* ED): But it's not a bit of bother. Ed!— (*Her voice drops to a loud whisper.*) Ed, tell Donald to run down to the A&P and get half a dozen bottles of beer, and —ah—some canned salmon— (*Her voice comes up again.*) Do you like canned salmon, Mr. Kirby?

KIRBY: Please don't trouble, Mrs. Sycamore. I have a little indigestion, anyway.

PENNY: Oh, I'm sorry. . . . How about you, Mrs. Kirby? Do you like canned salmon?

MRS. KIRBY (*you just know that she hates it*): Oh, I'm very fond of it.

PENNY: You can have frankfurters if you'd rather.

MRS. KIRBY (*regally*): Either one will do.

PENNY (*to* ED *again*): Well, make it frankfurters and some canned corn, and Campbell's soup— (ED *crosses to door,* PENNY *following.*) Got that, Ed?

ED (*going out kitchen door*): Okay!

PENNY (*calling after him*): And tell him to hurry! (PENNY *again addresses the* KIRBYS.) The A&P is just at the corner, and frankfurters don't take *any* time to boil.

GRANDPA (*as* PAUL *comes through cellar door*): And this is Alice's father, *Mr.* Sycamore. Mr. and Mrs. Kirby.

THE KIRBYS: How do you do?

PAUL: I hope you'll forgive my appearance.

(ALICE *starts downstairs.*)

PENNY: This is Mr. Sycamore's busiest time of the year. Just before the Fourth of July he always—

(*And then* ALICE *comes down. She is a step into the room before she realizes what has happened; then she fairly freezes in her tracks.*)

ALICE (*at arch*): Oh!

TONY (*crossing up to her*): Darling. I'm the most dull-witted person in the world. I thought it was tonight.

ALICE (*staggered*): Why, Tony, I thought you— (*To the KIRBYS.*) I'm so sorry—I can't imagine—why, I wasn't— have you all met each other?

KIRBY: Yes, indeed.

MRS. KIRBY: How do you do, Alice?

ALICE (*not even yet in control of herself*): How do you do, Mrs. Kirby? I'm afraid I'm not very—presentable.

TONY (*crossing to ALICE*): Darling, you look lovely.

KIRBY (*a step toward ALICE*): Of course she does. Don't let this upset you, my dear—we've all just met each other a night sooner, that's all.

MRS. KIRBY: Of course.

ALICE: But I was planning such a nice party tomorrow night. . . .

KIRBY (*being the good fellow*): Well, we'll come again tomorrow night.

TONY: There you are, Alice. Am I forgiven?

ALICE: I guess so. It's just that I— We'd better see about getting you some dinner.

PENNY: Oh, that's all done, Alice. (DONALD, *hat in hand, comes through kitchen door; hurries across room and out front way. He is followed into the room by ED, who joins the family circle. GRANDPA crosses to back of table.*) That's all been attended to.

(*Door slams on DONALD's exit.*)

ALICE (*sensing that DONALD is on way to round up a meal crosses over to PENNY*): But Mother—what did you send out for? Because Mr. Kirby suffers from indigestion—he can only eat certain things.

KIRBY: Oh, it's all right. It's all right.

TONY: Of course it is, darling.

PENNY: I asked him what he wanted, Alice.

ALICE (*doubtfully*): Yes, but—

KIRBY: Now, now, it's not as serious as all that. Just because I have a little indigestion.

KOLENKHOV: Perhaps it is not indigestion at all, Mr. Kirby. Perhaps you have stomach ulcers.

ALICE: Don't be absurd, Mr. Kolenkhov!

GRANDPA: You mustn't mind Mr. Kolenkhov, Mr. Kirby. He's a Russian, and Russians are inclined to look on the dark side.

KOLENKHOV: All right, I am a Russian. But a friend of mine, a Russian, *died* from stomach ulcers.

KIRBY: Really, I—

ALICE (*desperately*): Please, Mr. Kolenkhov! Mr. Kirby has indigestion and that's all.

KOLENKHOV (*with a Russian shrug*): All right, let him wait.

GRANDPA: Do sit down, Mr. Kirby. Make yourself comfortable.

KIRBY: Thank you. (*He sits left of table.*)

PENNY (*sitting above table*): Well— (*She sighs; a pause, a general shifting.*)

GRANDPA (*leaping into the breach*): Tell me, Mr. Kirby, how do you find business conditions? Are we pretty well out of the depression?

KIRBY: What? . . . Yes, I think so. Of course, it all depends.

GRANDPA: But you figure that things are going to keep on improving?

KIRBY: Broadly speaking, yes. As a matter of fact, industry is now operating at sixty-four per cent of full capacity, as against eighty-two per cent in 1925. (GAY *rises.*) Of course, in 1929—

GAY (*She weaves unsteadily across room singing—"There was a young lady from Wheeling who had a remarkable feeling." The imposing figure of* KIRBY *intrigues* GAY): Wo-o-o— (*She pinches his cheeks and with that lunges on her way upstairs.*)

PENNY: She—ah—

(*The* KIRBYS, *of course, are considerably astounded by this exhibition. The* SYCAMORES *have watched it with varying degrees of frozen horror.* ALICE *in particular is speechless; it is* GRANDPA *who comes to her rescue.*)

GRANDPA: That may seem a little strange to you people, but she's not quite accountable for her actions. A friend of Mrs. Sycamore's. She came to dinner and was overcome by the heat. (*Sits at table.*)

PENNY: Yes, some people feel it, you know, more than others. Perhaps I'd better see if she's all right. Excuse me please? (*She goes hastily upstairs.*)

ALICE: It *is* awfully hot. (*A fractional pause.*) You usually escape all this hot weather, don't you, Mrs. Kirby? Up in Maine?

MRS. KIRBY (*on the frigid side*): As a rule. I had to come down this week, however, for the flower show.

TONY: Mother wouldn't miss that for the world. That blue ribbon is the high spot of her year.

ESSIE: I won a ribbon at a flower show once. For raising onions. Remember, Alice?

ALICE (*quickly*): That was a garden show, Essie.

ESSIE (*crosses to couch*): Oh, yes. (PENNY *comes bustling downstairs again.* KIRBY *rises.*)

PENNY: I think she'll be all right now. . . . Has Donald come back yet?

ALICE: No, he hasn't.

PENNY: Well, he'll be right back, and it won't take any time at all. I'm afraid you must be starved.

KIRBY: Oh, no. Quite all right. (*He sees* PAUL's *Meccano boat model.*) Hello! What's this? I didn't know there were little children in the house.

PAUL: Oh, no. That's mine.

KIRBY: Really? Well, I suppose every man has his hobby. Or do you use this as a model of some kind?

PAUL: No, I just play with it.

KIRBY: I see.

TONY: Maybe you'd be better off if *you* had a hobby like that, Dad. Instead of raising orchids.

KIRBY (*indulgently*): Yes, I wouldn't be surprised.

ALICE (*leaping on this as a safe topic*): Oh, *do* tell us about your orchids, Mr. Kirby. (KIRBY *crosses to alcove.* ALICE *addresses others.*) You know, they take six years before they blossom, don't they? Think of that!

KIRBY (*addressing* GRANDPA *and* PENNY, *warming to his subject*): Oh, some of them take longer than that. I've got one coming along now that I've waited *ten* years for.

PENNY (*making a joke*): Believe it or not, I was waiting for an orchid. (PAUL *laughs.*)

KIRBY: Ah—yes. Of course during that time they require the most scrupulous care. (*The sound of hall door closing and* DONALD *suddenly bulges through archway, his arms full. The tops of beer bottles and two or three large cucumbers peep over the tops of the huge paper bag.*) I remember a bulb that I was very fond of—

ALICE (*crossing to* DONALD): Donald!

PENNY (*rising and going to* DONALD): Ah, here we are! Did you get everything, Donald?

DONALD: Yes'm. Only they didn't have any frankfurters, so I got pickled pigs' feet. (*Exits.*)

(KIRBY *blanches at the very idea.*)

ALICE (*following* DONALD *to kitchen door, taking command*): Never mind, Donald—just bring everything into the kitchen. (*She turns at kitchen door.*) Mr. Kirby, please tell them *all* about the orchids—I know they'd love to hear it. And— excuse me. (*She goes to rear of stage.* PENNY *crosses, looks off into the kitchen, and comes to right of table.*)

GRANDPA: Kind of an expensive hobby, isn't it, Mr. Kirby— raising orchids?

KIRBY (*sits at table*): Yes, it is, but I feel that if a hobby gives one sufficient pleasure, it's never expensive.

GRANDPA: That's very true. (PAUL, ESSIE *and* ED *are sitting on the couch.* TONY *is at the desk.*)

KIRBY: You see, I need something to relieve the daily nerve strain. After a week in Wall Street I'd go crazy if I didn't have something like that. Lot of men I know have yachts—just for that very reason.

GRANDPA (*mildly*): Why don't they give up Wall Street?

KIRBY: How's that?

GRANDPA: I was just joking.

MRS. KIRBY: I think it's necessary for everyone to have a hobby. Of course, it's more to me than a hobby, but my great solace is—spiritualism.

PENNY: Spiritualism? Now, Mrs. Kirby, everybody knows that's a fake.

MRS. KIRBY (*freezing*): To me, Mrs. Sycamore, spiritualism is—well—I would rather not discuss it, Mrs. Sycamore. (*She looks at* KIRBY. *He rises.*)

PAUL (*rising from couch and crossing to* PENNY): Remember, Penny, you've got one or two hobbies of your own.

PENNY: Yes, but not silly ones.

GRANDPA (*with a little cough*): I don't think it matters what the hobby is—the important thing is to have one.

KOLENKHOV: To be ideal, a hobby should improve the body as well as the mind. The Romans were a great people! Why? What was their hobby? Wrestling. In wrestling you have to think quick with the mind and act quick with the body.

KIRBY: Yes, but I'm afraid wrestling is not very practical for most of us. (*He gives a deprecating little laugh.*) I wouldn't make a very good showing as a wrestler.

KOLENKHOV: You could be a *great* wrestler. You are built for it. Look! (*With a startlingly quick movement* KOLENKHOV *grabs* KIRBY's *arms, knocks his legs from under him with a quick movement of a foot, and presto!* KIRBY *is flat on his whatsis. Not only that, but instantaneously* KOLENKHOV *is on top of him.* MRS. KIRBY *rises. Just at this moment*

ALICE *re-enters the room. Naturally, she stands petrified, then rushes immediately to the rescue.* TONY *and* ED *arrive at the scene of battle first. Amidst the general confusion they help* KIRBY *to his feet.*)

ALICE: Mr. Kirby! Are you—hurt?

TONY: Are you all right, Father?

KIRBY (*pulling himself together*): I—I—uh— (*He blinks, uncertainly.*) Where are my glasses?

ALICE: Here they are, Mr. Kirby. . . . Oh, Mr. Kirby, they're broken. (PAUL *turns to* PENNY.)

KOLENKHOV (*full of apology*): Oh, I am sorry. But when you wrestle again, Mr. Kirby, you will of course not wear glasses!

KIRBY (*coldly furious*): I do not intend to wrestle again, Mr. Kolenkhov. (*He draws himself up, stiffly, and in return gets a sharp pain in the back. He gives a little gasp.*)

TONY (*he assists his father to chair*): Better sit down, Father.

ALICE: Mr. Kolenkhov, how could you do such a thing? Why didn't somebody stop him?

MRS. KIRBY (*rises*): I think, if you don't mind, perhaps we had better be going. (*Gathers wraps.* GRANDPA *rises.*)

TONY: Mother!

ALICE (*close to tears*): Oh, Mrs. Kirby—please! Please don't go! Mr. Kirby—please! I—I've ordered some scrambled eggs for you, and—plain salad— Oh, please don't go!

KOLENKHOV: I am sorry if I did something wrong. And I apologize.

ALICE: I can't tell you how sorry I am, Mr. Kirby. If I'd been here—

KIRBY (*from a great height*): That's quite all right.

TONY: Of course it is. It's all right, Alice. (*To* MRS. KIRBY.) We're not going. (*Arm around* ALICE.)

(*A moment's silence—no one knows quite what to say. Then* MRS. KIRBY *looks at* KIRBY *and sits. Then* KIRBY *sits. Finally* GRANDPA *sits.*)

PENNY (*brightly*): Well! That was exciting for a minute, wasn't it?

GRANDPA (*quickly*): You were talking about your orchids, Mr. Kirby. Do you raise many different varieties?

KIRBY (*still unbending*): I'm afraid I've quite forgotten about my orchids. (*More silence, and everyone very uncomfortable.*)

ALICE: I'm—awfully sorry, Mr. Kirby.

KOLENKHOV (*exploding*): What did I do that was so terrible? I threw him on the floor! Did it kill him?

ALICE: Please, Mr. Kolenkhov. (*An annoyed gesture from KOLENKHOV. He sits in desk chair. Another general pause.*)

PENNY: I'm sure dinner won't be any time at all now. (*Looks off into kitchen. A pained smile from MRS. KIRBY.*)

ESSIE: Would you like some candy while you're waiting, Mr. Kirby? I've got some freshly made.

KIRBY: My doctor does not permit me to eat candy. Thank you.

ESSIE: But these are nothing, Mr. Kirby. Just coconut and marshmallow and fudge.

ALICE: Don't, Essie.

ESSIE: Well— (*Crosses to couch. They sit there again. Then RHEBA appears in kitchen doorway, beckoning violently to ALICE.*)

RHEBA (*in a loud whisper*): Miss Alice! Miss Alice!

ALICE: Excuse me. (*Starts toward RHEBA.*) What is it, Rheba? (*Quickly flies to RHEBA's side.*)

RHEBA: The eggs done fell down the sink.

ALICE (*desperately*): Make some more! Quick!

RHEBA: I ain't got any.

ALICE: Send Donald out for some!

RHEBA (*disappearing*): All right.

ALICE (*calling after her*): Tell him to hurry! (*She turns back to the KIRBYS.*) I'm so sorry. There'll be a little delay, but everything will be ready in just a minute. (*At this moment DONALD fairly shoots out of kitchen door and across living room, beating the Olympic record for all time. SLAM on*

DONALD's *exit. He exits through hall door.* PENNY *tries to ease situation with a gay little laugh. It doesn't quite come off, however.*)

TONY: I've certainly put you people to a lot of trouble, with my stupidity.

GRANDPA: Not at all, Tony.

PENNY: Look! Why don't we all play a game of some sort while we're waiting?

TONY: Oh, that'd be fine.

ALICE: Mother, I don't think Mr. and Mrs. Kirby—

KOLENKHOV (*rising from desk chair*): *I* have an idea. I know a wonderful trick with a glass of water. (*He reaches for a full glass that stands on desk. Crosses to* KIRBY *and holds it over* KIRBY's *head.*)

ALICE (*quickly*): No, Mr. Kolenkhov.

GRANDPA (*rises, shaking his head*): No-o, Mr. Kolenkhov. (*Sits. A shrug and* KOLENKHOV *returns glass to desk.*)

PENNY: But I'm sure Mr. and Mrs. Kirby would love this game. It's perfectly harmless.

ALICE: Please, Mother . . .

KIRBY: I'm not very good at games, Mrs. Sycamore.

PENNY: Oh, but *any* fool could play this game, Mr. Kirby. All you do is write your name on a piece of paper— (*Getting pads and pencils.* TONY *helps* KOLENKHOV *and himself to pads and pencils.*)

ALICE: But, Mother, Mr. Kirby doesn't want—

PENNY: Oh, he'll love it! (*Going right on distributing pencils, pads.*) Here you are, Mr. Kirby. Write your name on this piece of paper. And Mrs. Kirby, you do the same on this one. (PAUL, ESSIE, *and* ED *sit on couch.* ESSIE *takes pencils,* ED *pads.*)

ALICE: Mother, what *is* this game?

PENNY: I used to play it at school. It's called Forget-Me-Not. Here you are, Grandpa. Now, I'm going to call out five words—just anything at all—and as I say each word, you're to put down the first thing that comes into your mind. Is that clear? For instance, if I say, "grass," you might put down "green"—just whatever you think of, see? Or if I call out "chair," you might put down "table." It shows the reactions people have to different things. You see how simple it is, Mr. Kirby?

TONY: Come on, Father! Be a sport!

KIRBY (*stiffly*): Very well. I shall be happy to play it.

PENNY: You see, Alice? He *does* want to play.

ALICE: (*uneasily*): Well—

PENNY: Now, then! Are we ready?

KOLENKHOV: Ready!

PENNY: Now, remember—you must play fair. Put down the first thing that comes into your mind.

KIRBY (*pencil poised*): I understand.

PENNY: Everybody ready? . . . The first word is "potatoes." "Potatoes." . . . Ready for the next one? . . . "Bathroom." (ALICE *shifts rather uneasily.*)

ALICE: Mother! (*But seeing that no one else seems to mind, she relaxes again.*)

PENNY: "Bathroom"! Got that?

KOLENKHOV: Go ahead.

PENNY: All ready? . . . "Lust."

ALICE: Mother, this is not exactly what you—

PENNY: Nonsense, Alice—that word's all right.

ALICE: Mother, it's *not* all right.

MRS. KIRBY (*unexpectedly*): Oh, I don't know. (*To* ALICE.) It seems to me that's a perfectly fair word.

PENNY (*to* ALICE): You see? Now, you mustn't interrupt the game. (ALICE *drifts to the rear.*)

KIRBY: May I have that last word again, please?

PENNY: "Lust," Mr. Kirby.

KIRBY (*writing*): I've got it.

GRANDPA: This is quite a game, isn't it?

PENNY: Sssh, Grandpa. . . . All ready? . . . "Honeymoon." (ESSIE *snickers a little, which is all it takes to start* PENNY *off. Then she suddenly remembers herself.*) Now, Essie! . . . All right. The last word is "sex."

ALICE: (*under her breath*): Mother! (*Crossing to buffet.*)

PENNY: Everybody got "sex"? . . . All right— (*She takes* TONY'S *and* KOLENKHOV'S *papers.*) now give me all the papers. May I have your paper, Mr. Kirby? (*Gathers the pads. Three at table tear off sheets.* ED *hands three pads to* PENNY.)

GRANDPA: What happens now?

PENNY: Oh, this is the best part. Now I read out your re-actions.

KIRBY: I see. It's really quite an interesting game.

PENNY: I knew you'd like it. I'll read your paper first, Mr. Kirby. (*To the others.*) I'm going to read Mr. Kirby's paper first. Listen, everybody! This is Mr. Kirby. . . . "Potatoes—steak." That's very good. See how they go together? Steak and potatoes?

KIRBY (*modestly, but obviously pleased with himself*): I just happened to think of it. (ALICE *turns front.*)

PENNY: It's *very* good. . . . "Bathroom—toothpaste." Well! "Lust—unlawful." Isn't that nice? "Honeymoon—trip." Yes. (*Giggle.*) And "sex—male." Oh yes, of course . . . you are. That's really a wonderful paper, Mr. Kirby.

KIRBY (*taking a curtain call*): Thank you. . . . It's more than just a game, you know. It's sort of an experiment in psychology, isn't it?

PENNY: Yes, it is—it shows just how your *mind* works. Now we'll see how *Mrs.* Kirby's mind works. . . . Ready? . . . This is *Mrs.* Kirby. . . . "Potatoes—starch." I know just what you mean, Mrs. Kirby. M-m—oh dear! . . . "Bathroom —Mr. Kirby."

KIRBY: What's that?

PENNY: "Bathroom—Mr. Kirby."

KIRBY (*turning to his wife*): I don't quite *follow that*, my dear.

MRS. KIRBY: I don't know—I just thought of you in connection with it. After all, you *are* in there a good deal, Anthony. Bathing, and shaving—well, you *do* take a long time.

KIRBY: Indeed? I hadn't realized that I was being selfish in the matter. . . . Go on, Mrs. Sycamore.

ALICE (*worried, comes down to* KIRBY): I think it's a very silly game and we ought to stop it.

MRS. KIRBY: Yes.

KIRBY: No, no. Please go on, Mrs. Sycamore.

PENNY: Where was I? . . . Oh, yes. . . . "Lust—human."

KIRBY: Human? (*Thin-lipped.*) Really! Miriam!

MRS. KIRBY: I just meant, Anthony, that lust is after all a—human emotion.

KIRBY: I don't agree with you, Miriam. Lust is *not* a *human* emotion. It is depraved.

MRS. KIRBY: Very well, Anthony. I'm wrong.

ALICE: Really, it's the most pointless game. Suppose we play Twenty Questions?

MRS. KIRBY: Yes.

KIRBY (*raises hand as* ALICE *goes to the rear*): No, I find *this* game rather interesting. Will you go on, Mrs. Sycamore? What was the next word?

PENNY: (*reluctantly*): Honeymoon.

KIRBY: Oh, yes. And what was Mrs. Kirby's answer?

PENNY: Ah—"Honeymoon—dull."

KIRBY (*murderously calm*): Did you say—dull?

MRS. KIRBY: What I meant, Anthony, was that Hot Springs was not very gay that season. All those old people sitting on the porch all afternoon, and—nothing to do at night. (*Realizes she has gone too far.*)

KIRBY: That was not your reaction at the time, as I recall it.

TONY (*moves in a step*): Father, this is only a *game*.

KIRBY: A very illuminating game. Go on, Mrs. Sycamore!

PENNY (*brightly, having taken a look ahead*): This one's all right, Mr. Kirby. "Sex—Wall Street."

KIRBY: Wall Street? What do you mean by that, Miriam?

MRS. KIRBY (*nervously*): I don't know what I meant, Anthony. Nothing.

KIRBY: But you must have meant something, Miriam, or you wouldn't have put it down.

MRS. KIRBY: It was just the first thing that came into my head, that's all.

KIRBY: But what does it mean? Sex—Wall Street.

MRS. KIRBY (*annoyed*): Oh, I don't know what it means, Anthony. It's just that you're always talking about Wall Street, even when— (*She catches herself.*) I don't know what I meant. . . . Would you mind terribly, Alice, if we didn't stay for dinner? (*Rises.* GRANDPA *and* KOLENKHOV *rise. Also* ESSIE, ED, *and* PAUL.) I'm afraid this game has given me a headache.

ALICE (*quietly*): I understand, Mrs. Kirby.

KIRBY (*rises, clearing his throat*): Yes, possibly we'd better postpone the dinner, if you don't mind. (KOLENKHOV *drifts to the rear.*)

PENNY: But you're coming tomorrow night, aren't you?

MRS. KIRBY (*quickly*): I'm afraid we have an engagement tomorrow night. (*Wrap is half on shoulders.*)

KIRBY: Perhaps we'd better postpone the whole affair a little while. The hot weather and—ah—

TONY (*smoldering*): I think we're being very ungracious, Father. Of *course* we'll stay to dinner—tonight.

MRS. KIRBY (*unyielding*): I have a very bad headache, Tony.

KIRBY (*to* TONY): Come, come, Tony, I'm sure everyone understands.

TONY (*flaring*): Well, *I* don't. I think we ought to stay.

ALICE (*very low. She comes down to* TONY): No, Tony.

TONY: What?

ALICE: We were fools, Tony, ever to think it would work. It won't. Mr. Kirby, I won't be at the office tomorrow. I— won't be there at all any more. (*Moves to left in front of desk.*)

TONY (*follows her, puts his arm around her*): Alice, what are you talking about?

KIRBY (*to* ALICE): I'm sorry, my dear—very sorry. . . . Are you ready, Miriam?

MRS. KIRBY (*with enormous dignity; she crosses over to* KIRBY): Yes, Anthony.

TONY: Darling, you mustn't mind this.

KIRBY: Oh—it's been very nice to have met you all. (*With* MRS. KIRBY, *he goes as far as the archway.*)

MRS. KIRBY: Yes, lovely.

KIRBY: Are you coming, Tony?

TONY: No, Father, I'm not.

KIRBY (*crossing to arch with* MRS. KIRBY): I see. . . . Your mother and I will be waiting for you at home. . . . Good night.

PENNY AND ESSIE: Good night.

(*Before the* KIRBYS *can take more than a step toward the door, however, a new figure looms up in the archway. It is a quiet and competent-looking individual with a steely eye, and two more just like him loom up behind him.*)

THE MAN (*very quietly*): Stay right where you are, everybody. (*There is a little scream from* MRS. KIRBY, *an exclamation from* PENNY.) Don't move.

PENNY: Oh, good heavens!

KIRBY (*speaks when* THE MAN *says "Don't move"*): How dare you? Why, what does this mean?

GRANDPA: What is all this?

KIRBY: I demand an explanation!

THE MAN: Keep your mouth shut, you! (PENNY *turns to* PAUL. ED *backs up as G-man advances slowly into the room, looking the group over. Then he turns to one of his men.*) Which one is it?

THIRD MAN (*goes over and puts a hand on* ED'S *shoulder and brings him forward.* ESSIE *follows*): This is him.

ED: Heh! What are you doing?

ESSIE: Ed!

ED (*terrified*): Why, what do you mean?

ALICE (*crossing to* GRANDPA): Grandpa, what is it?

KIRBY: This is an outrage!

THE MAN: Shut up! (*He turns to* ED.) What's your name?

ED: Edward—Carmichael. I haven't done anything.

THE MAN: You haven't, huh?

GRANDPA (*not at all scared*): This seems rather high-handed to me. What's it all about?

THE MAN: Department of Justice.

PENNY: Oh, my goodness! J-men!

ESSIE: Ed, what have you done?

ED: I haven't done anything.

GRANDPA: What's the boy done, Officer?

ALICE: What is it? What's it all about?

THE MAN (*taking his time, and surveying the room*): That door lead to the cellar?

PENNY: Yes it does.

PAUL: Yes.

THE MAN (*ordering a man to investigate*): Mac . . . (THIRD G-MAN *exits.*) . . . Jim!

JIM: Yes, sir.

THE MAN: Take a look *upstairs* and see what you find.

JIM: Okay. (JIM *exits upstairs.*)

ED (*panicky*): I haven't done anything.

THE MAN: Come here, you! (*He takes some slips of paper out of his pocket.*) Ever see these before?

ED (*gulping*): They're my—circulars.

THE MAN: You print this stuff, huh?

ED: Yes, sir.

THE MAN: And you put 'em into boxes of candy to get 'em into people's homes.

ESSIE: The Love Dreams!

ED: But I didn't mean anything—

THE MAN: You didn't, huh? (*He reads circulars.*) "Dynamite the Capitol!" "Dynamite the White House!" "Dynamite the Supreme Court!" "God is the State; the State is God!"

ED: But I didn't mean that. I just like to print. Don't I, Grandpa? (DONALD *enters.*)

GRANDPA (*waves* ED *and* ESSIE *away*): Now, Officer, the Government's in no danger from Ed. Printing is just his hobby, that's all. He prints anything.

THE MAN: He does, eh?

PENNY: I never heard of such nonsense.

KIRBY: I refuse to stay here and—

(DE PINNA, *at this point, is shoved through cellar door by* MAC, *protesting as he comes.*)

DE PINNA: Hey, let me get my pipe, will you? Let me get my pipe!

MAC: Shut up, you! . . . We were right, Chief. They've got enough gunpowder down there to blow up the whole city.

PAUL: But we only use that—

THE MAN: Keep still! . . . Everybody in this house is under arrest.

KIRBY: What's that?

MRS. KIRBY: Oh, good heavens!

GRANDPA: Now look here, Officer—this is all nonsense.

DE PINNA: You'd better let me get my pipe. I left it—

THE MAN: Shut up, all of you!

KOLENKHOV: It seems to me, Officer—

THE MAN: Shut up!

(*From the stairs comes sound of drunken singing—"There was a young lady, etc." GAY, wrapped in* PENNY's *negligee, is being carried down stairway by a somewhat bewildered G-man.*)

JIM: Keep still, you! Stop that! Stop it!

THE MAN: Who's that?

GRANDPA: That is my mother! (*He sits.*)

KOLENKHOV: The fireworks! The fireworks! (*And then we hear from the cellar. A whole year's supply of fireworks just goes off.*)

RHEBA (*enters*): Donald! Donald!

(MRS. KIRBY's *scream is just a little louder than the explosion.*)

KIRBY: Miriam! Miriam! Are you all right? Are you all right?

TONY (*dashing to his mother*): It's all right! Mother! There's no danger.

ALICE: Grandpa! Grandpa! (*Crosses to* GRANDPA.)

GRANDPA (*ever so quietly*): Well, well, well!

DE PINNA (*wrenching himself loose from the G-man*): Let go of me! I've got to go down there!

PAUL: Good Lord! (*With* DE PINNA, *he dashes into the cellar.*)

PENNY: My manuscripts! I've got to save my manuscripts! (*She dashes to her desk.*)

ED: My xylophone! How will I get the xylophone out?

ESSIE: Mr. Kolenkhov! Mr. Kolenkhov!

KOLENKHOV: Do not worry! Do not worry!

DONALD (*rushing toward the kitchen*): It's all right, Rheba, it's all right!

THE G-MAN (*vainly trying to keep order*): Line up, you people! Line up, all of you!

(*And* GAY *just keeps singing.*)

Act III

The following day. Rheba *is in the midst of setting table for dinner, pausing occasionally in her labors to listen to the Edwin C. Hill of the moment—*Donald. *With intense interest and concentration, he is reading aloud from a newspaper.*

Donald: ". . . for appearance in the West Side Court this morning. After spending the night in jail, the defendants, thirteen in all, were brought before Judge Callahan and given suspended sentences for manufacturing fireworks without a permit."

Rheba (*puts plate down*): Yah. Kept me in the same cell with a strip teaser from a burlesque show.

Donald: I was in the cell with Mr. Kirby. My, he was mad!

Rheba (*sets knife and fork*): Mrs. Kirby and the strip teaser—they were fighting *all* night.

Donald: Whole lot about *Mr.* Kirby here. (Rheba *places napkins. Reading again.*) "Anthony W. Kirby, head of Kirby & Co., 62 Wall Street, who was among those apprehended, declared he was in no way interested in the manufacture of fireworks, but refused to state why he was on the premises at the time of the raid. Mr. Kirby is a member of the Union Club, the Racquet Club, the Harvard Club, and the National Geographic Society." My, he certainly is a joiner!

Rheba: All them rich men are Elks or something.

Donald (*looking up from his paper*): I suppose, after all this, Mr. Tony ain't ever going to marry Miss Alice, huh?

RHEBA: No, suh, and it's too bad, too. Miss Alice sure *loves* that boy.

DONALD: Ever notice how white folks always getting themselves in trouble?

RHEBA: Yassuh, I'm glad I'm colored.

DONALD: Me, too.

RHEBA (*sighs heavily*): I don't know what I'm going to do with all that food out in the kitchen. Ain't going to be no party tonight, that's sure.

DONALD: Ain't we going to eat it anyhow?

RHEBA (*gets salad plates from buffet*): Well, I'm cooking it, but I don't think anybody going to have an appetite.

DONALD: *I'm* hungry.

RHEBA (*setting salad forks*): Well, *they* ain't. They're all so broke up about Miss Alice.

DONALD: What's she want to go 'way for? Where's she going?

RHEBA (*puts half of salad plates on table*): I don't know— mountains some place. And she's *going*, all right, no matter what they say. I know Miss Alice when she gets that look in her eye.

DONALD: Too bad, ain't it?

RHEBA: Sure is.

(DE PINNA *comes up from cellar, bearing earmarks of the previous day's catastrophe. There is a small bandage around his head and over one eye, and another around his right hand. He also limps slightly.*)

DE PINNA: Not even a balloon left. Look. (*Pointing to exploded firecracker he is holding.*)

RHEBA: How's your hand, Mr. De Pinna? Better?

DE PINNA: Yes, it's better. (*A step toward kitchen.*) Is there some more olive oil out there?

RHEBA (*nods*): It's in the salad bowl.

DE PINNA: Thanks. (*He goes out kitchen door as* PENNY *comes downstairs. It is a new and rather subdued* PENNY. DONALD *rises.* RHEBA *turns to her.*)

PENNY (*with a sigh*): Well, she's going. Nothing anybody said could change her.

RHEBA: She ain't going to stay away long, is she, Mrs. Sycamore?

PENNY: I don't know, Rheba. She won't say.

RHEBA: My, going to be lonesome around here without her. (*She goes into kitchen.*)

DONALD: How *you* feel, Mrs. Sycamore?

PENNY: Oh, I'm all right, Donald. Just kind of upset. (*She is at her desk.*) Perhaps if I do some work maybe I'll feel better. (*Sits at her desk.*)

DONALD: Well, I won't bother you then, Mrs. Sycamore. (*He goes into kitchen.* PENNY *leans back and sits staring straight ahead.* PAUL *comes slowly downstairs; stands surveying room a moment; sighs.*)

PAUL: She's going, Penny.

PENNY: Yes. (*She is quiet for a moment; then she starts to weep softly.*)

PAUL (*going to her*): Now, now, Penny.

PENNY: I can't help it, Paul. Somehow I feel it's our fault.

PAUL: It's mine more than yours, Penny. All these years I've just been—going along, enjoying myself, when maybe I should have been thinking more about Alice.

PENNY: Don't say that, Paul. You've been a wonderful father. And husband, too.

PAUL: No, I haven't. Maybe if I'd gone ahead and been an architect—I don't know—something Alice could have been proud of. I felt that all last night, looking at Mr. Kirby.

PENNY: But we've been so happy, Paul.

PAUL: I know, but maybe that's not enough. I used to think it was, but—I'm kind of all mixed up now.

PENNY (*after a pause*): What time is she going?

PAUL: Pretty soon. Train leaves at half past seven.

PENNY: Oh, if only she'd see Tony. I'm sure he could persuade her.

PAUL: But she won't, Penny. He's been trying all day.

PENNY: Where is he now?

PAUL: I don't know—I suppose walking around the block again. Anyhow, she won't talk to him.

PENNY: Maybe Tony can catch her as she's leaving.

PAUL: It won't help, Penny.

PENNY: No, I don't suppose so. . . . I feel so sorry for Tony, too. (GRANDPA *comes downstairs, unsmiling but not too depressed by the situation.* PENNY, *anxiously, rises.*) Well? —Grandpa?

GRANDPA: Now, Penny, let the girl alone.

PENNY: But, Grandpa—

GRANDPA: Suppose she *goes* to the Adirondacks? She'll be back. You can take just so much Adirondacks, and then you come home.

PENNY (*sits at desk chair*): Oh, but it's all so terrible, Grandpa.

GRANDPA: In a way, but it has its bright side, too. (*Sits at table.*)

PAUL: How do you mean?

GRANDPA: Well, Mr. Kirby getting into the patrol wagon, for one thing, and the expression on his face when he and Donald had to take a bath together. I'll never forget that if I live to be a hundred, and I warn you people I intend to. If I can have things like that going on.

PENNY: Oh, it was even worse with Mrs. Kirby. When the matron stripped her. There was a burlesque dancer there and she kept singing a strip song while Mrs. Kirby undressed.

GRANDPA: I'll bet you Bar Harbor is going to seem pretty dull to the Kirbys this summer. (*With a determined step,* ALICE *comes swiftly downstairs. Over her arm she carries a couple of dresses. Looking neither to right nor left, she heads for kitchen.*) Need any help, Alice? (ED *starts downstairs carrying suitcase and hatbox.*)

ALICE (*in a strained voice*): No thanks, Grandpa. I'm just going to press these.

PENNY: Alice, dear—

GRANDPA: Now, Penny. (ED *has appeared in hallway with a hatbox, etc.,* ESSIE *behind him.*)

ED (*puts bags in hall*): I'll bring the big bag down as soon as you're ready, Alice.

ALICE: Thank you.

ESSIE: Do you want to take some candy along for the train, Alice?

ALICE: No, thanks, Essie.

PENNY: Really, Alice, you could be just as alone here as you could in the mountains. You could stay right in your room all the time.

ALICE (*quietly*): No, Mother, I want to be by myself—away from everybody. (*She includes the whole group. Crosses down to table—picks up a dart.*) I love you all—you know that. But I just have to go away for a while. I'll be all right. . . . Father, did you phone for a cab?

PAUL: No, I didn't know you wanted one.

PENNY: Oh, I told Mr. De Pinna to tell you, Paul. Didn't he tell you?

ED: Oh, he told *me*, but I forgot.

ALICE (*the final straw*): Oh, I wish I lived in a family that didn't always forget *every*thing. That—that behaved the way *other* people's families do. I'm sick of corn flakes, and —Donald, and—oh—(*unconsciously, in her impatience, is surprised to find dart suddenly in her hand*)—everything! (*She dashes dart to floor.*) Why can't we be like other people? Roast beef, and two green vegetables, and—doilies on the table and—a place you could bring your friends to— without— (*Unable to control herself further, she bursts out of room, into kitchen.*)

ESSIE: I'll—see if I can do anything. (*She goes into kitchen. The others look at each other for a moment, helplessly. PENNY, with a sigh, drops into her chair again. PAUL drifts to right. GRANDPA mechanically picks up dart from floor; smooths out the feathers, sits. ED crosses to xylophone with a futile gesture, runs his hammer idly over xylophone keys. He stops quickly as every head turns to look at him. The sound of the door opening, and* TONY *appears in archway—a worried and disheveled* TONY.)

PENNY (*rises quickly*): Tony, talk to her! She's in the kitchen.

TONY: Thanks. (*He goes immediately into kitchen. The family, galvanized, listens intently. Almost immediately* ALICE *emerges from kitchen again, followed by* TONY. *She crosses living room and starts quickly upstairs.*) Alice, won't you listen to me? Please!

ALICE (*not stopping*): Tony, it's no use.

TONY (*following her*): Alice, you're not being fair. At least let me talk to you. (*They are both gone—up the stairs.* ESSIE *comes out of kitchen.*)

ESSIE: Where'd they go?

ED (*with a gesture, indicates upstairs region*): Upstairs.

ESSIE (*looking upstairs*): She walked right out the minute he came in. (PENNY *sits at desk.* ESSIE *sits at table as* DE PINNA *also emerges from kitchen.*)

DE PINNA (*crossing to* GRANDPA): Knocked the olive oil right out of my hand. I'm going to smell kind of fishy.

GRANDPA: How're you feeling, Mr. De Pinna? Hand still hurting you?

DE PINNA: No, it's better.

PAUL: Everything burnt up, huh? Downstairs?

DE PINNA (*nodding, sadly*): Everything. And my Roman costume, too.

GRANDPA (*to* PENNY): M-m-m. I told you there was a bright side to everything. All except my twenty-three years' back income tax. (*He pulls an envelope out of his pocket.*) I get another letter every day.

DE PINNA: Say, what are you going to do about that, Grandpa?

GRANDPA: Well, I had a kind of idea yesterday. It may not work, but I'm trying it, anyhow.

DE PINNA (*eagerly*): What is it?

(*Suddenly* KOLENKHOV *appears in the arch.*)

KOLENKHOV: Good evening, everybody!

PENNY: Why, Mr. Kolenkhov!

GRANDPA: Hello, Kolenkhov.

KOLENKHOV: Forgive me. The door was open.

GRANDPA: Come on in.

KOLENKHOV (*comes into room*): You will excuse my coming today. I realize you are—upset.

PENNY: That's all right, Mr. Kolenkhov.

ESSIE: I don't think I can take a lesson, Mr. Kolenkhov. I don't feel up to it.

KOLENKHOV (*uncertainly*): Well, I—ah—

PENNY: Oh, but do stay to dinner, Mr. Kolenkhov. We've got all that food out there, and somebody's got to eat it.

KOLENKHOV: I will be happy to, Madame Sycamore.

PENNY: Fine.

KOLENKHOV: Thank you. . . . Now, I wonder if I know you well enough to ask of you a great favor.

PENNY: Why, of course, Mr. Kolenkhov. What is it?

KOLENKHOV: You have heard me talk about my friend, the Grand Duchess Olga Katrina.

PENNY: Yes?

KOLENKHOV: She is a great woman, the Grand Duchess. (*To group.*) Her cousin was the Czar of Russia, and today she is a waitress in Childs Restaurant, Times Square.

PENNY: Yes, I know. If there's anything at all that we can do, Mr. Kolenkhov . . .

KOLENKHOV: I tell you. The Grand Duchess Olga Katrina has not had a good meal since before the Revolution.

GRANDPA: She must be hungry.

KOLENKHOV: And today the Grand Duchess not only has her day off—Thursday—but it is also the anniversary of Peter the Great. A remarkable man!

PENNY (*rises*): Mr. Kolenkhov, if you mean you'd like the Grand Duchess to come to dinner, why, we'd be honored.

ESSIE (*rises*): Oh, yes!

KOLENKHOV (*with a bow*): In the name of the Grand Duchess, I thank you. (*Starts for door.*)

PENNY: I can hardly wait to meet her. Where is she now?

KOLENKHOV: She is outside in the street, waiting. I bring her in. (*And he goes out.* DE PINNA *rushes to the cellar door for his coat.*)

PENNY (*feverishly*): Ed, straighten your tie. Essie, your dress. How do *I* look? All right?

(KOLENKHOV *appears in hallway and stands at rigid attention.*)

GRANDPA: You know, if this keeps on I want to live to be a hundred and *fifty*.

KOLENKHOV (*his voice booming*): The Grand Duchess Olga Katrina! (*And* GRAND DUCHESS OLGA KATRINA, *wheat cakes and maple syrup out of her life for the day, sweeps into the room. She wears a dinner gown that has seen better days, and the whole is surmounted by an extremely tacky-looking evening wrap, trimmed with bits of ancient and moth-eaten fur. But once a Grand Duchess, always a Grand Duchess. She rises above everything—Childs, evening wrap, and all.*) Your Highness, permit me to present Madame Sycamore—(PENNY, *having seen a movie or two in her time, knows just what to do. She curtsies right to the floor, and catches hold of a chair just in time.*)—Madame Carmichael—(ESSIE *does a curtsy that begins where all others leave off. Starting on her toes, she merges "The Dying Swan" with an extremely elaborate genuflection*)—Grandpa—

GRANDPA (*with a little bow*): Madame.

KOLENKHOV: Mr. Carmichael, Mr. Sycamore, and Mr. De Pinna.

(PAUL *and* ED *content themselves with courteous little bows, but not so the social-minded* DE PINNA. *He curtsies to the floor—and stays there for a moment.*)

GRANDPA: All right now, Mr. De Pinna.

(DE PINNA *gets to his feet again.* ESSIE *crosses down to chair left of table.*)

PENNY: Will you be seated, Your Highness?

GRAND DUCHESS (*sits at table*): Thank you. You are most kind. (GRANDPA *sits.*)

PENNY (ESSIE *sits above table*): We are honored to receive you, Your Highness. (*Backing away.*)

GRAND DUCHESS: I am most happy to be here. (*To* PENNY.) How soon is dinner?

PENNY (*a little startled*): Oh, it'll be quite soon, Your Highness—very soon.

GRAND DUCHESS: I do not mean to be rude, but I must be back at the restaurant by eight o'clock. I am substituting for another waitress.

KOLENKHOV: I will make sure you are on time, Your Highness.

GRAND DUCHESS: Thank you, Kolenkhov.

DE PINNA: You know, Highness, I think you *waited on me* in Childs once. The Seventy-second Street place?

GRAND DUCHESS: No, no. That was my sister.

KOLENKHOV: The Grand Duchess Natasha.

GRAND DUCHESS: *I* work in Times Square.

DE PINNA: Oh!

GRANDPA: Quite a lot of your folks living over here now, aren't there?

GRAND DUCHESS: Oh, yes—many. My uncle, the Grand Duke Sergei—he is an *elevator man* at Macy's. A very nice man. Then there is my cousin, Prince Alexis. He will not speak to the rest of us because he works at Hattie Carnegie. He is in ladies' underwear.

KOLENKHOV: When he was selling hot dogs at Coney Island he was willing to talk to you.

GRAND DUCHESS: Ah Kolenkhov, our time is coming. My sister, Natasha, is studying to be a manicurist, Uncle Sergei they have promised to make floorwalker, and next month I get transferred to the *Fifth Avenue* Childs. From there it is only a step to *Schrafft's,* and (*to* GRANDPA) *then* we will see what Prince Alexis says!

GRANDPA (*nodding*): I think you've got him.

GRAND DUCHESS: You are telling *me?* (*She laughs in a triumphant Russian laugh, in which* KOLENKHOV *joins.*)

PENNY: Your Highness—did you know the Czar? Personally, I mean.

GRAND DUCHESS: Of course—he was my cousin. It was terrible, what happened, but perhaps it was for the best. Where could he get a job now?

KOLENKHOV: Pravda, Pravda. That is true.

GRAND DUCHESS (*philosophically*): And poor relations are poor relations. It is the same in every family. My cousin, the King of Sweden—he was very nice to us for about ten years. Every once in a while he would send a money order. But then he said (*to* GRANDPA), I just cannot go on. I am not doing so well myself. I do not blame him.

PENNY: No, of course not. . . . Would you excuse me for just a moment? (*She goes to foot of stairs and stands peering up anxiously, hoping for news of* ALICE.)

DE PINNA (*the historian at heart, crosses in a step*): Tell me, Grand Duchess, is it true what they say about Rasputin?

GRAND DUCHESS: Everyone wants to know about Rasputin. . . . Yes, my dear sir, it is true. And how.

DE PINNA: You don't say?

KOLENKHOV: Your Highness, we have to watch the time.

GRAND DUCHESS: Yes, I must not be late. The manager does not like me. He is a Communist. (*To* PENNY.)

PENNY: We'll hurry things up. Essie, why don't you go out in the kitchen and see if you can help Rheba?

GRAND DUCHESS (*rising;* ESSIE *and* GRANDPA *also rise,* ED *backs away*): I will help, too. I am a very good cook.

PENNY: Oh, but Your Highness! Not on your day off!

GRAND DUCHESS: I do not mind. Where is your kitchen? (KOLENKHOV *takes her wrap to hatrack.*)

ESSIE: Right through here, but you're the guest of honor, Your Highness.

GRAND DUCHESS: But I love to cook! Come, Kolenkhov! (*Beckons to* KOLENKHOV.) If they have got sour cream and pot cheese I will make you some blintzes! (*And sweeps through kitchen door.*)

KOLENKHOV: Ah! Blintzes! . . . Come, Pavlowa! We show you something! (*With* ESSIE, *he goes into the kitchen.*)

DE PINNA: Say! The Duchess is all right, isn't she? Hey, Duchess! Can I help? (*And into the kitchen.*)

ED: Gee! She's got a wonderful face for a mask, hasn't she?

PENNY: Really, she's a very nice woman, you know. Considering she's a Grand Duchess.

GRANDPA: Wonderful what some people go through, isn't it? And still keep kind of gay, too.

PENNY: M-m. She made me forget about everything for a minute. (*She returns to stairs and stands listening.*)

PAUL: I'd better call that cab, I suppose.

PENNY: No, wait, Paul. Here they are. Maybe Tony has— (*She stops as* ALICE'S *step is heard on stair. She enters—dressed for traveling.* TONY *looms up behind her.*)

ALICE (*crossing to table*): Ed, will you go up and bring my bag down?

TONY (*quickly*): Don't you do it, Ed! (ED *hesitates, uncertain.*)

ALICE: Ed, please!

TONY (*a moment's pause; then he gives up*): All right, Ed. Bring it down. (ED *goes upstairs.*) Do you know that you've got the stubbornest daughter in all forty-eight states? (*The doorbell rings.*)

ALICE: That must be the cab. (*She goes to door.*)

GRANDPA: If it is, it's certainly wonderful service.

(*To the considerable surprise of everyone, the voice of* KIRBY *is heard at the front door.* GRANDPA *rises, goes to back of his chair.*)

KIRBY: Is Tony here, Alice?

ALICE: Yes. Yes, he is. Come in, Mr. Kirby. (KIRBY *comes in.*)

GRANDPA: How do you do?

KIRBY (*uncomfortably*): Ah—good evening.

PENNY: Good evening.

KIRBY: Forgive my intruding. . . . Tony, I want you to come home with me. Your mother is very upset.

TONY (*he looks at* ALICE): Very well, Father. . . . Good-by, Alice.

ALICE (*very low*): Good-by, Tony.

KIRBY (*trying to ease the situation*): I need hardly say that this is as painful to Mrs. Kirby and myself as it is to you people. I—I'm sorry, but I'm sure you understand.

GRANDPA (*coming down to table*): Well, yes—and in a way, no. Now, I'm not the kind of person tries to run other people's lives, but the fact is, Mr. Kirby, I don't think these two young people have got as much sense as—ah—you and I have.

ALICE (*tense*): Grandpa, will you please not do this?

GRANDPA (*disarmingly*): I'm just talking to Mr. Kirby. A cat can look at a king, can't he? (ALICE, *with no further words, takes up phone and dials. There is finality in her every movement.*)

PENNY: You—you want me to do that for you, Alice?

ALICE: No, thanks, Mother.

PAUL (*looks at* PENNY): You've got quite a while before the train goes, Alice.

ALICE (*into phone*): Will you send a cab to seven-sixty-one Claremont, right away, please? . . . That's right. Thank you. (*She hangs up. Starts to right.*)

PAUL: Alice!

ALICE (*embrace*): Father!

KIRBY: Are you ready, Tony?

GRANDPA: Mr. Kirby, I suppose after last night you think this family is kind of crazy?

KIRBY: No, I would not say that, although I am not accustomed to going out to dinner and spending the night in jail.

GRANDPA: Well, you've got to remember, Mr. Kirby, you came on the wrong night. Now tonight, I'll bet you, nothing'll happen at all. Maybe.

KIRBY: Mr. Vanderhof, it was not merely last night that convinced Mrs. Kirby and myself that this engagement would be unwise.

TONY: Father, I can handle my own affairs. (*He crosses to* ALICE.) Alice, for the last time, will you marry me?

ALICE: No, Tony. I know exactly what your father means, and he's right.

TONY: No, he's *not*, Alice.

GRANDPA (*crosses to them*): Alice, you're in love with this boy, and you're not marrying him because we're the kind of people we are.

ALICE: Grandpa—

GRANDPA: I know. You think the two families wouldn't get along. Well, maybe they wouldn't—but who says they're right and we're wrong?

ALICE: I didn't say that, Grandpa. I only feel—

GRANDPA: Well, what *I* feel is that Tony's too nice a boy to wake up twenty years from now with nothing in his life but stocks and bonds. (ALICE *and* TONY *drift upstage.*)

KIRBY: How's that?

GRANDPA (*turning to* KIRBY *and moving in front of table*): Yes. Mixed up and unhappy, the way you are.

KIRBY (*outraged*): I beg your pardon, Mr. Vanderhof. I am a very happy man. (ALICE *crosses to printing press.*)

GRANDPA: Are you?

KIRBY: Certainly I am.

GRANDPA (*sits*): I don't think so. What do you think you get your indigestion from? Happiness? No, sir. You get it because most of your time is spent in doing things you don't want to do.

KIRBY: I don't do anything I don't want to do.

GRANDPA: Yes, you do. You said last night that at the end of a week in Wall Street you're pretty near crazy. Why do you keep on doing it?

307

KIRBY: Why do I keep on—why, that's my *business*. A man can't give up his business.

GRANDPA: Why not? You've got all the money you need. You can't take it with you.

KIRBY: That's a very easy thing to say, Mr. Vanderhof. But I have spent my entire life building up my business.

GRANDPA: And what's it got you? Same kind of mail every morning, same kind of deals, same kind of meetings, same dinners at night, same indigestion. Where does the fun come in? Don't you think there ought to be something *more*, Mr. Kirby? You must have wanted more than that when you started out. We haven't got too much time, you know—any of us.

KIRBY: What do you expect me to do? Live the way *you* do? Do nothing?

GRANDPA: Well, I have a lot of fun. Time enough for everything—read, talk, visit the zoo now and then, practice my darts, even have time to notice when spring comes around. Don't see anybody I don't want to, don't have six hours of things I *have* to do every day before I get *one* hour to do what I like in—and I haven't taken bicarbonate of soda in thirty-five years. What's the matter with that?

KIRBY: The matter with that? Suppose we *all* did it? A fine world we'd have, everybody going to *zoos*. Don't be ridiculous, Mr. Vanderhof. Who would do the work?

GRANDPA: There's always people that like to work—you can't *stop* them. Inventions, and they fly the ocean. There're always people to go down to Wall Street, too—because they *like* it. But from what I've seen of you I don't think you're one of them. I think you're missing something.

KIRBY (*crossing toward* PENNY): I am not aware of missing anything.

GRANDPA: I wasn't either, till I quit. I used to get down to that office nine o'clock sharp no matter how I felt. Lay awake nights for fear I wouldn't get that contract. Used to worry about the world, too. Got all worked up about whether Cleveland or Blaine was going to be elected

President—seemed awful important at the time, but who cares now? What I'm trying to say, Mr. Kirby, is that I've had thirty-five years that nobody can take away from me, no matter what they do to the world. See?

KIRBY (*crossing to table*): Yes, I do see. And it's a very dangerous philosophy, Mr. Vanderhof. It's—it's un-American. And it's exactly why I'm opposed to this marriage. (ALICE *turns.*) I don't want Tony to come under its influence.

TONY (*a gleam in his eye*): What's the matter with it, Father?

KIRBY: Matter with it? Why, it's—it's downright Communism, that's what it is.

TONY: You didn't always think so.

KIRBY: I most certainly did. What are you talking about?

TONY: I'll tell you what I'm talking about. You didn't always think so, because there was a time when you wanted to be a trapeze artist. (ALICE *comes forward.*)

KIRBY: Why—why, don't be an idiot, Tony.

TONY: Oh, yes, you did. I came across those letters you wrote to Grandfather. Do you remember those?

KIRBY: NO! . . . (*Turns away.*) How dared you read those letters? How dared you?

PENNY: Why, isn't that wonderful? Did you wear tights, Mr. Kirby?

KIRBY: Certainly not! The whole thing is absurd. I was fourteen years old at the time.

TONY (*crosses a step*): Yes, but at *eighteen* you wanted to be a saxophone player, didn't you?

KIRBY: Tony!

TONY: And at twenty-one you ran away from home because Grandfather wanted you to go into the business. It's all down there in black and white. You didn't always think so.

GRANDPA: Well, well, well!

KIRBY: I may have had silly notions in my youth, but thank God my father knocked them out of me. I went into the business and forgot about them.

TONY (*crossing back to* KIRBY): Not altogether, Father. There's still a saxophone in the back of your clothes closet.

GRANDPA: There is?

KIRBY (*quietly*): That's enough, Tony. We'll discuss this later.

TONY: No, I want to talk about it *now*. I think Mr. Vanderhof is right—dead right. I'm never going back to that office. I've always hated it, and I'm not going on with it. And I'll tell you something else. (ED *starts down the stairs and crosses to* PENNY.) I didn't make a mistake last night. I knew it was the wrong night. I brought you here on purpose.

ALICE: Tony!

PENNY: Well, for heaven's—

TONY: Because I wanted to wake you up. I wanted you to see a real family—as they really *were*. A family that loved and understood each other. You don't understand *me*. You've never had time. Well, I'm not going to make *your* mistake. I'm clearing out.

KIRBY: Clearing out? What do you mean?

TONY: I mean I'm not going to be pushed into the business just because I'm your son. I'm getting out while there's still time.

KIRBY: But, Tony, what are you going to do?

TONY: I don't know. Maybe I'll be a bricklayer, but at least I'll be doing something *I want to do*. (*Doorbell.*)

PENNY: That must be the cab.

GRANDPA (*rises and crosses a step to the right*): Ask him to wait a minute, Ed. (ED *exits hall door.*)

ALICE: Grandpa!

GRANDPA: Do you mind, Alice? (ALICE *goes to alcove, her back to the group.* GRANDPA *rises, crosses to* TONY.) You know, Mr. Kirby, Tony is going through just what you and I did when we were his age. I think if you listen hard enough you can hear yourself saying the same things to *your* father twenty-five years ago. We all did it. And we were right. How many of us would be willing to settle when we're young for what we eventually get? All those plans we make

. . . what happens to them? It's only a handful of the lucky ones that can look back and say that they even came close. (ALICE *turns.* GRANDPA *has hit home.* KIRBY *turns slowly to look at his son, as though seeing him for the first time.* GRANDPA *continues.*) So . . . before they clean out that closet, Mr. Kirby, I think I'd get in a few good hours on that saxophone. (*Moves to his chair.* ED *returns.* GRAND DUCHESS, *an apron over her evening dress, comes in from kitchen.*)

GRAND DUCHESS: I beg your pardon, but before I make the blintzes, how many will there be for dinner?

GRANDPA: Your Highness, may I present Mr. Anthony Kirby, and Mr. Kirby, Jr.? The Grand Duchess Olga Katrina.

KIRBY: How's that?

GRAND DUCHESS: How do you do? Before I make the blintzes, how many will there be to dinner?

GRANDPA: Oh, I'd make quite a stack of them, Your Highness. Can't ever tell.

GRAND DUCHESS: Good! The Czar always said to me, Olga, do not be stingy with the blintzes. (*She returns to kitchen leaving a somewhat stunned* KIRBY *behind her.* GRANDPA *laughs.*)

KIRBY: Ah . . . who did you say that was, Mr. Vanderhof?

GRANDPA (*very offhand, comes down in front of table*): The Grand Duchess Olga Katrina. She's cooking the dinner.

KIRBY: Oh!

GRANDPA: And speaking of dinner, Mr. Kirby, why don't you and Tony both stay?

PENNY: Oh, please do, Mr. Kirby. We've got all that stuff we were going to have last night. I mean tonight.

GRANDPA (*sits at table*): Looks like a pretty good dinner, Mr. Kirby, and'll kind of give us a chance to get acquainted. Why not stay?

TONY: How about it, Father? Are we staying for dinner?

KIRBY (*shifting*): Why, if you'd care to, Tony, I'd like to, very much.

TONY (*going to* ALICE): Now if Alice will send away that cab, Mr. Vanderhof . . .

GRANDPA: How about it, Alice? Going to be a nice crowd. Don't you think you ought to stay for dinner? (ALICE *is hesitant.*)

KIRBY: I'm staying, Alice. The families ought to get to know each other, don't you think?

ALICE: Mr. Kirby . . . Tony . . . oh, Tony!

TONY: Darling. (*They embrace.*)

ALICE (*kissing* GRANDPA): Grandpa, you're wonderful!

GRANDPA: I've been telling you that for years.

ESSIE (*entering from kitchen, carrying letter and butter dish, she goes to* GRANDPA): Grandpa, here's a letter for you. It was in the icebox.

GRANDPA: Let me see. (*Looking at envelope.*) The Government again.

ESSIE: How do you do, Mr. Kirby?

KIRBY: How do you do?

TONY: Won't you step into the office, Miss Sycamore? I'd like to do a little dictating.

ED: I'd better tell that cab. (*Exits.*)

GRANDPA: Well, well, well! (ED *enters.*)

PENNY (*crossing to table*): What is it, Grandpa?

GRANDPA: The United States Government apologizes. I don't owe 'em a nickel; it seems I died eight years ago. (ED *crosses to center of buffet.*)

ESSIE: Why, what do they mean, Grandpa?

GRANDPA: Remember Charlie, the milkman? Buried under my name?

PENNY: Yes.

GRANDPA: Well, I just told them they made a mistake and I was Martin Vanderhof, Jr. So they're very sorry and I may even get a refund. (ED *crosses to xylophone.*)

ALICE: Why, Grandpa, you're an old crook. (*She moves to alcove with* TONY.)

GRANDPA: Sure!

KIRBY (*interested*): Pardon me, how did you say you escaped the income tax, Mr. Vanderhof?

KOLENKHOV (*bursting through kitchen door, bringing a chair with him*): Tonight, my friends, you are going to eat . . . (*He stops short as he catches sight of* KIRBY.)

KIRBY (*heartily*): Hello, there!

KOLENKHOV (*stunned*): How do you do?

KIRBY: Fine! Fine! Glad to see you!

KOLENKHOV (*to* GRANDPA): What has happened?

GRANDPA: He's relaxing. (ED *strikes keys of xylophone.*) That's right, play something, Ed. (ED *starts to play.* ESSIE *is immediately up on her toes as* KOLENKHOV *goes up to xylophone and sings "Goody-Goody!"* PENNY *applauds.* KIRBY *joins group at xylophone.*)

GRAND DUCHESS (*entering from kitchen*): Everything will be ready in a minute. You can sit down.

PENNY (*pulling her desk chair over*): Come on, everybody. Dinner! (*They start to pull up chairs.*) Come on, Mr. Kirby! (DE PINNA *enters from kitchen.*)

KIRBY (*still interested in xylophone*): Yes, yes, I'm coming.

PENNY: Essie, stop dancing and come to dinner. (ESSIE *brings a chair from hall, dances to table.*)

KOLENKHOV: You will like Russian food, Mr. Kirby.

PENNY: But you must be careful of your indigestion.

KIRBY: Nonsense! I haven't any indigestion.

TONY: Well, Miss Sycamore, how was your trip to the Adirondacks?

ALICE: Shut your face, Mr. Kirby.

KOLENKHOV: In Russia when they sit down to dinner . . .

GRANDPA (*tapping on his plate*): Quiet! everybody! Quiet! (*Immediately the talk ceases. All heads are lowered as* GRANDPA *starts to say Grace.*) Well, Sir, here we are again. We want to say thanks once more for everything You've done for us. Things seem to be going along fine. Alice is going to marry Tony, and it looks as if they're going to be very happy. Of course the fireworks blew up, but that was Mr. De Pinna's fault (DE PINNA *raises his head*), not

Yours. We've all got our health and as far as anything else is concerned we'll leave it to You. Thank You. (*The heads come up again.* RHEBA *and* DONALD *in fresh uniforms come through kitchen door with a goose on a large platter and a huge stack of blintzes.*)

KOLENKHOV: Grandpa, I have heard from my friend in Siberia. He has escaped again!

GRANDPA: Save the stamp for me!

PENNY (*when* KOLENKHOV *says "friend in Siberia."*): Mr. Kirby, do you like roast goose? We have roast goose for dinner.

KIRBY: Like it? Why, it's my favorite dish.

ESSIE: Mr. Kirby, I'm going to dance for you later. I've got a new mazurka.

ED: I've written some special music for it.

DE PINNA: Tell me, Mr. Kirby . . . what do you think of The Securities Commission?

PAUL: Mr. De Pinna, we've got to start thinking about next year's fireworks.

ALICE: Well, here goes the Adirondacks.

TONY: And a very good thing, too.